WAR OR PEACE IN THE SOUTH CHINA SEA?

NIAS – Nordic Institute of Asian Studies
Recent NIAS Reports

36. David D. Wang: Clouds over Tianshan. Essays on Social Disturbance in Xinjiang in the 1940s

37. Erik Paul: Australia in Southeast Asia. Regionalisation and Democracy

38. Dang Phong and Melanie Beresford: Authority Relations and Economic Decision-Making in Vietnam

39. Mason C. Hoadley (ed.): Southeast Asian-Centred Economies or Economics?

40. Cecilia Nathansen Milwertz: Beijing Women Organizing for Change

41. Santosh Soren: Santalia. Catalogue of Santali Manuscripts in Oslo

42. Robert Thörlind: Development, Decentralization and Democracy

43. Tarab Tulku: A Brief History of Tibetan Academic Degrees in Buddhist Philosophy

44. Donald B. Wagner: The State and the Iron Industry in Han China

45. Timo Kivimäki (ed.): War or Peace in the South China Sea?

46. Ellen Bangsbo: Teaching and Learning in Tibet. A Review of Research and Policy Publications

47. Andrew Martin Fischer: State Growth and Social Exclusion in Tibet. Challenges of Recent Economic Growth

48. Jens Kovsted, John Rand and Finn Tarp: From Monobank to Commercial Banking. Financial Sector Reforms in Vietnam

49. Mikaela Nyman: Democratizing Indonesia. The Challenges of Civil Society in the Era of Reformasi

50. Anak Agung Banyu Perwita: Indonesia and the Muslim World. Islam and Secularism in the Foreign Policy of Soeharto and Beyond

NIAS Press is the autonomous publishing arm of NIAS – Nordic Institute of Asian Studies, a research institute located at the University of Copenhagen. NIAS is partially funded by the governments of Denmark, Finland, Iceland, Norway and Sweden via the Nordic Council of Ministers, and works to encourage and support Asian studies in the Nordic countries. In so doing, NIAS has been publishing books since 1969, with more than two hundred titles produced in the past few years.

UNIVERSITY OF COPENHAGEN

Nordic Council of Ministers

WAR OR PEACE IN THE SOUTH CHINA SEA?

Edited by Timo Kivimäki

NIAS – Nordic Institute of Asian Studies
NIAS Reports, No. 45

First published in 2002 by NIAS Press
Reprinted in 2015
Nordic Institute of Asian Studies
Øster Farimagsgade 5, 1353 Copenhagen K, Denmark
tel: (+45) 3532 9501 • fax: (+45) 3532 9549
E–mail: books@nias.ku.dk • Website: http://www.niaspress.dk/

1.   *British Library Cataloguing in Publication Data*
War or peace in the South China sea?. - (NIAS reports ; no. 45)
    International relations 2.South China Sea - Strategic aspects
    I.Kivimaki, Timo II.Nordic Institute of Asian Studies
    327.1'6'0916472

ISBN 978-87-91114-01-4

Typesetting by NIAS Press
Printed and bound in Great Britain
by Marston Book Services, Oxfordshire

CONTENTS

Contributors ... 7

PART I: INTRODUCTION

1. Introduction *by Timo Kivimäki* ... 1

2. The History of the Dispute *by Stein Tønnesson* ... 6

3. Claims and Conflict Situations *by Ramses Amer* ... 24

PART II: DIMENSIONS

4. Dangers to the Environment *by Tom Næss* ... 43

5. The Economic Dimension: Natural Resources and Sea Lanes *by Stein Tønnesson* ... 54

6. The Military Aspects of the Disputes *by Bjørn Møller* ... 62

7. The Political Dimension: Sources of Conflict and Stability *by Ramses Amer and Timo Kivimäki* ... 87

PART III: PEACE PROSPECTS

8. Ongoing Efforts in Conflict Management *by Ramses Amer* ... 117

9. What Could Be Done? *by Timo Kivimäki, Liselotte Odgaard and Stein Tønnesson* ... 131

10. Conclusions *by Timo Kivimäki* ... 165

Bibliography ... 171

Index ... 211

FIGURES

3:1   Definitions of the maximum extent of EEZ, continental shelf and territorial sea ... 25

7.10   Number of inter-state disputes and conflicts among the South China Sea nations ... 90

MAP

3:1   Map of the South China Sea ... 26

TABLES

6:1   Military installations in the Spratly Islands ... 64

6:2   PLA naval facilities ... 67–68

6:3   The naval military balance in the South China Sea ... 78

7:1   Disputes since the 1950s (or since independence) among countries with territorial claims in the South China Sea ... 88

CONTRIBUTORS

Dr Ramses Amer is an associate professor and co-ordinator of the Southeast Asia Programme (SEAP) at Uppsala University.

Dr Timo Kivimäki is a senior researcher at the Nordic Institute of Asian Studies (NIAS).

Dr Bjørn Møller is a senior fellow and project director of the Research Program on Non-Offensive Defense, Copenhagen Peace Research Institute (COPRI).

Mr Tom Næss is a researcher at the Fridtjof Nansen Institute (FNI), Norway.

Dr Liselotte Odgaard is an assistant professor at the Department of Political Science, University of Århus.

Dr Stein Tønnesson is director of the International Peace Research Institute, Oslo (PRIO).

PART I

INTRODUCTION

1

INTRODUCTION

Timo Kivimäki

The South China Sea area is often portrayed as a theatre of military tension and dangerous conflict potential. A recent proof of the possibility that the territorial disputes there could trigger conflict could be witnessed in April 2001, as a US Navy EP-3 Aries intelligence aircraft collided with a Chinese F-8 fighter plane over waters that the People's Republic of China (PRC) was claiming, but the United States considered international. While the resulting diplomatic confrontation was about safety of aviation and military technology, the disagreement over the sovereignty of the waters played an important part in the argumentation.

The South China Sea disputes are, however, a much more complex matter, involving environmental values, economic security and political developments, and so cannot be reduced to traditional military security alone. For the ordinary people in the countries that take part in the disputes, the area is first and foremost a source of seafood and a sea-lane of transportation. Both the safety of sea lanes and the management of fisheries are fundamentally affected by the disputes of sovereignty over territories in the South China Sea.

The interest of the disputant nations in the territorial disputes in the South China Sea is tied to their political, economic, environmental and military concerns. In terms of military security, there are reasons to claim that for many of these nations the disputes over territories in the South China Sea constitute 'the least unlikely' trigger for inter-state war. In general, territorial disputes have proved to be the principal motive for inter-state warfare,[1] while more specifically the statistics of militarised inter-state disputes[2] show the area to be no exception in this regard. The importance of these disputes in regional security considerations is paramount. Indeed, while institutionalisation of the security arrangements in the South China Sea area is rather underdeveloped, the disputes of South China Sea have motivated collective security arrangements even among some of the non-aligned nations. As early as November 1983, General Benny Murdani, then Commander of the Indonesian Armed Forces, stated that Indonesia was ready to give military assistance to Malaysia if the latter were attacked. He promised that Indonesia would assist Malaysia militarily if the atoll Terumbu Layang-Layang, one of the disputed Spratly Island groups held by Malaysia but also claimed by Vietnam and China, came under attack.[3] Economically and ecologically, fisheries constitute a major interest as around 70 per cent of the Southeast Asian population live by the sea and the South China Sea fisheries represent almost one quarter of the total Asian catch. Also the importance of the sea-lanes in the South China Sea is a key factor in economic, diplomatic, military and environmental policies.

For the external involved powers, such as the United States and Japan, the South China Sea presents a problem of economic, diplomatic, environmental and military stability. With the exception of direct military threat, many of the same worries experienced by the disputants are also felt, albeit to a lesser extent, by the United States and Japan. This has been clearly expressed in the military and diplomatic tension, as well as in the qualified nervousness of the markets dependent on the South China Sea.

The South China Sea has become meaningful also for the non-involved nations such as those in the European Union. This interest is often based on considerations of *global security policies*: the economic, ecological and social threats caused by the prospect of war or ecological disaster in the area.

First, new global security policies are based on national security considerations. Political, economic and military interests are interlinked with global security interests and this is why even faraway countries have to follow developments in places like the South China Sea. National security policies of most nations are today more than ever based on a broad, comprehensive and *global* concept of security. National security policies are concretely influenced by the development of global international tension. International tension is also seen to reflect on regional tensions and global threats of war. Moreover today the threat of uncontrolled migration, refugee problems, international criminality, the spread of drugs and small arms, epidemics and religious fundamentalism are seen as factors influencing national security, often created by global insecurity and wars. Furthermore, national economic security can easily be affected by conflicts at the major hubs of international trade routes, such as the South China Sea. Comprehensive global security policy issues, such as global environmental challenges, directly affect the national security of all countries. While global environmental challenges as such might be security threats, the disputes in the South China Sea also prove how they might very well be connected with more traditional security threats: while the sovereignty of the areas is disputed, this unclear situation is rapidly giving rise to environmental challenges, as will be shown in Tom Næss's chapter in this volume.

Second, global security policies have been developed outside the national security policy context in the framework of the promotion of peace via the instruments offered by development cooperation. By supporting democracy, human rights and economic development, as well as helping developing countries to build institutions for dispute settlement and conflict transformation, aid donor countries have attempted to contribute to global security. Many countries and agencies with a serious commitment to development cooperation have already started to draw up their conflict prevention strategies as part of their development cooperation.[4]

The aim of the present study is to introduce the reader to the various dimensions of the disputes. Here the South China Sea is interpreted as encompassing not only the South China Sea proper, but also the Gulf of Thailand. When looking at generalisations, references are also made to areas bordering the area in focus.

A conscious effort in this volume is to avoid the tendency of media reports and many scholarly works of reducing all the dimensions of the disputes to strategic issues. Many aspects of the disputes emphasise the common interests rather than reinforcing the common perception of the setting as a zero-sum game over sovereignty and energy resources. In addition, by showing the richness of the different facets of the disputes, the book also advocates the creation of a strategic understanding to aid diplomatic efforts for peace in the area.

The first part of the volume is introductory. The genesis of the disputes is first presented and analysed by Stein Tønnesson in Chapter 2. Another introductory chapter (Chapter 3) by Ramses Amer defines the claims and presents the conflicts between the disputants in the South China Sea.

After presenting the background of the dispute, the study proceeds to the various dimensions of the dispute. Environmental aspects – the question of the protection of biodiversity, the prevention of water pollution, protection of the reefs and prevention of the overexploitation of the fisheries – are presented by Tom Næss in 'Dangers to the Environment'. The economic aspects of natural resources and trade routes are discussed by Stein Tønnesson in 'Natural Resources and Sea Lanes'. Finally, the traditional security question is covered in Chapters 6 and 7: Bjørn Møller concentrates on the military dimension of the South China Sea problem, while Kivimäki and Amer look more generally at the political conflict potential. These two chapters analyse the dimensions most directly relevant to traditional global security, including the potential of tension, war and escalation and the military magnitude of potential conflicts. Here, the pillars of political and military crisis stability are studied as well as the elements of uncertainty.

From the background and analysis of the dimensions and conflict potential, the study proceeds to an analysis of the potentials of conflict management.[5] The name of this third part of the project is 'Peace Prospects'. The development of conflict management is analysed in Amer's chapter on 'Ongoing Efforts in Conflict Management'. He studies the existing mechanism of conflict management and dispute resolution, while the next chapter, 'What Could Be Done?', outlines suggestions on the basis of the academic analysis of conflict management. Three levels of conflict management are presented: containment of violence, dispute resolution and conflict transformation. The presentation proceeds from the level of violence, by looking at the minimum measures to contain violence in the form of deterrence to the possibilities of resolving the disputes behind the conflict behaviour (dispute resolution) and concludes with an analysis of the potential possibilities to manipulate the structures of interaction by means of conflict transformation. The first approach is presented by Liselotte Odgaard and Stein Tønnesson, the second by Stein Tønnesson alone and the last by Timo Kivimäki (all in Chapter 9). The analysis of solution models – existing political processes and abstract solution principles by scholars – aims at giving an overview of the alternative strategy options for policies towards conflict in the South China Sea.

In brief, the aims of this study can be described by using a game metaphor. The study will provide the reader with an introduction to the South China Sea game, with the first part offering an explanation of the game setting with players and their positions (history by Tønnesson and claims by Amer). The second part presents the strategic environment of the game with powers, interests and stakes of the players as well as the rules of the game (chapters on environmental [Næss], economic [Tønnesson] and military dimensions [Møller] and the conflict potential [Amer and Kivimäki]). Finally, alternative strategy options available for the diplomacy of conflict prevention are analysed in the last two chapters (Amer [Chapter 8] and Kivimäki, Odgaard and Tønnesson [Chapter 9]).

NOTES

1   Holsti, Kalevi, 1991. *Peace and War: Armed Conflicts and International Order 1648–1989*. Cambridge Studies in International Relations, vol. 14. Cambridge: Cambridge University Press.

2   Jones, Daniel M., Stuart A. Bremer and J. David Singer, 1996. 'Militarized Interstate Disputes, 1816–1992: Rationale, Coding Rules, and Empirical Patterns', *Conflict Management and Peace Science*, vol. 15 no. 2 (Fall), pp. 163–213.

3   *Kompas*, 17 November 1983.

4   The UN contribution to the debate already in 1995 contained policy lines to taking conflict prevention seriously in development cooperation, see Boutros-Ghali, Boutros 1995. *Agenda for Peace*. 2nd edition with the supplement and related UN documents. United Nations, New York; see also OECD/DAC 1997. *Conflict Peace and Development Cooperation on the Threshold of the 21st Century*, Policy Statement, May 1997. OECD, Paris 1997; UNDP, forthcoming. *UNDP in Crisis, Post-Conflict and Recovery Situations*. UNDP, New York, NY; OECD/DAC 1997. *DAC Guidelines on Conflict, Peace and Development Cooperation*. OECD, Paris 1997; World Bank, Post-Conflict Unit and Belgian Ministry of Foreign Affairs 1999. *Security, Poverty Reduction and Sustainable Development, Challenges for the New Millennium*, September 1999; Swedish Foreign Ministry 1999. *Preventing Violent Conflict – A Swedish Action Plan*. Ds. 1999, p. 24, The Printing Works of the Government Offices, Stockholm; Danish Foreign Ministry 1999. *Prevention and Resolution of Violent Conflicts in Developing Countries*, a public draft paper, Copenhagen; International Alert, n.d. *Code of Conduct. Conflict Transformation Work*. International Alert, London; International IDEA 1999. *Democratic Institutions and Conflict Management*. Background Paper. IDEA, Stockholm; Finnish Foreign Ministry (Olli Ruohomäki and Timo Kivimäki) 2000. *Peaceful Solutions. Navigating Prevention and Mitigation of Conflicts*, Finland's Ministry for Foreign Affairs, Department for International Development Cooperation, Helsinki.

5   Conflict management in this volume means a broad variety of measures to contain violence, resolve disputes that motivate violence, and measures to transform structures that give rise to disputes. For a more detailed definition, see Chapter 9 in this volume.

2

THE HISTORY OF THE DISPUTE

Stein Tønnesson

Basically there are three ways of writing a history of the disputes in the South China Sea.[1] The first is to apply a national perspective, go as far back in history as possible in order to find evidence that the sea and its islands have been inviolable parts of one's own national patrimony.[2] The second is to compose a non-partisan legal treatise, present the chronology of conflicting claims to sovereignty, and evaluate their relative merits on the basis of international law.[3] The third is to write an international history, where events and trends are analysed on the basis of changes in the international system and the balance-of-power.[4]

Here we shall mostly follow the third approach, but with a side glance to the second. Although history does not need to be as important for the legal resolution of the dispute as is often imagined, it will play a certain role. Thus it does seem necessary to mention the critical dates when treaties, decrees or actions established the various claims to sovereignty over the Spratly and Paracel Islands.[5] Such dates can be found in the years 1877, 1909, 1930–33, 1946–47, 1951, 1956, 1974 or 1988. Readers who are interested in finding the optimal basis for settling the sovereignty disputes should look out for these years in the text below.

The main focus of the chapter will be on the central area of the South China Sea, which includes the Spratly and Paracel Islands (as well as Scarborough Reef, Macclesfield Bank and Pratas Island and Reef), but developments in the Gulf of Tonkin and the Gulf of Thailand will also be taken into consideration.

BEFORE NATIONAL SOVEREIGNTY

Although the concept of national sovereignty only really came to East Asia in the 19th century, 20th-century regimes would often read their claims to national sovereignty over islands, reefs and territorial waters much further back in time. They tried to sustain their claims by referring to archaeological finds and ancient documents. Chinese archaeologists have found Chinese objects in the islands of the South China Sea dating back more than 2,000 years. The degree to which these objects are 'Chinese' can, however, be disputed. Although an object may be Chinese in style or originally have been made in China, it was not necessarily brought to the island by someone representing China as a state. Then also, for almost a thousand years, much of today's Vietnam was part of the Chinese empire, and retained a tributary relationship to China until the French conquest in 1884.

Since China has the richest historical literature, it is Chinese written sources that contain the first and most frequent mentions of the South China Sea and its islands. The islands were frequented by collectors of feathers and tortoise shells, later also by fishermen, but when Chinese authors named the reefs in the South China Sea and tried to describe their location, the main purpose was to warn against them. These barely visible coral islands represented a great danger to ships sailing up and down the coast of Vietnam or along northern Borneo and the western coast of Palawan and Luzon. Ancient books also reveal the presence of ghastly demons both in the Paracel and the Spratly Islands.[6]

The South China Sea had two main ancient sailing routes, both going in a north–south direction: one along the eastern, the other along the western side of the sea. For captains navigating these routes, it was essential to stay clear of the Spratlys and the Paracels, which at the time were probably not clearly distinguished from each other, but instead considered as one continuous danger zone. When heavy winds blew ships off course, they would sometimes endow the reefs with added value in the form of shipwrecks and precious merchandise, thus producing fields of excavation for 20th-century national archaeologists. There were instances also in the old days when emperors or kings claimed the sole right to issue concessions to plunder shipwrecks. These claims have since been used as a historical argument for contemporary claims to sovereignty. This seems a dubious enterprise since international law requires not only discovery or economic exploitation but also a continuous exercise of sovereignty in order to establish a legitimate sovereignty claim.

From the 12th to the mid-15th centuries, Chinese ships dominated trade in the South China Sea. However, before that, traders from the Southeast Asian state of Sri Vijaya, who in turn had been linked to Muslim merchants of Persian, Arab and other origins, had played the dominant role. It was in this era that the Malay language was established as a lingua franca in long-distance trade. Chinese silk and ceramics were exchanged for Southeast Asian spices or Arab frankincense. Chinese commercial and naval shipping went through a period of intense expansion in the 14th to early 15th centuries, leading one expedition all the way to Africa. Then suddenly the emperor ordered an end to the building of ocean-going ships. His decision provided new opportunities for other maritime nations, such as the Ryukuyu Kingdom in Okinawa and later, the Portuguese who took Melaka in 1511 and Macao in 1557, and later the Dutch. The Dutch dominated the lucrative spice trade during the 17th century. In the 18th and 19th centuries there was a resurgence of Chinese and also Vietnamese shipping; the first of the Vietnamese Nguyen kings, Gia Long (1802–20) and Minh Mang (1820–47), pursued an active maritime policy, and claimed sovereignty to the Paracels which, probably on the basis of erroneous Western maps, they believed to be a far more significant group of islands than it was in reality.[7]

After the 1830s, when the Europeans started systematic surveys of the tiny Spratlys and Paracels and produced more accurate maps, there is little evidence that the Nguyen dynasty upheld its claim through declarations, effective occupation or utilisation.

The British and French now arrived with increasing frequency, with superior ships and notably better cannons than the local naval powers. The British constructed Singapore as a port city, launched the Opium War (1839–42), acquired Hong Kong and established protectorates in Malaya and northern Borneo. The French displayed their naval supremacy by sinking a number of Vietnamese war junks off Da Nang in 1847. They colonised the whole of Indochina (Vietnam, Cambodia, Laos) in 1863–84, and leased a territory on the Liaozhou peninsula (north of Hainan) from the 1890s to the 1940s.

THE COLONIAL POWERS AND CHINA

The Europeans brought fire power, silver, gold and opium, but also concepts such as 'sovereignty' and 'freedom of navigation'. They drew a crucial distinction between land and sea. Land was to be divided into territories with mapped and demarcated borders. The sea should be free for all, except for a narrow band of territorial waters along the coasts. Most of the countries around the South China Sea were made into British, French and Spanish colonies (the Spanish Philippines became American in 1898), and treaties were drawn up to separate them from each other. The monarchies in China, Japan and Thailand were not fully subjugated, but forced to open themselves up while also being invited to join the European international society. Thus they would have the right to sign treaties of their own and act as sovereign states. Their governments had to learn European ways: to map and demarcate land borders, delineate territorial waters, plant flags and set up sovereignty markers on islands, and tear down markers erected by others.[8]

The Sino–French treaty of 1887 decided the land border between China and French Indochina, and the dividing line between Chinese and Indochinese coastal islands in the Gulf of Tonkin. The land border between French Indochina and Siam, and also the maritime border in the Gulf of Thailand, remained contested for much of the 20th century. The border established between the French protectorate Cambodia and Siam, and between Cambodia and the French colony Cochinchina (southernmost Vietnam) left Cambodia with a very short coast. This would put Cambodia at a serious disadvantage later, when maritime zones were calculated on the basis of distance from the coast. From the Cambodian perspective, it was a serious problem that it was deprived of the big offshore island Phu Quoc, which the French placed under the administration of Cochinchina.

The Europeans and Americans were not much interested in the Paracels and the Spratlys. Just as in the old Chinese books, on European maps the Spratlys were called 'Dangerous Grounds'. Nomadic fishermen, who mostly spoke Hainanese dialects and lived in Hainan during the monsoon, inhabited the larger islands during parts of the year. To Europeans the reefs and islets were mainly a danger to navigation, but British ships explored them and gave them British names (such as 'Spratly'). In the 1870s a group of merchants in northern Borneo wanted to exploit guano (bird dung used as fertiliser and for producing soap) on Spratly Island and Amboyna Cay. As a consequence, these two islands were claimed formally by the British crown in 1877. This was probably the first time that any state made a modern, Western-style legal claim to any of the Paracels or Spratly Islands. From then until 1933 Spratly Island and Amboyna Cay were regularly included in the British colonial list, but little was done to exploit them or sustain the British sovereignty claim.[9]

Although the Paracels occupied a strategic position along the shipping route between Singapore and Hong Kong, and were positioned between French Indochina and Hainan, neither Britain nor France took any steps to claim the archipelago before the 1930s. In the first decades of the 20th century, only the Chinese empire displayed an interest in the Paracels, notably by sending a mission to claim the island group in 1909, two years before the Qing dynasty succumbed to the Chinese Revolution. In the next three decades, China fell apart and suffered a series of civil wars, and was not in a position to uphold its claims to the islands through effective occupation or utilisation.

The factor that would generate a much keener interest in the Paracels and Spratlys was the arrival on the scene of a new naval power: Japan.

THE COMING OF JAPAN

Japan had destroyed the Chinese navy in the war of 1894–95 and established a presence in the South China Sea through the annexation of Taiwan (Formosa). Japanese merchant companies competed with the Europeans and Americans in the China trade, and in the years following the Great European War (1914–18), Japanese companies in Taiwan started a systematic exploitation of guano both in the Paracels and the Spratlys, but without making formal claims. These operations were probably strategically motivated. The Japanese navy thought the islands would provide useful support points for a southward naval expansion.

It was the fear of Japanese expansion that led France to gain an interest both in the Spratlys and the Paracels. In 1930–33, France claimed the Spratlys for itself, and also occupied some of them. In 1938 it established a permanent presence in the Paracels, which were now being claimed on behalf of the protectorate Annam (today's central Vietnam), with basis in the claims made by the Nguyen dynasty in the early 19th century. France recognised, however, that there was a rival Chinese claim, and told the Chinese government that the stationing of a French garrison in the Paracels had a defensive purpose and would not prejudice the legal resolution of the dispute. Britain chose not to oppose the French actions in either the Spratlys or the Paracels, although it did not abandon its own claim to the Spratly Islands and Amboyna Cay from 1877, but merely let the claim stay dormant. Japan protested officially against the French actions.

In 1939, before it occupied Hainan, Japan established a military presence both in the Paracels and the Spratlys. To the dismay of Great Britain, who had relied on France to defend Western interests in the area, the French did not offer active resistance. Japan now launched its own formal claim to the two archipelagos as parts of the Japanese empire. Within the Japanese administrative system, the Spratlys depended on Taiwan and the Paracels on Hainan. The Western powers, including the United States, delivered protests in Manila, but the USA did not protest on anyone else's behalf, just against the unilateral Japanese action. China, ravaged by civil war, could not let its interests be heard, although the provincial Guangdong government was involved in rival demands for concessions to exploit guano in the Paracels.[10]

The Japanese dug out a submarine base in Itu Aba (the largest of the Spratly Islands) and this base is reported to have served as one of the vantage points for the Japanese invasion of the Philippines in 1942. In the previous year, Japan had entered into a treaty of cooperation with the French (Vichy) regime in Indochina. During much of the Second World War, French (in fact Vietnamese) and Japanese (in fact Taiwanese) troops lived side by side both in the Paracels and the Spratlys. Only in 1945 was the French garrison withdrawn from the Paracels.

SINO–FRENCH RIVALRY

Towards the end of the Second World War, the United States became the dominant naval power in the region, but the Americans showed little interest in the rocky islets in the South China Sea, except as targets for shooting exercises. The most active claimant at the end of the Second World War was the Republic of China (the government of Chiang Kai-shek) who sent naval expeditions both to the Paracels and the Spratlys in 1945–46, set up sovereignty markers, and established a permanent presence on Woody Island and Itu Aba, respectively the largest island in each group. In 1947–48, Chiang Kai-shek's government also published a map with a dotted U-shaped line encompassing virtually all of the South China Sea. This map would later become standard both in Taiwan and in mainland China, but its legal status has never been clarified. It remains unclear if it is meant as a claim only to all the islands within the line, or if it also should be seen as a claim to the sea and sea-bed, as Chinese 'historical waters'.[11] Legal scholars and politicians in Taipei have quarrelled bitterly about this question.

France also sent expeditions to the Spratlys and the Paracels in 1946–47, reiterated its claims to both archipelagos, and made an unsuccessful attempt to force a Chinese garrison to depart from Woody Island in the eastern Paracels. After the failure France established a permanent presence instead, on behalf of Vietnam, on Pattle Island in the western part of the Paracels.

In 1949, Chiang Kai-shek's government fled to Taiwan, and mainland China became a people's republic (PRC). In May 1950, Chiang's forces were chased from Hainan as well, and shortly afterwards the troops on Itu Aba and Woody Island were withdrawn to Taiwan. This gave France an opportunity to take over the Chinese possessions. Paris decided *not* to use the opportunity, in order not to further compromise its interests in China. Thus Itu Aba and Woody Island, as well as the other Spratly and Paracel islands, remained unoccupied for a period of six years.

DECOLONISATION AND COLD WAR

In the following decades, the conflicts in the South China Sea were affected by the two dominant political processes of the period: decolonisation and the Cold War. The first decolonised states to emerge in the region were the Philippines and Vietnam. The Philippines gained independence in 1946, but when nationalists within the Philippine government wanted to claim the Spratlys, their American advisors discouraged them. The Spanish–American treaty of 1898 made it clear that the western limit of the Philippine islands did not include the Spratlys, and the United States was not keen to carry the cost of a Philippine irredentist adventure that might bring conflict with Chiang Kai-shek's regime in China.

The Democratic Republic of Vietnam (DRV) was proclaimed on 2 September 1945, and was recognised by France as a 'free state' on 6 March 1946, but war broke out between France and the communist-led

11

Democratic Republic of Vietnam in November–December of the same year. When Vietnam was recognised as an independent state in 1950, it had two rival regimes. The Democratic Republic (under President Ho Chi Minh) was recognised by the PRC, the Soviet Union and the East European states. The State of Vietnam (under former emperor Bao Dai) was recognised by Britain and the United States, although for most practical purposes it remained a French colony. Ho Chi Minh depended on support from the PRC and was not in a position to oppose the view of the socialist camp, which held that the Paracels and Spratlys belonged to the PRC. Hainanese fishermen in the Paracels also seem to have assisted North Vietnam in transporting arms and other provisions to the guerrilla forces in South Vietnam.[12]

The leaders of the State of Vietnam tried to push France towards a more active irredentism on behalf of Vietnam both in the Paracels and the Spratlys. France held that the whole of the Paracels was Vietnamese, but claimed the Spratlys to be a French possession, not Vietnamese.

At the peace conference in San Francisco in 1951, Japan formally abandoned its claims to Hainan, Taiwan and all other islands in the South China Sea, but the treaty did not say to whom the other islands were ceded, although it was clear that Taiwan and Hainan would be Chinese. Neither of the two Chinese regimes was present in San Francisco. At this stage the whole socialist camp supported the PRC's claim, but France and the State of Vietnam (who were both represented in San Francisco) maintained their own claims to the two island groups. The USA (which had both France's and Chiang Kai-shek's interests in mind) and Britain (who still had its own claim to Spratly Island and Amboyna Cay, and had to think about its possessions in northern Borneo) preferred to let the matter remain unsettled. Sabah and Sarawak were relieved of British rule only in 1963, as constituent states within the Malaysian Federation, and the Sultan of Brunei did not want independence until 1984. Britain did little to push the interests of North Borneo, Brunei and Sarawak in the Spratly area. In 1950, at the instigation of Australia, the British government examined the strategic importance of the Spratlys and the Paracels in order to decide if something ought to be done to prevent them from coming under the rule of a communist state. The conclusion was that the islands were of little economic or strategic value and that the Commonwealth could safely maintain its passive stance.

To compensate for its absence in San Francisco, the Republic of China on Taiwan negotiated its own peace treaty with Japan in 1952, and persuaded Japan to accept a clause about the Paracels and Spratlys that differed from the one in San Francisco in that Japan 'renounced all right, title and claim to Taiwan (Formosa) and P'eng-hu (Pescadores) as well as the Spratly and the Paracel Islands'. The fact that the Spratlys and Paracels were mentioned along with Taiwan and the P'eng-hu, which are close to Taiwan, gave the impression that they all formed a Chinese whole. However, shortly afterwards, France and Japan exchanged letters to the effect that the new treaty had not, in the view of Japan, entailed any change in relation to the San Francisco treaty. The French government thus felt it had annulled the Taiwanese gain.

1956

1956 was a decisive year not only in Suez and Budapest, but also in the South China Sea. A group of Philippine maritime activists, led by the brothers Thomas and Filemon Cloma, had grown tired of their government's passivity with regard to the western islands. With encouragement from the Philippine vice-president, and claiming that the islands west of Palawan had become *res nullius* after Japan had abandoned them, they sent an expedition to occupy a number of them and proclaimed a new *Kalaya'an* (Freedomland). Thomas Cloma introduced a distinction between his Freedomland and 'the Spratly Islands' further to the west. This distinction, which later became a part of the Philippines policy, was never fully clarified, but it seems that Freedomland encompasses most of what others call the Spratly Islands, but not Spratly Island itself and the banks and reefs lying west of it.[13]

The action of the Cloma brothers triggered a stream of protests, claims and counter-claims. Taiwan reacted strongly and sent a force to expel the Filipinos, but when the Taiwanese arrived, the Cloma party had already left. Not long after, Taiwan proceeded to reoccupy Itu Aba (which it had abandoned in 1950) and has since retained a regular presence, from 1971 a permanent occupation.

The PRC also restated its own claim. Its navy could not yet project power as far south as the Spratlys, but the PRC established a permanent presence in Woody Island of the eastern Paracels, which had only been seasonally inhabited by Hainanese fishermen since Chiang's troops left in 1950. The Vietnamese garrison in Pattle Island in the western Paracels was around the same time relieved of its French command and shifted to US logistical support. South Vietnam also pronounced its own claim to the Spratlys, issued a protest against the Cloma action, and sent an expedition to the Spratlys to erect Vietnamese markers. France did not support the Vietnamese protest, but delivered its own protest in Manila, in defence of its own claim. Britain, Japan and the USA did not take any official position. In 1957 the French government decided to do the same with its Spratly claim as Britain had done in the 1930s: neither officially abandon it nor try to defend it further.[14]

OIL AND THE LAW OF THE SEA

By the mid-1950s British and US oil companies had started to show interest in the possibility of discovering oil in the Spratly area, as an extension of their activities in northern Borneo. Yet oil only really became a factor in the sovereignty dispute in the years 1969–73, at the height of the Vietnam War. The prospect of finding oil provided a new motive for pursuing sovereignty claims, and made it more acceptable to spend resources on keeping troops and other personnel in these unfriend-ly places.

In 1967 an initiative was taken on the global level to open negoti-ations about the fate of those parts of the world's continental shelf that lie beyond national jurisdiction. In 1969 the International Court of Justice in the Hague adjudicated the North Sea Continental Shelf cases by enunciating the natural prolongation principle, i.e., that national jurisdiction of the continental shelf could extend beyond the territorial waters limit. This led to the opening of the Third United Nations Conference on the Law of the Sea in 1973 (UNCLOS III, 1973–82), the year of the oil crisis. This refocused attention on how far national jurisdiction of the continental shelf could extend from the shore of a coastal state. In the light of these discussions it seemed increasingly important to possess all kinds of islands, since they could serve as arguments to claim an extensive continental shelf.[15]

The temptation to be more aggressive in pursuing claims in the Spratlys was reinforced when the coastal states participating in UNCLOS III started to push for the creation of so-called Exclusive Economic Zones (EEZs), where the coastal states would have sovereign rights to exploit the marine resources (notably fish). Kenya proposed a 200-nautical-mile EEZ as early as 1972, and although this was highly controversial, it won out in the end and became part of the United Nations Convention on the Law of the Sea (LOS Convention) that was signed in 1982. The 200 nautical-mile limit was made to apply not only to the sea, but to the sea-bed as well. The LOS Convention established that every coastal state could claim a continental shelf out to the same limit as the EEZ, regardless of the depth of the sea (and to a maximum of 350 nautical miles if the natural shelf was naturally prolonged that far). The states around the South China Sea supported these principles, and of course started to position themselves already in the 1970s in order to benefit as much as possible from the emerging legal regime. The LOS Convention was signed in 1982, and entered into force in November 1994, when the 60th state had deposited its instrument of ratification. It has now been ratified by all the states with claims in the Spratly area – except Taiwan – but not the UK or the USA.

In 1971, clearly motivated by the prospect of finding oil, the Philippines officially declared the *Kalaya'an* (the eastern part of the

Spratlys) to be part of the Philippines. In 1974, while awarding a concession to a consortium of companies to explore for oil, the Philippines occupied five islets in the Reed Bank area. The claim to Kalaya'an was reiterated in 1978, when the Philippines occupied two additional features.

In 1973, the same year as UNCLOS III started, South Vietnam awarded a number of oil exploration contracts to US companies in the area west of the Spratlys, and at the same time took steps to include the Spratlys under the administration of a South Vietnamese province. At the same time, South Vietnam, Cambodia and Thailand made huge overlapping claims to continental shelf areas in the Gulf of Thailand. As we shall see below, the unified Socialist Republic of Vietnam, which was founded in 1976, took over the South Vietnamese claims. In 1982, when the Law of the Sea Convention was signed (and three years after Vietnam had invaded and occupied Cambodia), Vietnam drew a system of straight baselines along most of its coast, as a basis for claiming a vast continental shelf and EEZ, and also established a principle (in agreement with its client regime in Cambodia) of a shared Cambodian–Vietnamese historical waters zone in the Gulf of Thailand.[16]

After Sabah and Sarawak left British rule to become part of the Malaysian Federation in 1963, Kuala Lumpur started preparing to make its own claims north of Borneo. A continental shelf act was passed in 1966 and 1969, and in 1979 Malaysia published a controversial map with an extensive continental shelf claim north of Borneo. It also claimed a number of islands and reefs within the area of the continental shelf claim, and sent troops to permanently occupy one of them in 1983, another in 1986. In the Gulf of Thailand, Malaysia and Thailand agreed in 1979 to establish a Joint Development Zone (JDZ) in the area where their continental shelf claims overlapped. It would, however, take 14 years before the zone could be formally established in 1993, and it was only at the end of the 1990s that gas production could begin under a joint legal regime.

The prospects of finding oil and the new law of the sea regime thus prompted a scramble for claiming continental shelf areas and for possessing reefs and islands. The most hotly contested area was the Spratlys. Vietnam moved in from the west, the Philippines from the east and Malaysia from the south, while Taiwan kept Itu Aba. By the mid-1980s, these four states had occupied virtually all such features that were permanently above the sea (high tide elevations). None of the states tried to drive other countries' troops off islands that were already occupied, but were satisfied to occupy new features. After Taiwan lost China's seat in the United Nations in 1971 and Japan and the USA switched their recognition to the PRC in 1979, Taiwan continued to occupy Itu Aba on behalf of China as a whole, not of a separate Taiwan.

The loser in the scramble for occupation of the Spratlys was the PRC, who came too late for the better pieces. However, a new factor would gradually increase the PRC's leverage: the regional isolation of Vietnam.

VIETNAM'S ISOLATION

Since it was recognised by the socialist camp in 1950, the DRV (North Vietnam) had given the impression of supporting the Chinese claims in the South China Sea, not through explicit official declarations, but through the publication of maps, personal communications, and an official declaration in 1956 that fully supported the PRC's recent declaration of territorial waters (without taking exception to the fact that the declaration had specifically mentioned the Paracels and Spratlys as Chinese).[17] It was South, not North Vietnam who pushed Vietnamese maritime irredentism in the South China Sea. During the last years of the Vietnam War, the relationship between the PRC and North Vietnam deteriorated, and Hanoi switched to the South Vietnamese stance. The South China Sea policy pursued by the unified Socialist Republic of Vietnam (SRV) from its founding in 1976 has been a continuation of South Vietnam's policy, not North Vietnam's.

In 1972, the PRC received President Nixon in Beijing, in the same year as the United States carried out its heaviest bombing of Hanoi. In January 1974, after the Paris peace accords which provided for US withdrawal from Vietnam and a year before the Ho Chi Minh offensive, which resulted in the North Vietnamese conquest of Saigon, the PRC attacked and drove out the South Vietnamese troops from the western Paracels. The United States did not intervene. Thus the PRC had ended the equivocal situation that had lasted since 1947, with Chinese troops occupying the eastern Paracels and Vietnamese troops holding the western (until 1956 under French command). Since 1974 the PRC has exercised full military control of the whole of the Paracels. There can be little doubt that the Chinese action in the Paracels in 1974 did much to arouse Hanoi's animosity towards Beijing, and to isolate the pro-Chinese faction in the Vietnamese communist leadership.

In response to the loss of the western Paracels, South Vietnam rushed to permanently occupy several Spratly Islands, using the same troops that had been driven out of the Paracels. In April 1975, even before the final conquest of Saigon, a North Vietnamese task force arrived in the Spratlys and took command of the Vietnamese garrisons there. Since then, Vietnam has gradually expanded its garrisons in the Spratlys and has always occupied more reefs and islands than any other power – despite the cost this must have entailed.

After the end of the Vietnam War, Vietnam and the PRC were rivals in trying to normalise their relations with the member states of the

Association of Southeast Asian Nations (ASEAN), which had been formed by Indonesia, Malaysia, the Philippines, Singapore and Thailand in 1967. The PRC won, and the Vietnamese invasion of Cambodia in 1978 isolated Vietnam from most other countries in the region. Vietnam came to depend on the Soviet Union, not least in naval matters. The former Japanese, French and American base in Cam Ranh Bay was now leased out to the Soviet Navy, and a joint venture with Soviet oil companies (Vietsovpetro) took over the oilfields that American companies had explored on the continental shelf of South Vietnam. For some years the South China Sea was an important theatre in the Soviet–American naval rivalry.[18] This made it difficult for the PRC to further improve its position, although it was in this period that the Chinese government started to allocate more resources to the PLA navy and to prepare for an assertive maritime policy.

Brunei and the PRC were the only claimant states not to control any features in the Spratly area during the 1980s. This changed when Gorbachev scaled down the costly Soviet deployments abroad and signalled serious reductions in Soviet support to Vietnam. Hanoi now found itself without any powerful allies, and the PRC utilised the situation to move into the Spratlys. A scientific expedition surveyed the area in 1987, and the following year the PRC occupied several reefs. One such reef was close to an island held by Vietnamese forces. The circumstances are disputed, but a battle occurred in March 1988, at which three Vietnamese ships were sunk and more than 70 troops killed or drowned.[19]

The PRC refrained, however, from ousting the Vietnamese forces from any of the positions they were holding. Some Chinese naval circles would later regret this, thinking a chance had been lost to establish hegemony in the Spratly area. As long as Vietnam was occupying Cambodia, it was unlikely that anyone would support Vietnam against the PRC. By 1989, Vietnam withdrew its troops from Cambodia, thus providing the basis for a peace settlement. This made it possible to improve Hanoi's relationship with Beijing (normalisation of relations 1991) as well as with the countries of ASEAN (full membership 1995) and the United States (normalisation 1995 and normal trade relations 2000).

ASEAN VERSUS CHINA

In the 1990s, the main constellation was ASEAN versus China (with Taiwan still maintaining the same claims on behalf of 'China' as the PRC). At the same time the general relations between the states in the region tended to improve. This increased the possibilities of conflict management and dispute resolution, although little progress was made in the central part of the South China Sea. Progress was mainly made in the Gulf of Thailand and the Gulf of Tonkin.

Thailand has the world's fifth largest trawling fleet, and incidents between Vietnamese coastguards and Thai fishing vessels formed an important part of the hostile relationship between the two countries in the 1980s. These incidents continued in the 1990s, and became so serious that both parties sought a solution. The breakthrough came in 1996 when Vietnam and Thailand reached an agreement both on fishery cooperation and on the delineation of the continental shelf. By then, Vietnam had also reached an agreement with Malaysia on establishing a Joint Development Zone in the area where their continental shelf claims overlapped. At the time of writing (2002), the remaining problem in the Gulf of Thailand is to negotiate agreements between Cambodia and its neighbour states. Cambodia has declared a wish to have a Joint Development Zone in the area where its claim overlaps that of Thailand. However, Cambodia no longer seems to accept the joint historical waters zone with Vietnam, which was established in 1982. Cambodia remains geographically disadvantaged, and it will therefore be difficult to find solutions that satisfy the Cambodians.

While negotiating with Thailand, Vietnam also engaged in negotiations with China about both the land border and the maritime border in the Gulf of Tonkin. A land border treaty was signed in December 1999, and treaties on fishery cooperation and maritime delimitation followed in December 2000. The latter treaties seem, however, to have been signed a little prematurely. Negotiations continued after the treaties were officially signed, and it took a long time before the delimitation treaty was made public.[20]

With regard to the disputes in the central part of the South China Sea, there were frequent informal and formal talks throughout the 1990s, and also a great number of incidents between naval forces, coastguards and fishermen, but no progress was made towards conflict resolution. The foreign ministers of ASEAN agreed on a joint declaration on the South China Sea in July 1992 and surprised the PRC by strongly supporting the Philippines in a dispute with the PRC over Mischief Reef in March 1995. The Philippines had discovered new Chinese military installations on this submerged reef, which is located in the eastern part of the Spratlys. Mischief Reef remained a serious bone of contention between the PRC and the Philippines throughout the decade.

ASEAN's unity was less firm towards the end of the decade. As a result of the dramatic political events resulting from the Asian crisis of 1997–98 in Indonesia and Malaysia, Malaysia's relations with the Philippines, Indonesia and Singapore worsened. In 1999, Malaysia pursued its own course in the Spratlys, occupying new features and moving closer to the PRC. An effort was made to maintain ASEAN unity, with Thailand taking over some of Indonesia's former role in brokering between the member states.

In the first half of the 1990s, the PRC refused to discuss the South China Sea with ASEAN, and said that it would only discuss the problem bilaterally with each of the states concerned. The PRC later softened its attitude and allowed the matter to be raised in the ASEAN Regional Forum (ARF), as well as in meetings between Chinese and ASEAN representatives. In 1999, ASEAN agreed on a draft 'code of conduct' with the aim of preventing occupation of additional features and preventing conflict in disputed areas. The PRC agreed to negotiate with ASEAN about such a 'code of conduct', but came up with its own proposal, emphasising joint cooperation more than conflict prevention. There were several rounds of negotiations in 2000–01, with the aim of merging the two proposals into a common text. However, when the ASEAN leaders met with China to discuss the South China Sea at the ASEAN summit in Hanoi in July 2001, the disagreement between Malaysia and the other ASEAN states seemed more acute than the disagreements between the ASEAN states and China.[21]

It took time before issues related to the disputes in the South China Sea could be raised in formal international forums. However, throughout the 1990s, Indonesian Ambassador Hasjim Djalal and Canadian law professor Ian Townsend-Gault organised annual informal track 2 'Managing Potential Conflicts in the South China Sea' workshops. Indonesia hosted them and Canada funded them. All the states around the South China Sea participated (including Taiwan) both in the annual workshops themselves and in a number of technical working groups.[22]

Djalal failed, however, to gain support from the PRC to create a Joint Development Zone in the central part of the South China Sea. In principle, China was in favour of joint cooperation schemes, but never came up with – or endorsed – concrete proposals. The main effect of the workshops was to pave the way for multilateral talks within the forums established by ASEAN and, possibly, for other regional mechanisms in the future. The legal, environmental and maritime experts in the region came to know one another. They also improved their understanding of the Law of the Sea.

Many commentators believed that China's reason for refusing to enter serious discussions about the South China Sea disputes was based on an expectation of gradually establishing a naval hegemony. When the Soviet naval presence at Cam Ranh Bay was scaled down and the US naval and air bases in the Philippines were closed in 1992, there was a feeling that a regional power vacuum had emerged and that a regional arms race might follow. A scare spread of 'creeping Chinese assertiveness'.[23] The PRC contributed to the scare by its naval build-up, by pressuring Taiwan, and by expanding its facilities in the Spratly area, notably its constructions on Mischief Reef. However, with the US naval demonstration in the Taiwan Strait in 1996, Singapore's construction of new base facilities for the US Navy at Changi, and a new visiting-forces agreement between the USA and the Philippines in 1998, it became clear that the USA was not pulling out. The US Commander-in-Chief Pacific (CINCPAC), who was a major player in US diplomacy in East Asia under the Clinton administration, managed a discreet but persistent effort to demonstrate US technological supremacy and foster confidence-building measures. The main aim was to discourage 'rogue states' and to 'engage' the PRC. The new administration of President George W. Bush seemed in 2001 to give up 'engagement' and instead pursue a policy of strategic competition with China. This might lead to a more active posture of the USA also in the South China Sea, where a US spy plane collided with a Chinese fighter jet in April 2001. The fighter jet was lost, whereas the US spy plane was forced to land on Hainan Island. At the time of writing this chapter, the Bush administration's China policy does not yet seem to have been fully clarified, but China clearly tries its best to avoid open conflict.

Throughout the 1990s, both China and Vietnam tried to draw the attention of US oil companies to the exploration opportunities in the South China Sea, albeit with little success. In 1992, the PRC awarded a concession for oil exploration to the small US company Crestone within an area that Vietnam considers to be part of its continental shelf. Vietnamese naval vessels prevented the Sino-American exploration activities, and the Vietnamese government responded in 1996 by awarding a concession in the same area to another far more important US firm (Conoco). However, none of the American companies seemed eager to drill for oil as long as the area was disputed. Generally disappointing results from oil exploration on the Vietnamese continental shelf also reduced the oil industry's expectations of finding huge quantities of oil and gas under the Spratlys.[24]

Oil, however, was not the main bone of contention. The most dangerous incidents in the 1990s were related to fishing activities. Philippine patrol boats would regularly intervene to prevent 'illegal' Chinese fishing. On several occasions they shot at Chinese vessels, in 2000 killing a captain. Each time the PRC protested vehemently. In 1999, there were also Sino–Philippine incidents around Scarborough Shoal, a disputed feature that is not part of either the Paracels or the Spratlys, but situated between Luzon and the Paracels, not far from the former US naval base at Subic Bay.

Fishing disputes have a long tradition in the South China Sea, but a new aspect of the disputes in the 1990s was an increasing awareness of the danger that fish stocks may become depleted, and of other serious threats to the marine environment. This was reflected at the track 2 workshops in Indonesia, since the environment was something everyone could agree to talk about. The participating countries agreed to cooperate in scientific research and in the monitoring of biological diversity. The United Nations Environment Programme (UNEP) also drew up an ambitious Strategic Action Plan for protecting the environment in the South China Sea. For a long time the PRC refused to participate, but gave the green light in late 2000, with the proviso that the programme must not concern disputed areas. Chinese environmental agencies, and also some coastal provinces, have themselves become deeply worried by diminishing fish stocks. The PRC launched a unilateral temporary ban on fishing in 1999, and the protection of fish stocks formed an essential part of the Sino-Vietnamese negotiations leading to the treaty on fishery co-operation in the Gulf of Tonkin in December 2000. The treaty will hopefully be a step forward in terms of both environmental awareness and maritime conflict resolution.

The overall impression is, at the threshold of the 21st century, that most of the countries of ASEAN are readier than ever before to enter a process of conflict resolution, despite some internal disagreements, notably with Malaysia. China has also recently been more forthcoming, but its main priorities still lie elsewhere: to benefit from its WTO membership, reunify with Taiwan, and prevent a US-dominated re-unified Korea. If China decides to enter a process of conflict resolution in the South China Sea, one of the main motives will be to forestall active US involvement. Another motive might be to establish a foreign policy area where Chinese Taibei could be invited to play a role – as a part of China. There is still ample room for pessimism, but it has also been stated, in a recent doctoral thesis, that the seeds of a regional order in the South China Sea have been sown. This possible order would be based partly on continued US naval supremacy, and partly on growing regional cooperation between ASEAN and China.[25]

NOTES

1   This chapter has been written on the basis of Stein Tønnesson: 'An international history of the dispute in the South China sea', *East Asian Institute Working Paper* No. 71, 16 March 2001, which also served as basis for an article submitted to the *Asian Journal of Social Science.*

2   Chinese and Vietnamese historians are here the main practitioners.

3   Good examples of the second kind of history can be found in Greg Austin, *China's Ocean Frontier. International Law, Military Force and National Development,* St Leonards: Allen & Unwin, Australia, 1998. See also Mark J. Valencia, John Van Dyke and Noel Ludwig, *Sharing the Resources of the South China Sea,* The Hague: Kluwer Law International, 1997 (pbk Hawaii University Press, 1999).

4   A source of inspiration for such a history is Michael Yahuda, *The International Politics of the Asia-Pacific, 1945–1995,* London: Routledge, 1996.

5   The Spratly Islands are called the Nanshan Islands in Chinese, Truong Sa in Vietnamese and Kalayaan in the Philippines. Similarly, the Paracels are called Xisha in Chinese and Hoang Sa in Vietnamese. In this volume the English names will be used throughout.

6   Roderich Ptak. 'Die Paracel- und Spratly-Inseln in Sung-, Yüan- und frühen Ming-Texten: Ein maritimes Grenzgebiet?' in Sabine Dabringham and Roderich Ptak (eds), *China and Her Neighbours: Borders, Visions of the Other, Foreign Policy. 10th to 19th Century.* Wiesbaden: Harrassowitz Verlag, 1997.

7   Vietnamese and Chinese historians disagree concerning the meaning of certain names for the islands on Vietnamese maps and in Vietnamese documents from the first four decades of the 19th century. For an 1838 Vietnamese map that clearly includes the Paracels, but not the Spratlys, see Lu Ning. *Flashpoint Spratlys!*, Singapore: Dolphin Books, 1995, p. 184.

8   Thongchai Winichakul, *Siam Mapped. A History of the Geo-body of a Nation.* Honolulu: University of Hawaii Press, 1994.

9   For the history of the British claim, see Geoffrey Marston, 'Abandonment of Territorial Claims: the Cases of Bouvet and Spratly Islands'. *British Yearbook of International Law,* 1986, pp. 337–356.

10 The best general account of this period in the history of the South China Sea disputes remains Marvyn S. Samuels, *Contest for the South China Sea.* New York: Methuen, 1982. The author of this chapter is currently editing a book to be published by Otto Harrassowitz Verlag in Munich in 2002, with historical approaches to the conflicts in the South China Sea. This will include a chapter by Stein Tønnesson on the 1930–56 period.

11 Zou Keyuan, 'The Chinese Traditional Maritime Boundary Line in the South China Sea and Its Legal Consequences for the Resolution of the Dispute over the Spratly Islands'. *The International Journal of Marine and Coastal Law,* vol. 14, no. 1 (March 1999), pp. 27–54.

12 The forthcoming edited volume with historical approaches to the conflict in the South China Sea (see note 9) will include a chapter by Christopher Goscha on the 'Maritime Ho Chi Minh Trail'.

13 *The Philippines and the South China Sea Islands: Overview and Documents,* Manila: Center for International Relations and Strategic Studies, Foreign Service Institute, CIRSS Papers no. 1, December 1993; Ruben C. Carranza Jr, 'The Kalayaan Islands Group: Legal Issues and Problems for the Philippines', *World Bulletin,* vol. 10, no. 5–6 (September–December 1994), p. 49; Wilfrido V. Villacorta, 'The Philippine Territorial Claim in the South China Sea'. In R. D. Hill, Norman G. Owen and E.V. Roberts (eds), *Fishing in Troubled Waters. Proceedings of an Academic Conference on Territorial Claims in the South China Sea.* Hong Kong: University of Hong Kong, Centre of Asian Studies Occasional Papers and Monographs no. 97 (1991), p. 210.

14 Note a/s: Îles Spratley, MAE Direction Générale des Affaires Politiques, Asie-Océanie, 8.3.57, pp. 401–409; Note a/s: des Spratly, MAE, Direction Générale des Affaires Politiques, Asie-Océanie, 15.3.57, pp. 412–413, dos. 522, sous-série Chine 1956–1967, série Asie-Océanie 1944–1955, Ministère des Affaires Etrangères (Paris).

15 A highly readable account of the history of the Law of the Sea, and particularly of UNCLOS III, is Clyde Sanger, *Ordering the Oceans. The Making of the Law of the Sea*. Toronto: University of Toronto Press, 1987.

16 Daniel J. Dzurek, 'Maritime Agreements and Oil Exploration in the Gulf of Thailand'. In Gerald Blake, Martin Pratt, Clive Schofield and Janet Allison Brown (eds), *Boundaries and Energy: Problems and Prospects*. The Hague: Kluwer Law International, 1998, pp. 117–135.

17 A summary of the North Vietnamese statements that are often said to represent a legal *estoppal* of Vietnamese sovereignty claims can be found in Greg Austin, *China's Ocean Frontier*, pp. 126–130.

18 Derek da Cunha, *Soviet Naval Power in the Pacific*. Boulder, CO: Lynne Rienner, 1990.

19 Chang Pao-min, 'A New Scramble for the South China Sea Islands'. *Contemporary Southeast Asia*, vol. 12, no. 1 (June 1990), pp. 24–29; Sheng Lijun, 'Beijing and the Spratlys'. *Issues and Studies*, vol. 31, no. 7 (July 1995), pp. 18(45 (p. 26); Chen Hurng-yu, 'The PRC's South China Sea Policy and Strategies of Occupation in the Paracel and Spratly Islands'. *Issues and Studies*, vol. 36, no. 4 (July/August 2000), pp. 95–131 (pp. 100–102).

20 An English translation of the treaty on fishery cooperation, including a discussion of it, can be found in Zou Keyuan, 'Sino-Vietnamese Fishery Agreement in the Gulf of Tonkin'. *East Asia Institute Working Paper*, no. 77. Singapore, 23 May 2001.

21 Communication 1 Sept. 2001 from Do Hung (Radio France Internationale), who was present in Hanoi during the summit and interviewed several foreign ministers and their advisors. For the code of conduct, see Chapter 9 in this volume.

22 Hasjim Djalal, 'Indonesia and the South China Sea Initiative'. *Ocean Development and International Law*, vol. 32, no. 2, April–June 2001, p. 97–103; Ian Townsend-Gault, 'Preventive Diplomacy and Pro-activity in the South China Sea', *Contemporary Southeast Asia*, vol. 20, no. 2 (August 1998), pp. 171–189; Lee Lai To, *China and the South China Sea Dialogues*. Westport CO: Praeger, 1999.

23 Ian James Storey, 'Creeping Assertiveness: China, the Philippines and the South China Sea Dispute'. *Contemporary Southeast Asia*, vol. 21, no. 1 (April 1999), pp. 95–118.

24 Robert A. Manning, *The Asian Energy Factor*. New York: Palgrave, 2000, pp. viii–ix.

25 Liselotte Odgaard, 'Deterrence and Cooperation in the South China Sea. An Analysis of the Spratly Dispute and the Implications for Regional Order between the PRC and Southeast Asia after the Cold War'. PhD dissertation, Department of Political Science, University of Aarhus, Denmark, December 1999.

3

CLAIMS AND CONFLICT SITUATIONS[1]

Ramses Amer

INTRODUCTION

The purpose of this chapter is twofold: first, to outline the claims made by the countries bordering the South China Sea and second, to identify the areas of overlapping claims and assess the existing conflict situations in the area.

The conflict identification process aims to move beyond a narrow focus on the multilateral conflict over the Spratly archipelago and to display the complex conflict situation in the area. In order to identify the conflict situations in the South China Sea, the emphasis will be on the areas in which there are overlapping claims. As part of the identification process, existing boundary agreements will be taken into consideration. The final step in the identification process will be a discussion relating to the prevailing degree of conflict between the various claimants.

GEOGRAPHICAL SCOPE[2]

Water areas

This study encompasses the South China Sea proper as well as adjacent water areas which can be seen as natural prolongation of the South China Sea proper. In terms of land, the South China Sea proper is bordered by the People's Republic of China (PRC) to the north, Vietnam to the west, Peninsular Malaysia to the southwest, Brunei Darussalam and the two Malaysian states of Sabah and Sarawak to the south, and, finally, the Philippines to the east. The adjacent water areas which can be viewed as a natural prolongation of the South China Sea proper encompass the Gulf of Tonkin located between Vietnam to the west and northwest, mainland China to the north and northeast, the island of Hainan to the east and the South China Sea proper to the south. In the southwest, the Gulf of Thailand lies between Thailand to the west and northwest, Cambodia and Vietnam to the north, Malaysia to the southwest and the South China Sea proper to the west.

Island groups

In the literature on the South China Sea proper it is customary to refer to three groups of islands and to one submerged bank when the different features in the area are discussed and described; namely the Paracel archipelago, the Spratly archipelago, the Pratas Islands and the Maccles-field Bank.

There are four other island groups in the southwestern part of the South China Sea – the Anambas, Badas, Natuna and Tambelan Islands. They are probably not given the same attention as the ones mentioned earlier because Indonesia's ownership is generally recognised.

There are also a number of features, i e. islands, cays and reefs, in the Gulf of Tonkin and in the Gulf of Thailand, but they are not customarily identified as forming island groups as in the South China Sea proper.

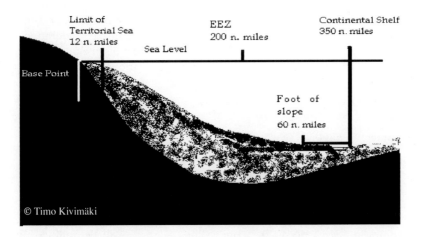

Figure 3.1: Definitions of the maximum extent of EEZ, continental shelf and territorial sea (drawn on the basis of UNCLOS article 76, para 4 (a)(ii) and para 5)

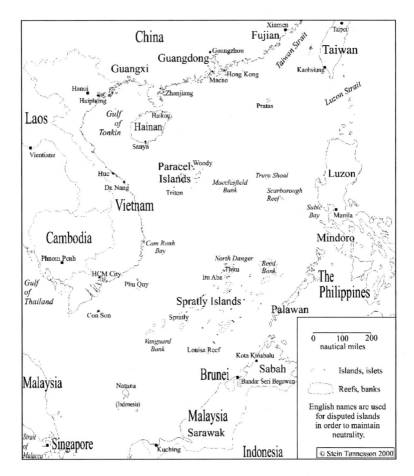

Map 3.1: Map of the South China Sea

Source: *Security Dialogue* 3/2000

CLAIMS BY THE COUNTRIES BORDERING THE SOUTH CHINA SEA[3]

Introduction

In the following analysis the basis and extent of the claims of the various countries bordering on the South China Sea area will be outlined. It should be noted that although the claims and arguments presented have been formulated and used by the various countries, their specific extent has not always been outlined on maps. Furthermore, some of the claims displayed on maps were put forward by earlier governments in some of the countries, in some cases decades ago. The text is formulated in such a way as to reveal ambiguities in some of the lines of argumen-tation. Furthermore, the fact that all claimants refer to international law should not be interpreted as evidence that their respective inter-pretations are well founded.

Brunei's claims

In the southern part of the South China Sea, Brunei Darussalam claims an exclusive economic zone (EEZ) of 200 nautical miles and the natural prolongation of its continental shelf. Brunei also claims sovereignty over Louisa Reef in the Spratly archipelago, but Brunei does not control that reef. Brunei argues in terms of modern international law, i.e. the 1982 United Nations Convention on Law of the Sea (1982 UNCLOS) to sustain its claims to EEZ and continental shelf areas in the South China Sea. Brunei's claim to Louisa Reef seems to be based on the fact that it is located within the continental shelf area claimed by Brunei.

Cambodia's claims

Cambodia has sovereignty claims to islands, cays and reefs in the Gulf of Thailand and controls many of these features. Cambodia also claims an EEZ of 200 nautical miles and the natural prolongation of the continental shelf in the Gulf of Thailand off the Cambodian coast extending southwest to southward in the Gulf of Thailand. The extent of Cam-bodia's claims has gradually been defined since the late 1960s. Cambodia argues in terms of modern international law, i.e. the 1982 UNCLOS, to sustain its claims to EEZ and continental shelf areas in the Gulf of Thailand. The basis of the sovereignty claims to features in the Gulf seems to be historical.

The PRC's claims

The PRC, alongside Taiwan, has the most extensive claims in the South China Sea. The PRC claims sovereignty over the Paracel and Spratly archipelagos and the Pratas Islands. As shown by official Chinese maps, the PRC claims the major parts of the sea areas of the South China Sea as 'historical waters' in a U-shaped area southwards to the east of the Vietnamese coastline, turning eastwards to the northeast of the Indo-nesian controlled Natuna Islands, and to the north of the Malaysian state of Sarawak, then turning northeastwards along the coast of Brunei Darussalam and the Malaysian state of Sabah, and finally northwards to the west of the Philippines. The PRC also claims an EEZ of 200 nautical miles and the natural prolongation of the continental shelf in the Gulf of Tonkin.

Currently the PRC controls the whole Paracel archipelago. It took control of the eastern part of the Paracels in 1956 and the western part in 1974. The PRC gained its first foothold in the Spratly archipelago in 1988. Since then it has continued to expand its control over islands and reefs in the archipelago. It is estimated that the PRC currently controls some ten islands, cays and reefs in the Spratlys. The Pratas Islands are under Taiwanese control.

The PRC's claims in the South China Sea are based on historical records and maps which are used to sustain two kinds of claims. First, they show that China discovered the island groups in the South China Sea, and second, they show how Chinese people occupied the islands and developed them. More recently, the PRC has also increasingly been arguing in terms of modern international law, i.e. the 1982 UNCLOS, to substantiate its claims to water and continental shelf areas in the South China Sea.

Indonesia's claims

Indonesia controls the Anambas, Badas, Natuna and Tambelan Islands. Indonesia also claims an EEZ of 200 nautical miles and the natural prolongation of the continental shelf extending into the South China Sea proper to the north of the Anambas Islands and to the north and east of the Natuna Islands.

Indonesia regards itself as an archipelagic state and therefore it follows the Archipelagic Principle, which implies that water areas within the straight baselines joining 'appropriate' points of the outermost islands in the Indonesian archipelago are to be considered as territorial waters and the claims to EEZ and continental shelf areas are measured from the outermost islands of the Indonesian archipelago.

Indonesian control over the islands is based on the notion that they form part of the Indonesian archipelago. To sustain its views on the Archipelagic Principle and claims to water and continental shelf areas in the South China Sea, Indonesia argues in terms of modern international law, i.e. the 1982 UNCLOS.

Malaysia's claims

Malaysia claims sovereignty over the southern part of the Spratly archi-pelago. It also claims an EEZ of 200 miles and the natural prolongation of the continental shelf in the South China Sea off the east coast of Peninsular Malaysia and off the coasts of the states of Sabah and Sarawak. Malaysia also claims an EEZ of 200 miles and the natural prolongation of the continental shelf in the Gulf of Thailand off the northeast coast of Peninsular Malaysia. The extent of its claims has gradually been defined since the 1960s.

Currently Malaysia controls at least three islands and reefs in the Spratly archipelago. Malaysia first took control of Swallow Reef in 1983 and has since then expanded its control.

Malaysia argues in terms of modern international law (i.e. the 1982 UNCLOS) to uphold its claims to EEZ and continental shelf areas in the South China Sea. Malaysia's claim to part of the Spratlys seems to be based on the fact that these features are located within the continental shelf area claimed by Malaysia.

The Philippines' claims

The Philippines claims sovereignty over almost the whole Spratly archipelago with the exception of Spratly Island itself, Royal Charlotte Reef, Swallow Reef and Louisa Reef. The nation also claims an EEZ of 200 nautical miles and the natural prolongation of the continental shelf in the South China Sea to the west of the country.

The Philippines controls some eight islands, cays and reefs in the Spratly archipelago. The nation first took control of five islands, cays and reefs in the early 1970s and has since expanded its control.

The Philippines regards itself as an archipelagic state and therefore follows the Archipelagic Principle, which implies that claims to EEZ and continental shelf areas are measured from the outermost islands of the Filipino archipelago.

The claims of sovereignty over the major part of the Spratly archipelago are based on the notion of discovery. To sustain its views on the Archipelagic Principle and claims to EEZ and continental shelf areas in the South China Sea, the Philippines argues in terms of modern international law, i.e. the 1982 UNCLOS.

Taiwan's claims

Taiwan pursues the same claims as the PRC in the South China Sea.[4] It can be argued that both the PRC and Taiwan are pursuing a 'Chinese' claim. Among the islands in the South China Sea, Taiwan claims sovereignty over the Paracel and Spratly archipelagos and the Pratas Islands. Taiwan also claims the major parts of the sea areas of the South China Sea as 'historical waters' in a U-shaped area southwards to the east of the Vietnamese coastline turning eastwards to the northeast of the Indonesian controlled Natuna Islands and to the north of the Malaysian state of Sarawak, then turning northeastwards along the coast of Brunei Darussalam and the Malaysian State of Sabah, and finally northwards to the west of the Philippines. Taiwan also claims an EEZ of 200 nautical miles and the natural prolongation of the continental shelf in the Gulf of Tonkin.

Taiwan controls Itu Aban Island in the Spratly archipelago and the Pratas Islands. Taiwan does not control any island, cay or reef in the Paracel archipelago, which is fully under the PRC's control.

Taiwan's claims in the South China Sea are based on historical records and maps which are used to uphold two kinds of claims. First, they show that China discovered the island groups in the South China Sea, and second, they show how Chinese people occupied the islands and developed them. In more recent times Taiwan has also increasingly been arguing in terms of modern international law, i.e. the 1982 UNCLOS, to substantiate its claims to water and continental shelf areas in the South China Sea.

Thailand's claims

Thailand has sovereignty claims to islands, cays and reefs in the Gulf of Thailand and controls most of these features. Thailand also claims an EEZ of 200 nautical miles and the natural prolongation of the continental shelf in the Gulf of Thailand corresponding to the northern and western parts of the Gulf. The claim to the northern part of the Gulf, i.e. the Bight of Thailand, is a historical claim as established by a Royal Proclamation in 1959. The extent of Thailand's claims in the Gulf of Thailand has gradually been defined since the early 1970s. Thailand argues in terms of historic rights and in terms of modern international law, i.e. the 1982 UNCLOS, to uphold its claims.

Vietnam's claims

Vietnam claims sovereignty over the whole of the Paracel and Spratly archipelagos. It has claims to an EEZ of 200 nautical miles and to the natural prolongation of the continental shelf in the South China Sea to the east and the southeast of the Vietnamese coastline and in the Gulf of Tonkin. Vietnam also has sovereignty claims to islands, cays and reefs, to an EEZ of 200 nautical miles, and to the natural prolongation of the continental shelf in the Gulf of Thailand.

Vietnam currently controls more then 20 islands, cays and reefs in the Spratly archipelago. The control over features in the archipelago has gradually been expanded since the mid-1970s when Vietnam controlled six of the features. Vietnam does not control any island, cay or reef in the Paracel archipelago, which is fully under the PRC's control. Vietnam also controls islands, cays and reefs in the Gulf of Thailand.

Vietnam's sovereignty claims to the Paracel and Spratly archipelagos are based on historical records from pre-colonial times and from the French colonial period. Interestingly enough, the unified Vietnam also relies on documentation from the former Republic of Vietnam to substantiate its claims. Also the sovereignty claim to features in the Gulf of Thailand seems to be historical. In more recent times, Vietnam has increasingly been arguing in terms of modern international law, i.e. the 1982 UNCLOS, to substantiate its claims to EEZ and continental shelf areas in the South China Sea proper, in the Gulf of Thailand and in the Gulf of Tonkin.

OVERLAPPING CLAIMS

Introduction

In order to give the overview of the overlapping claims more structure, the discussion begins with the northern part of the South China Sea and then moves southwards. The overview will be divided into two parts: one deals with the overlapping claims to water and continental shelf areas, while the other deals with overlapping sovereignty claims to islands, cays and reefs. The overview does not take into consideration any existing boundary agreement as they will be outlined in the next section.

Water, EEZ and continental shelf areas

- In the northwestern part of the South China Sea, the Philippines and Taiwan have overlapping claims to EEZ and continental shelf areas to the north of the Philippines and to the south of Taiwan.
- The PRC, Taiwan and Vietnam have overlapping claims to EEZ and continental shelf areas in the Gulf of Tonkin.
- The PRC's and Taiwan's claims to so-called 'historical waters' in the South China Sea overlap to varying degrees with claims to EEZ and continental shelf areas made by Vietnam to the east of the Vietnamese coast, by Indonesia to the northeast of the Natuna Islands, by Malaysia to the north of the coast of the state of Sarawak and to the northwest of the state of Sabah, by Brunei Darussalam to north of its coast, and by the Philippines to the west of the Filipino archipelago.
- Brunei and Malaysia have overlapping claims to EEZ and continental shelf areas off the coast of Brunei and Sarawak.
- Vietnam's continental shelf claims to the south and southeast of its coast overlap with Indonesia's continental shelf claims to the north of the Natuna Islands.
- Indonesia and Malaysia have overlapping claims to EEZ and continental shelf areas in an area to the east of Peninsular Malaysia and to the west and north of the Anambas Islands as well as to the east-northeast of the Natuna Islands and to the northwest of Kalimantan (Indonesian part of Borneo) and to the west of Sarawak.
- Another area of overlapping claims to EEZ and continental shelf areas can be found to the southwest of Vietnam, to the east-northeast of the east coast of Peninsular Malaysia and to the southeast of the coast of Thailand. The claims of Malaysia, Thailand

and Vietnam overlap in one area. In other areas bilateral claims overlap between Malaysia and Thailand, Malaysia and Vietnam, and between Thailand and Vietnam, respectively.

- There are overlapping claims to EEZ and continental shelf areas in the Gulf of Thailand off the coasts of Cambodia, Thailand and Vietnam. The claims of Cambodia, Thailand and Vietnam overlap in one area. In other areas bilateral claims overlap between Cambodia and Thailand, Cambodia and Vietnam, and between Thailand and Vietnam, respectively.

Islands, cays and reefs

- The first area with overlapping sovereignty claims to islands, cays and reefs are the Pratas Islands located in the northwestern part of the South China Sea, both the PRC and Taiwan claim sovereignty over these.
- The second area is the Paracel archipelago to which the PRC, Taiwan and Vietnam have overlapping sovereignty claims.
- There are also overlapping sovereignty claims to the whole or parts of the Spratly archipelago with the PRC, Taiwan and Vietnam claiming the whole archipelago, the Philippines claiming the major part of it, Malaysia claiming the southern part, and Brunei Darussalam claiming Louisa Reef.
- In the Gulf of Thailand there are overlapping sovereignty claims by Cambodia and Vietnam to islands, cays and reefs located off the Cambodian and Vietnamese coasts.
- Different claims to water, EEZ and continental shelf areas based on either claims to island groups or de facto control of such island groups or of some islands, cays and reefs expand the areas with potentially overlapping claims.

Boundary agreements

The following agreements have been reached relating to areas of overlapping claims in the South China Sea:

- On 27 October 1969 Indonesia and Malaysia signed an agreement delimiting their continental shelf boundary. The agreement was ratified on 7 November 1969. The agreement separates Indonesian waters and continental shelf areas around the Anambas and Natuna Islands and the northwest of Kalimantan (Indonesian part of Borneo) from Malaysian waters and continental shelf areas to the east of Peninsular Malaysia and to the west of Sarawak. [5]
- On 21 February 1979 Malaysia and Thailand signed a Memorandum of Understanding on the delimitation of their continental shelf

boundary in the Gulf of Thailand. The Memorandum did not specify the exact location of the boundary but it stipulated that negotiations should continue to complete the delimitation of the boundary. In this context another Memorandum of Understanding reached by the two countries on the same day is of relevance, namely on the establishment of a joint authority for the exploitation of the sea-bed in a 'defined' area of the continental shelf in the Gulf of Thailand. The two countries agreed to exploit the resources of the sea-bed in the disputed area through mutual cooperation and they decided to establish a Joint Authority to be known as *Malaysia–Thailand Joint Authority*.[6] Malaysia and Thailand also signed a Treaty on 24 October 1979 relating to the delimitation of the territorial seas between the two countries in the Gulf of Thailand.[7]

- Vietnam and the then People's Republic of Kampuchea (PRK) signed an agreement on 'historic waters' on 7 July 1982. These 'historic waters' were defined as being located between the coast of Kien Giang Province, Phu Quoc Island and the Tho Chu islands on the Vietnamese side and the coast of Kampot Province and the Poulo Wai islands on the Cambodian side. The agreement stipulated that the two countries would hold, 'at a suitable time', negotiations to determine the maritime frontier in the 'historic waters'. Pending such a settlement, the two countries would continue to regard the Brévié Line drawn in 1939 as the dividing line for the islands within the 'historic waters' and the exploitation of the zone would be decided by 'common agreement'.[8] This was followed by the signing of a treaty on the settlement of border problems between Cambodia and Vietnam and an agreement on border regulations on 20 July 1983 in Phnom Penh.[9] Finally, on 27 December 1985, the Treaty on the Delimitation of the Vietnam–Kampuchea Frontier was signed by the two countries and ratified by the Council of the State of Vietnam on 30 January 1986 and by the National Assembly of the PRK on 7 February 1986. The principle governing the settlement of the border disputes between the two countries was to be the respect for the 'present demarcation line', specified as 'the line that was in existence at the time' of independence. This 'line' was retained by the two countries, following the principle *uti possidetis* (as you possess). It was also stated that the common border 'on land and on their historical waters' was based on the borderline drawn on a 1/100,000 map in use before 1954 or up to that year.[10]

- Between Malaysia and Vietnam an agreement was reached on 5 June 1992 to engage in joint development in areas of overlapping claims to continental shelf areas in the Gulf of Thailand to the southwest of Vietnam and to the east-northeast off the east coast of Peninsular Malaysia.[11]

- Thailand and Vietnam reached an agreement delimiting their continental shelf and EEZ boundaries in a disputed area in the Gulf of Thailand to the southwest of Vietnam and to the northeast of Thailand on 9 August 1997.[12]

- The PRC and Vietnam signed an agreement on the demarcation of the territorial waters, the EEZs and the continental shelves of the two countries in the Gulf of Tonkin on 25 December 2000.[13]

CONFLICT SITUATIONS

As outlined above, formal bilateral agreements on boundary delimitation have been reached between: Indonesia and Malaysia; Malaysia and Thailand; Vietnam and the then PRK (Cambodia); Thailand and Vietnam; the PRC and Vietnam. Agreements on joint development in disputed areas have been reached between Malaysia and Thailand and between Malaysia and Vietnam, respectively. In the context of this study, the two cases in the second category will not be identified as conflict situations despite the fact that the disputes have not been formally settled. This is because the disputes are formally managed for the time being.

The agreements between Vietnam and Cambodia were not recognised by all parties within Cambodia for most of the 1990s, but in recent years Cambodia has indicated an acceptance of the agreements. However, new bilateral talks on the status of their borders between the countries have been initiated to reach a solution to remaining disputed issues.[14] Therefore, in the context of this study, the border disputes between Vietnam and Cambodia in the Gulf of Thailand are not classified as settled, and there is a bilateral conflict situation between the two countries.

In this section the existing territorial disputes will be identified with a view to further narrowing down the number of potential conflicts. This will be done through a process of assessing general political factors.

The overlapping claims which cover the most extensive area are those between the PRC and Taiwan, since both of them claim sovereignty over the Paracel archipelago, the Spratly archipelago, the Pratas Islands, most of the water areas in the South China Sea proper, and EEZ and continental shelf areas in the Gulf of Tonkin. In fact, the PRC and Taiwan are pursuing similar claims in the South China Sea area.[15] Should this state of affairs be perceived as an extensive territorial conflict between the PRC and Taiwan? First, it should be observed that both the PRC and Taiwan are pursuing what could be termed a 'Chinese' claim and there is therefore no incompatibility between them as both parties are in agreement that the areas in question are 'Chinese' territory.

Second, the overall relations between the PRC and Taiwan have been characterised by animosity and a high degree of tension for reasons other than the overlapping claims in the South China Sea area. These tensions date all the way back to the victory of the Communist Party in the Chinese civil war and the establishment of the PRC in 1949. Following this line of argument, it can be claimed that there is no activated conflict situation between the PRC and Taiwan in the South China Sea area.[16]

The PRC's claim to 'historical waters' in the South China Sea proper overlaps with the claims to EEZ and continental shelf areas of Vietnam, Indonesia, Malaysia, Brunei and the Philippines. Thus there are bilateral disputes between the PRC and each of the other five countries. The PRC's sovereignty claim to the Paracel archipelago is also a bilateral dispute with Vietnam. The PRC's sovereignty claim to the whole Spratly archipelago creates another bilateral dispute with Vietnam over various areas that are not claimed by other Southeast Asian countries. In addition to the disputed areas with Vietnam, the PRC's claim results in a major multilateral dispute which also involves Brunei, Malaysia and the Philippines. In short, all areas of overlapping claims identified above involving the PRC and the Southeast Asian countries can be classified as territorial disputes.

It has been established that Taiwan's claims in the South China Sea area overlap with the claims of the following countries: Brunei Darusalam, Indonesia, Malaysia, the Philippines and Vietnam. Furthermore, Taiwan's claims to EEZ and continental shelf areas in the Gulf of Tonkin overlap with Vietnam's claims in the Gulf. To discuss Taiwan's overlapping claims with these countries presents two intriguing problems. The first one has been identified above, i.e. the fact that Taiwan is pursuing similar claims to the PRC in the South China Sea. Second, in political terms, none of the Southeast Asian claimants recognises Taiwan as anything but a province of the PRC, i.e. the one-China policy, and from this follows that no formal diplomatic relations exist between these countries and Taiwan. Taking these two factors into consideration, is it possible to argue that the afore-mentioned Southeast Asian countries have territorial disputes with Taiwan, or should it be argued that they are facing 'Chinese' claims and that the disputes have to be viewed as Sino–Bruneian, Sino–Indonesian, Sino–Malaysian, Sino–Filipino or Sino–Vietnamese conflicts? In the context of this study, the Taiwanese presence in any of the areas in which it has a claim will be viewed as creating a territorial dispute between Taiwan and the Southeast Asian countries involved.

There is no Taiwanese presence in the Paracel archipelago, therefore the overlapping sovereignty claims by Taiwan and Vietnam to the archipelago is not regarded as a dispute in the context of this study. Taiwan's and

Vietnam's overlapping claims in the Gulf of Tonkin will not be classified as a conflict situation since Taiwan does not have a presence in the area.

The situation in the Spratly archipelago is different, since Malaysia, the Philippines and Vietnam, respectively, control several islands, cays and reefs and Taiwan controls Itu Aban Island. There are therefore territorial disputes with overlapping sovereignty claims to the whole or parts of the Spratly archipelago between Taiwan and those three countries, as well as between Taiwan and Brunei with its sovereignty claims to Louisa Reef.

Taiwan's extensive claims to 'historical waters' in the South China Sea proper overlap with claims made by Brunei, Indonesia, Malaysia, Vietnam and the Philippines, thus there are bilateral disputes between Taiwan and each of these countries. Furthermore, the overlapping claims in the area south of Taiwan and north of the Philippines create a bilateral conflict situation in its own right.

From the above discussion relating to both the PRC and Taiwan it can be concluded that overlapping sovereignty claims to the whole or parts of the Spratly archipelago create a multilateral conflict situation involving the following countries: Brunei Darussalam, Malaysia, the Philippines, the PRC, Taiwan and Vietnam.

A pertinent question emerges: Between which countries could the Spratly conflict potentially surface as an issue in the context of other bilateral territorial disputes? Most such situations have already been identified above in connection with the analyses relating to the PRC and Taiwan, respectively, but the discussion can be expanded further. First, between the PRC and Vietnam with their overlapping claims to the whole Paracel archipelago and to water and continental shelf areas to the east of the Vietnamese coast. In this context it can be noted that the PRC and Vietnam reached an agreement relating to their boundary issues in the Tonkin Gulf in late December 2000.[17] Second, between Brunei Darussalam and Malaysia with overlapping claims to water and continental shelf areas off the coast of Brunei and the Malaysian state of Sarawak.

There are two additional areas of overlapping claims to water and/or continental shelf areas. The first area is to the northeast of Indonesia's Natuna Islands, where Indonesia's claims overlap with the PRC's and Taiwan's claims to 'historical waters'. Thus there is a Sino–Indonesian conflict situation. The second area is to the north of the Natuna Islands and to the south to southeast of Vietnam, where Indonesia and Vietnam are pursuing claims to continental shelf areas.

In the Gulf of Thailand it has been noted that the bilateral dispute between Thailand and Vietnam has been formally resolved and the bilateral disputes between Malaysia and Thailand and between Malaysia and Vietnam, respectively, have been handled through joint develop-ment agreements. However, these three countries are still involved in a trilateral conflict situation in one area of the Gulf of Thailand where their claims overlap. Furthermore, Cambodia still has bilateral disputes with Thailand and Vietnam, respectively, in other parts of the Gulf of Thailand. However, no trilateral conflict situation exists involving Cambodia, Thailand and Vietnam since the latter two have resolved their bilateral dispute in the area.

To sum up, the above analysis has suggested a way of overcoming some conflict situations, most importantly the potential one based on overlapping claims between the PRC and Taiwan. Another example is Taiwan's and Vietnam's overlapping sovereignty claims to the Paracel archipelago. Nevertheless, the majority of the areas of overlapping claims have been classified as conflict situations. Most are bilateral territorial disputes with two exceptions: first, the multilateral Spratly conflict with overlapping sovereignty claims to the whole or parts of the Spratly archipelago by six countries and, second, the trilateral dispute in the Gulf of Thailand involving Malaysia, Thailand and Vietnam. The other identified conflict situations are bilateral and they encompass the following: Brunei–Malaysia, Brunei–PRC, Brunei–Taiwan, Cambodia–Thailand, Cambodia–Vietnam, PRC–Indonesia, PRC–Malaysia, PRC–Philippines, PRC–Vietnam, Indonesia–Taiwan, Indonesia–Vietnam, Malaysia–Taiwan, Malaysia–Vietnam, Philippines–Taiwan, Philippines–Vietnam and Taiwan–Vietnam.

This overview has displayed the complex conflict situation in the South China Sea by highlighting the extent of overlapping territorial claims in the area. It has shown that the Spratly conflict is the most extensive in terms of the number of involved claimants, but there are also many bilateral disputes in the South China Sea. To determine how activated these bilateral conflict situations are is beyond the scope of this study as it would involve a detailed examination of the diplomatic interaction between the involved countries in each dispute.[18]

NOTES

1   The approach used in this chapter is derived from Ramses Amer, 'The "Oil Factor" and the Conflicts in the South China Sea'. In Farid Abbaszadegan and Franz Wennberg (eds), *Olja – en förbannelse?* [Oil – a curse?], Skrifter utgivna av Sällskapet för asienstudier 9 (Uppsala, 1999), pp. 35–60; and, from Ramses Amer, *Conflict Situations and Conflict Management in the South China Sea*, UPSK Occasional Paper, no. 5/00 (Bangi, Selangor: Unit Pengajian Strategi and Keselamatan [Strategic and Security Studies Unit], Universiti Kebangsaan Malaysia, 2000).

2   For details, see Dieter Heinzig, *Disputed Islands in the South China Sea. Paracels – Spratlys – Pratas – Macclesfield Bank* (Wiesbaden: Otto Harrassowitz

and the Institute of Asian Affairs in Hamburg, 1976); Merwyn S. Samuels, *Contest for the South China Sea* (New York and London: Methuen, 1982).

3   For studies dealing with the overall situations and claims, see among others: Bob Catley and Malmur Keliat, *Spratlys: The Dispute in the South China Sea* (Aldershot, Brookfield, Singapore and Sydney: Ashgate, 1997); John Chao K.T., 'South China Sea: Boundary Problems Relating to the Nansha and Hsisha Islands', in Hungdah Chiu (ed.), *Chinese Yearbook of International Law and Affairs*, vol. 9, (1989–90), pp. 66–156; Jorge R. Coquia, 'Maritime Boundary Problems in the South China Sea', *University of British Columbia Law Review*, vol. 24, no. 1 (1990), pp. 117–125; Daniel J. Dzurek, *The Spratly Islands Dispute: Who's On First?* Maritime Briefing vol. 2, no. 1 (Durham: International Boundaries Research Unit, University of Durham, 1996); B.A. Hamzah, 'Jurisdictional Issues and Conflicting Claims in the Spratlys', *Foreign Relations Journal*, vol. V, no. 1 (March 1990), pp. 1–26; Victor Prescott, *The South China Sea: Limits of National Claims*, MIMA Paper (Kuala Lumpur: Maritime Institute of Malaysia [MIMA], 1996); Victor Prescott, *The Gulf of Thailand* (Kuala Lumpur: Maritime Institute of Malaysia (MIMA), 1998). For studies dealing with specific countries, see among others: Hermogenes C. Fernandez, *The Philippine 200-Mile Economic Zone. Sources of Possible Cooperation or Disputes with Other Countries*, Series One Monograph, no. 3 (October 1982) (Makati, Metro Manila: Development Academy of the Philippine Press, for the Secretariat to the Cabinet Committee on the Law of the Sea Treaty); Lo Chi-kin, *China's Policy towards Territorial Disputes. The Case of the South China Sea Islands* (London and New York: Routledge, 1989); Kuan-Ming Sun, 'Policy of the Republic of China towards the South China Sea. Recent Developments', *Marine Policy*, vol. 19, no. 5 (September 1995), pp. 401–409; Sheng Lijun; *China's Policy towards the Spratly Islands in the 1990s*, Working Paper no. 287 (Canberra: Strategic and Defence Studies Centre, The Australian National University, June 1995); The Hoang Sa and Truong Sa, *Archipelagoes and International Law* (Hanoi: Ministry of Foreign Affairs, Socialist Republic of Vietnam, April 1988); The Hoang Sa and Truong Sa, *Archipelagoes Vietnamese Territories* (Hanoi: Ministry of Foreign Affairs, Socialist Republic of Vietnam, 1981); *The Philippines and the South China Sea Islands: Overview and Documents*, CIRSS Papers, no. 1 (December 1993) (Pasay City, Metro Manila: Center for International Relations and Strategic Studies, Foreign Service Institute); Mark J. Valencia, *Malaysia and the Law of the Sea. The Foreign Policy Issues, the Options and their Implications* (Kuala Lumpur: Institute of Strategic and International Studies [ISIS Malaysia], 1991); Mark J. Valencia, *China and the South China Sea Disputes*, Adelphi Paper, no. 298 (Oxford: Oxford University Press and the International Institute for Strategic Studies [IISS], 1995).

4   For a detailed comparison between the PRC's and Taiwan's claims and policies, see Chen Hurng-yu, 'A Comparison between Taipei and Peking in their Policies and Concepts Regarding the South China Sea', *Issues and Studies*, vol. 29, no. 9 (1993), pp. 22–58.

5   Vivian L. Forbes, *Indonesia's Maritime Boundaries*, A Malaysian Institute of Maritime Affairs Monograph (Kuala Lumpur: Malaysian Institute of Maritime Affairs [MIMA], 1995), pp. 20–22 and Annex E.1.

6   Kriangsak Kittichaisaree, *The Law of the Sea and Maritime Boundary Delimitation in South-East Asia* (Singapore, Oxford and New York: Oxford University Press, 1987), pp. 100–103 and 189–194; 'Malaysia-Thailand (Gulf of Thailand Continental Shelf) (1979)', in Jonathan I. Charney and Lewis M. Alexander (eds), *International Maritime Boundaries*, Vol. I (Dordrecht, Boston and London: Martinus Nijhoff Publishers and the American Society of International Law, 1993), pp. 1099–1110.

7   'Malaysia-Thailand (Territorial Sea) (1979)', ibid., pp. 1091–1098; and, Kittichaisaree, *op. cit.*, pp. 186–188.

8   For the full text of the Agreement of 7 July 1982 see British Broadcasting Corporation, Summary of World Broadcasts, Part Three, Far East 7074 A3/7–8 (10 July 1982) (hereafter 'BBC/FE'). The text of the Agreement has also been reproduced in an English-language version as 'Appendix 2' in Kittichaisaree, *op. cit.*, pp. 180–181. Interestingly enough the 'full text' of the Agreement transmitted by the official Cambodian news agency (SPK) on July 8 omitted the sentence: 'Patrolling and surveillance in these historical waters will be jointly conducted by the two sides', which was included in Article 3 of the version published by the Vietnamese News Agency and reproduced in Kittichaisaree's study (BBC/FE/7074 A3/8, 7076/A3/7 [13 July 1982]; and, Kittichaisaree, op. cit., pp. 180–181).

9   BBC/FE/7393 A3/1 (23 July 1983). See also Quang Nghia; 'Vietnam–Kampuchea Border Issue Settled', *Vietnam Courier*, no. 4 (1986), pp. 8–9.

10 For reports from Vietnam and the PRK announcing the signing of the Treaty and for details see BBC/FE/8143 A3/1–3 (30 December 1985). See also Quang, *op. cit.*, pp. 8–9.

11 Ramses Amer, 'Vietnam and Its Neighbours: The Border Dispute Dimension', *Contemporary Southeast Asia*, vol. 17, no. 3 (December 1995), p. 306.

12 BBC/FE/2996 B/4–5 (13 August 1997). See also Nguyen Hong Thao, 'Vietnam's First Maritime Boundary Agreement', *Boundary and Security Bulletin*, vol. 5, no. 3 (1997), pp. 74–79; Nguyen Hong Thao, 'Vietnam and Thailand Settle Maritime Disputes in the Gulf of Thailand', *The MIMA Bulletin*, vol. 2/98 (1998), pp. 7–10.

13 Information about the agreement can be found in the text of the joint statement on comprehensive cooperation issued on 25 December 2000 in connection with a high-level Sino–Vietnamese summit in Beijing. The joint statement has been reproduced in: 'Déclaration Vietnam–China sur la coopération au nouveau siècle', Agence vietnamienne de l'information (AVI) (25 Dec. 2000); and in 'Joint Viet Nam–China Statement for Comprehensive Cooperation (take two)', Vietnam News Agency (VNA) (26 December 2000. From the web site of Vietnam News Agency (http://www.vnagency.com.vn/).

14 During the 1990s there have been periods of deep tension relating to the border issues in relations between Cambodia and Vietnam. For details on the ongoing talks and the periods of tension, see Ramses Amer, 'The Border Conflicts between Cambodia and Vietnam', *Boundary and Security Bulletin*, vol. 5, no. 2 (Summer 1997), pp. 80–91; Ramses Amer, 'Expanding ASEAN's Conflict Management Framework in Southeast Asia: The Border Dispute

Dimension', *Asian Journal of Political Science*, vol. 6, no. 2 (December 1998), pp. 47–48 (hereafter Amer, 'Expanding ASEAN'); Ramses Amer, 'Managing Border Disputes in Southeast Asia', *Kajian Malaysia, Journal of Malaysian Studies*, Special Issue on Conflict and Conflict Management in Southeast Asia, vol. 23, nos. 1-2 (June-December 2000), pp.40-42 (hereafter Amer, 'Managing Border Disputes').

15 For a detailed comparison between the PRC's and Taiwan's claims and policies, see Chen 1993, op. cit, pp. 22–58.

16 In this context it can be observed that the political changes within Taiwan and the potential scenario of Taiwan declaring independence could have a significant impact also on the situation in the South China Sea. An activated conflict situation between the PRC and Taiwan could emerge if an independent Taiwan were to pursue the present extensive claims in the South China Sea as it would no longer be a 'Chinese' claim in the area.

17 For details about the Sino–Vietnamese territorial disputes see Ramses Amer, 'The Territorial Disputes between China and Vietnam and Regional Stability', *Contemporary Southeast Asia*, vol. 19, no. 1 (1997), pp. 86–113; Ramses Amer, 'The Challenge of Managing the Border Disputes between China and Vietnam', *EAI Working Paper*, no. 16 (24 November 1998) (Singapore: East Asian Institute [EAI], National University of Singapore); Ramses Amer, 'The Management of the Border Disputes Between China and Vietnam and its Regional Implications', EIAS Publications, *Briefing Papers*, BP 00/03 (Brussels: European Institute for Asian Studies [EIAS], October 2000); Ramses Amer, 'The Sino-Vietnamese Approach to Managing Border Disputes', *Maritime Briefing*, vol. 3, no. 5, Durham: International Boundaries Research Unit, University of Durham (forthcoming 2002).

18 For detailed analysis of the territorial disputes among the ASEAN members, see Amer, *Expanding ASEAN*, pp. 33–56; and Amer, 'Managing Border Disputes'.

PART II: DIMENSIONS

4

DANGERS TO THE ENVIRONMENT

Tom Næss

THE SOUTH CHINA SEA MARITIME ENVIRONMENT

The South China Sea is an integrated ecosystem. It is one of the richest seas in the world in terms of marine flora and fauna; coral reefs, mangroves, seagrass beds, fish and plants (Bateman 1999:1).[1] For the littorals, and especially for archipelagic states like Indonesia and the Philippines, fishing and marine-based tourism provide valuable foreign exchange earnings and job opportunities. But, at the same time, population pressure and rapid economic growth threaten the coastal and marine habitats upon which the populations of this region so heavily depend. In fact, fisheries alone contribute approximately 65% of the animal protein consumed in the Philippines, Malaysia and Indonesia, with the highest dependency being found among the poorest coastal dwellers. With economic growth on the one side and socio-economic problems on the other, there exist a number of threats to the marine environment. Overfishing, sedimentation, sewage, industrial waste, oil spills, habitat destruction, and depletion of mangroves and coral reefs due to particular fishing techniques are some of the problems to be addressed if the South China Sea is not to become a dumping ground for regional pollution and industrial waste.[2]

The linkages to the South China Sea conflict might not be that obvious, as the conflict seems to centre on sovereignty and judicial claims to central parts of the sea, rather than fishing quotas or biodiversity. However, even though the South China Sea conflict may appear to be irreconcilable, this should not prevent claimants from pursuing responsible and sustainable environmental policies. National, regional and international environmental initiatives co-exist within the region, but what is lacking is an integrated regional approach to the totality of problems in the area. The first part of this chapter will deal with the environmental challenges; in the second part an overview of existing environmental initiatives will be presented.

RESOURCE MANAGEMENT: FISHERIES

Fish is an important source of food and income for Southeast and East Asians. The Southeast Asian region alone produces over 8.0 million metric tons live weight of marine fish annually; this represents about 10% of the total world catch and 23% of the total catch in Asia. The South China Sea ranks fourth among the world's 19 fishing zones in terms of total annual marine production. Because economic activities and productive ecosystems – coral reefs, mangroves and estuaries – are situated in coastal areas, some 70% of the Southeast Asian population are coastal dwellers, representing approximately 270 million, or roughly 5% of the world's population.[3]

The development of efficient fishing fleets and industries is seen as an important task by most governments in the region. However, increased fishing also threatens the environment. The pressure on coastal fish stocks is growing as a result of the introduction of modern fishing techniques like trawling. Trawls are often dragged along the sea-bed destroying corals; and because they are so efficient, coastal fish stocks are depleted. Little remains to be caught by smaller fishing boats. At the same time, primitive destructive fishing methods are still used in Indonesia, Vietnam, the PRC and the Philippines, and also to a limited extent in Thailand and Malaysia. The use of explosives and chemicals destroys coral reefs and habitats of species as well as their breeding grounds. Recent surveys conducted in Indonesia, which is the world''s centre of coral reef diversity with some 75,000 sq km of coral, reveal that only 29% of coral reefs are in a good condition (i.e. with more than 50% live coral cover), 46% are in a poor condition and 14% in a critical condition.[4] The littoral areas, mostly developing countries, recognise that fish is a resource that may be threatened if the current trend continues, but they also need fish to feed their populations and to uphold industries based on fishery products. East Asia was not only the fastest growing economic region in the world in the 1980s and 1990s, it was also one of the most heavily populated regions. The governments have to provide food for hungry masses, and seafood is the main animal protein source for most Asians; two-thirds of the animal protein consumed in Asia comes from fish and crustaceans. Thus, there exists a struggle between socio-economic and environmental concerns, with the former often winning, as food and economic income are more important to the individual than sustainable use of coastal resources.

BIODIVERSITY MANAGEMENT: CORAL REEFS, MANGROVES, SEAGRASS, ESTUARIES AND WETLANDS

Roughly 30% of the world's coral reefs are found in Southeast Asia. The diversity is very high and the coral reefs are important because they are nursery and breeding grounds for 12% of the world's total fish catch. Indeed, it has been estimated that coral reefs contribute 30% of East Malaysia's total catch, 25% in the Philippines.[5]

Coral reefs are in many ways similar to tropical rainforests. Biodiversity is high, reefs fix nitrogen and remove carbon, and they provide a visual display of colour and life unmatched anywhere on earth, thereby constituting a tourist magnet that has been exploited for many years, especially in Thailand, Malaysia, Indonesia and the Philippines. Future income from tourism and fisheries are important factors in the further development of coastal nations.

Thirty per cent of the world's mangrove forest, covering 50,000 sq km of coastal areas, can be found in the South China Sea region. The types of mangrove forest found in this area represent the most diverse in terms of numbers of species existing on our planet. But mangroves do not only represent rich biodiversity, they are also important in terms of economic and environmental value. Mangrove trees are harvested for use as fuel, building materials, etc., but they are also important because they support productive fisheries (as nursery grounds) and prawn production, and protect coastal areas from erosion and the impact of storms.[6] Products and ecological services provided by the mangrove systems of the South China Sea are estimated to be worth about 15.984 million USD a year.[7]

Seagrass is a basis for many complex marine ecosystems and provides a valuable nursery for commercially important fish and other living resources (shrimp, crab, etc.). Seagrass binds sediment to the bottom, thereby preventing erosion of the sea floor. Estuaries and wetlands are normally associated with river deltas and coastal areas where land and sea meet. These areas may include mangrove forests, swamps and fens. Wetlands and estuaries are seasonal homes to migratory birds; they have their own animal and plant diversity, and serve as nursing ground for fish and crabs. They also trap nutrients and prevent erosion, as well as being used for aquaculture and agricultural purposes. The estimated value of these areas in the South China Sea region is 190.726 million USD a year.

Environmental problems in the region threaten these diverse natural living resources. The loss of coral reefs, mangroves, estuaries and seagrass beds can have serious long-term consequences because of the time needed for these ecosystems to recover after damage. A case in point is the rapid degradation of coral reefs and mangroves. The original area of mangroves has decreased by 70% during the last 70 years, and estimated rates of mangrove loss in each country of the region range from around

0.5 to 3.5% of the total area per annum. If the current trend of mangrove loss continues at the present rate, it could result in a total loss of this sort of habitat in the region by around 2030.[8] Estimates made by Chou *et al.*, claim that 82% of the coral reefs surveyed in the South China Sea display evidence of degradation.[9] Fifty per cent of the Philippine and 85% of Indonesian reefs are at high risk. From the PRC we know that 95% of the coral reefs around Hainan are damaged, an unknown amount along the coast of Vietnam, and 10–40% of reefs in Thailand and Malaysia. Scientists and experts in the region all agree that action is urgently needed to halt the destruction of the marine environment.

For many years the South China Sea dispute has prevented coastal nations from cooperating on any issue referring to the sea itself. The focus on sovereignty over reefs and small islands has blocked any attempt at reaching formal agreement on other issues, issues of importance to the entire region and its population. The most important of these non-contentious issues is, of course, to protect the precious South China Sea environment. But in 2000, a long awaited breakthrough was achieved on environmental issues. The first formal agreement on South China Sea issues by claimant states was reached in September 2000 on a UNEP administrated and GEF funded Strategic Action Programme for the South China Sea.[10] The Strategic Action Programme will be a catalyst in the process towards a UNEP Regional Seas Programme for the South China Sea, which eventually might force the concerned countries to put sensitive issues aside and start cooperation on saving fisheries and other vital living resources of the South China Sea environment.

Although an Action Plan[11] for the East Asian Seas was agreed upon as early as 1981, this plan has had minor effects on the South China Sea region, because of a lack of commitment by the signatory states to fund and undertake activities in accordance with the initial concept of the plan.[12] The governing body of the UNEP-financed Action Plan, the Coordinating Body on the Seas of East Asia (COBSEA),[13] has for nearly 20 years seen little interest or funding from its participating countries Singapore, Thailand, Indonesia, Malaysia, Vietnam, Cambodia, the Philippines, the PRC and Indonesia. Thus the scope of the East Asian Seas Action Plan has remained limited. Up until now, management of the marine environment has been dependent on how the individual state, or a sub-regional group of states, carries out environmental policies.

This is not to say that nothing has been accomplished since 1981. Numerous sub-regional projects have been established without help from the COBSEA. And ASEAN has achieved a lot in terms of bringing the ASEAN member states together in maritime environmental projects.[14] The capacity building effect of these projects should not be underestimated, and should be recognised as a manifest willingness to cooperate on the part of marine scientists, decision-makers and foreign aid agencies within the ASEAN group. The efforts made by NGOs, IGOs or international aid agencies have also been considerable.[15] However, no formal initiative aiming at embracing all South China Sea littoral countries in a UNEP-administered environmental action plan has yet succeeded; this is due to the sensitive and conflict-ridden issue of sovereignty over islets/islands.

REGIONAL COOPERATION IN THE SOUTH CHINA SEA

The ethnic, cultural and political differences among the South China Sea littoral countries, and especially between the PRC and the ASEAN countries, seem to defy resolution, even in the technical areas of marine scientific research. Although the PRC is participating in a UNDP/GEF/ IMO project administered from the Philippines, as well as an ADB-funded project which also covers Cambodia and Vietnam, the PRC has been reluctant to take part formally in any multilateral endeavour connected with the South China Sea. As the overlapping claims to central parts of the sea continue to cause repeated political skirmishes between the PRC and various ASEAN members, the political climate has not seemed ripe for establishing formal legal agreements. But, as the South China Sea littoral nations started to meet at the beginning of the 1990s at a series of informal meetings (initiated by Indonesia) called 'Managing Potential Conflicts in the South China Sea Workshops', major political interaction also increased within several forums (notably the ASEAN Regional Forum, the Council for Security Co-operation in the Asia-Pacific and APEC). Spill-over effects on the field of marine scientific research cooperation can be seen in both the Managing Potential Conflicts in the South China Sea Workshops and in UNEP's Strategic Action Programme for the South China Sea. A slow but steady change of policy has happened, with occasional steps backwards from time to time. This process culminated in September 2000 with the signing of the Strategic Action Programme by all parties to COBSEA.

THE UNEP EAS/RCU SOUTH CHINA SEA STRATEGIC ACTION PROGRAMME

Indonesia, Malaysia, the Philippines, Singapore and Thailand adopted the East Asian Seas Action Plan in 1981 for the development and protection of the marine environment and coastal areas in the region. The Coordinating Body for the Seas of East Asia (COBSEA) is the decision-making body, whereas the UNEP East Asian Sea Regional Coordinating Unit (EAS/RCU) is the secretariat responsible for the implementation of scientific programmes and integration of national activities. COBSEA was established in the early 1980s to coordinate the implementation of the UNEP East Asian Action Plan. COBSEA started out by arranging annual meetings, but soon realised that it needed scientific expertise and data as a basis for its work. COBSEA, consisting of selected government representatives, therefore decided to organise meetings of experts from the region in order to obtain scientific advice on the environmental problems of the East Asian Seas region.[16] COBSEA undertakes a wide range of projects that aim to support management of the coastal marine environment and marine protected areas.[17] According to a scientist from the region, Dr Edgardo Gomez, participating countries have evolved fairly efficient mechanisms for programme management and project implementation with technical assistance from UNEP. They have also established a trust fund that provides partial support for the programme activities.[18]

The UNEP EAS/RCU has been working for the establishment of a South China Sea Strategic Action Programme since 1994, when Australia, Cambodia, South Korea, the PRC and Vietnam joined COBSEA. COBSEA decided to revise its East Asian Sea Action Plan to encompass the new participants, and in 1996 it finally decided to act when they 'sought the assistance of UNEP and GEF in preparing a Transboundary Diagnostic Analysis of the issues and problems and their societal root causes as the basis for development of ... a Strategic Action Programme' (UNEP 1999: 4) for the South China Sea. Seven countries participated: Thailand, Vietnam, Cambodia, the Philippines, Indonesia, the PRC and Malaysia. For two years, the South China Sea littoral nations collaborated on national interagency, cross-disciplinary reports on the marine environment. These reports were used as a basis for the formulation of a Transboundary Diagnostic Analysis (TDA), where marine environmental problems were analysed and important transboundary environmental problems were addressed and brought to the attention of the governments of the region. The problems associated with fisheries and the trade of fish and fisheries products represented the first step to obtain funding from the Global Environment Facility (GEF), as GEF only funds projects that are of a transboundary or global nature.[19]

The work laid down in first the Transboundary Diagnostic Analysis, and then secondly in the South China Sea SAP when the funding was secured from GEF, was a major effort by national governments as well as the marine scientific experts who took part in the preparation stages. Such a project has in fact never been done before in the region. According to Liana Talaue-McManus, the UNEP Task Manager responsible for formulating the Transboundary Diagnostic Analysis, this work is not easy. It is not difficult to prove that each nation in the South China Sea region is suffering from marine environmental problems; the difficulty lies in proving that the problems are transboundary, she claims. The lack of data, and the fact that reports on transboundary environmental problems in the South China Sea have not been written before, made the task even more difficult. However, once the Transboundary Diagnostic Analysis and the first draft of the South China Sea Strategic Action Programme had been finished, the funding agency, the Global Environment Facility (GEF), said it was the best international waters project ever.[20]

THE PEOPLE'S REPUBLIC OF CHINA

When the Strategic Action Programme was finally ready and the seven countries who took part in the preparation stages were about to sign and adopt the proposals laid down in it, political problems prevented its implementation. Thailand, Cambodia, Vietnam, the Philippines, Indonesia and Malaysia all signed the Strategic Action Programme, but the PRC refused. According to the coordinator of UNEP's regional seas office in Thailand, Hugh Kirkman (interview, 1999), Chinese government agencies involved in the preparation stages, the Ministries of Harbour, Fisheries, Forestry, Finance, the State Environmental Protection Agency and the State Oceanic Administration, could not agree on whether to sign the plan or not. The Ministry of Foreign Affairs therefore made the final decision, in November 1999, to block the plan (Talaue-McManus 1999, interview). The UNEP initiative ran into difficulties because of the South China Sea dispute. There can be no other answer; this kind of behaviour has been experienced by the ASEAN countries before. ASEAN has made efforts at engaging the PRC in peaceful and confidence-building talks both through the ASEAN Regional Forum and through the Managing Potential Conflicts in the South China Sea Workshops, but the PRC 'often douses cold water on the various ASEAN initiatives to resolve the South China Sea dispute within a multilateral framework'.[21] But when the PRC first refused to sign, UNEP did not accept that as an end to the entire process. Senior officials from the UNEP headquarters in Nairobi, Kenya, have negotiated the text of the Strategic Action Programme with the PRC, and on how to reach a final agreement. And the final document is indeed marked by the PRC. It is made clear in the document that only UNEP and no other international, or UN-related organisations, are to be involved in the execution of the Programme. The PRC has also made it clear that there shall be no reference to the South China Sea dispute, and littoral countries are not allowed to carry out any research in disputed areas. With these modifications the UNEP Strategic Action Programme was signed by the PRC at a COBSEA meeting in September 2000.

ENVIRONMENTAL INSTITUTIONS

Although there is still a clear lack of institutional capacity for national and regional enforcement of environmental legislation in the Southeast and East Asian region, a gradual change has been evident since the beginning of the 1980s.[22] Environmental ministries and environmental laws have been established and adopted in most countries, international organisations are present, and the number of environmentally oriented NGOs has increased, although it differs from one country to another. NGOs have become an important factor in promoting environmental concern and putting pressure on politicians throughout the region.

There has been a gradual institutionalisation of efforts within ASEAN. The first ASEAN Environment Programme appeared in 1977. As COBSEA was established in 1981, UNEP became more involved in ASEAN's environmental efforts, and this has helped ASEAN to establish its environment programmes. ASEAN later established the ASEAN Experts' Group on Environment (AEGE), upgraded to the ASEAN Senior Officials on Environment around 1990. In 1988, UNEP, COBSEA and AEGE formulated the ASEAN Environment Programme III (ASEP III), which was to be implemented in the period 1988–92, and was a continuation of ASEP I (1978–82) and ASEP II (1983–87). ASEP III culminated in the formulation of a new ASEAN Strategic Action Plan on the Environment that was adopted by the Sixth ASEAN Ministerial Meeting on the Environment in April 1994. The capacity building on marine-environment related affairs in the region, together with the gradual integration and upgrading of environmental issues within ASEAN, are in large part due to the involvement of UNEP. UNEP and many other organisations have made governments of the region aware of the growing environmental problems in the region. Together with the international focus on the environment after the establishment of Agenda 21 from the UN Conference on Human Environment (UNCED) and the UN Law of the Sea Convention, which both emphasised the need for regional and sub-regional cooperative environmental programmes, a gradual change has been accomplished.[23]

There has also been a gradual build-up of institutions handling marine environmental problems. The UNEP East Asian Seas Action Plan of 1981 was one of the earliest steps in a continuing process towards integration and diffusion of marine environmental knowledge and policy in the Southeast Asian region. As stated by Edgardo Gomez (1988: 13):

> In the implementation of the action plan, several dozen national institutions have been involved and nearly five hundred national experts have benefited from training activities. Consequently, there has been an improvement in government awareness of environmental

concerns in the marine realm which is slowly being translated into policies and measures in concordance with the objectives of the action plan.

But even though there has been an increase in the number of initiatives and projects aimed at improving management and protection of marine resources, they reflect a lack of coordination and a lack of clout which is typical of the current situation in the South China Sea. Chou Loke Ming, a senior marine scientist from Singapore, sums up the situation:

> Information has resulted from a growing number of national, bilateral and regional research programmes designed to increase understanding of the periphery of the South China Sea. Various mechanisms for information exchange exist in the region and these are usually associated with established networking programmes, some of which are initiated by regional or international intergovernmental agencies. The number of newsletters, technical reports, and scientific data generated from these programmes shows that much information is available. Numerous conferences in all fields of marine science held in the region demonstrate the interest of scientists and policy makers. Training opportunities in marine science are also expanding within the region. In order to strengthen the region's management of the South China Sea, what may be needed is an effective mechanism to coordinate and integrate all aspects of marine science training, networking and information exchange.[24]

There remains a lack of coordination between the numerous initiatives, projects and programmes. Moreover, the PRC continues to be sceptical about allowing its scientists to participate in ASEAN-related activities. Consequently, there has been little actual political change resulting from the knowledge forwarded by the scientists. The endorsement of the UNEP Strategic Action Programme may be the first step in a direction where the environment will enjoy more support and protection from the countries of the South China Sea region.

NOTES

1   See Coulter, Daniel Y. (1996): 'South China Sea Fisheries: Countdown to Calamity', *Contemporary Southeast Asia*, vol. 17, no. 4.

2   See Brookfield, Harold and Yvonne Byron (eds) (1993): *South-East Asia's Environmental Future: the Search for Sustainability*, United Nations University, Kuala Lumpur: Oxford University Press.

3   See UNEP (2000): Strategic Action Programme for the South China Sea, Draft Version 3, http://www.roap.unep.org/easrcu/publication/sapV3.doc [03.01.2001].

4   See Soegiarto, Aprilani (1994): 'Sustainable Fisheries, Environment and the Prospects of Regional Cooperation in Southeast Asia'. Paper presented to the Monterey Institute of International Studies Workshop on 'Trade and

Environment in Asia-Pacific: Prospects for Regional Cooperation', East–West Centre, Honolulu, Hawaii, 23–25 September 1994.

5 See Gomez, Edgardo D.: 'Coastal Zone Management and Conservation in the South China Sea', in B. Morton ed. (1998): *The Marine Biology of the South China Sea*. Proceedings of the Third International Conference on the Marine Biology of the South China Sea, Hong Kong, 28 October–1 November 1996. Hong Kong: Hong Kong University Press.

6 See Low, Jeffrey K.Y., Beverly P.L. Goh and L.M. Chou (1996): 'Regional Cooperation in Prevention and Response to Marine Pollution in the South China Sea'. Paper presented to the Second ASEAMS Scientific Symposium, UNEP, Bangkok, 1996.

7 See UNEP (2000), *op. cit.*

8 Ibid.

9 See Chou Loke Ming and Hong Woo Khoo (1993): 'Marine Science Training, Networking and Information in the South China Sea Region'. Paper presented to the First Working Group Meeting on Marine Scientific Research in the South China Sea, Manila, Philippines, 30 May–3 June 1993.

10 See UNEP (2000), *op. cit.*

11 An Action Plan is normally the first plan made by littoral countries surrounding a semi-enclosed sea in cooperation with UNEP. According to the East Asian Seas Action Plan of 1981, Ch. 5: 'The principal objective of the action plan is the protection and sustainable development of the marine environment and the coastal areas for the promotion of the health and well-being of present and future generations. The action plan is intended to provide a framework for an environmentally-sound and comprehensive approach to coastal area development particularly appropriate to the needs of the region.'

12 Vanderzwaag, Davis and Douglas M. Johnston (1998): 'Toward the Management of the Gulf of Thailand: Charting the Course of Cooperation', in Douglas M. Johnston (ed.): *SEAPOl Integrated Studies of the Gulf of Thailand*, vol. 1, 1998. Bangkok: Innomedia Co.

13 COBSEA's role in the implementation of the East Asian Seas Action Plan is to set policies and the general direction for type and level of activities and projects. Most projects are delegated to a participating institution, which is given responsibility for the project (Chou Loke Ming and Hong Woo Khoo 1993: 175–176).

14 The ASEAN Subcommittee on Marine Science (ASCMS) and the ASEAN Senior Officials on Environment (ASOEN) have been responsible for cooperative projects with Australia (the ASEAN–Australia Marine Science Programme), Canada (ASEAN–Canadian Marine Pollution Programme), the USA (ASEAN–US AID Coastal Resources Management Programme), Japan, the Republic of Korea and the European Community (UNEP 1997: 16). In addition, the Asian Development Bank has a project on the marine environment.

15 For an excellent overview of projects, programmes and development of environment-related work in the South China Sea region, see Edgardo D.

Gomez: 'Coastal Zone Management and Conservation in the South China Sea', in B. Morton (ed.) (1998): *The Marine Biology of the South China Sea*. Proceedings of the Third International Conference on the Marine Biology of the South China Sea, Hong Kong, 28 October–1 November 1996. Hong Kong: Hong Kong University Press.

16 Goh, B.P.L. and Chou Loke Ming (eds) (1996): *UNEP Regional Co-ordinating Unit/East Asian Seas Action Plan: Proceedings of the Second ASEAMS Scientific Symposium*. Bangkok: UNEP. RCU/EAS Technical Reports Series no. 10.

17 COBSEA was established by governments of the Southeast Asian region with the mandate of coordinating, initiating, reviewing and approving activities related to the Action Plan.

18 Gomez, Edgardo (1988): 'Achievements of the Action Plan for the East Asian Seas', in UNEP (1988): *Cooperation for Environmental Protection in the Pacific*. Bangkok: UNEP Regional Seas Reports and Studies no. 97.

19 Interview with the editor of the UNEP Strategic Action Manager, Dr Liana Talaue McManus 9.7.1999.

20 Interview with Programme Director, Dr Hugh Kirkman, UNEP, Regional Coordinating Unit for East Asian Seas, Bangkok, Thailand, and Talaue McManus (*op. cit.*).

21 Samuel Kim (1994): 'Mainland China in a Changing Asia-Pacific Regional Order', *Issues and Studies* vol. 30, no. 10, pp. 36–38: cited in Castro, Renato Cruz de (1998): 'The Controversy in the Spratlys: Exploring the Limits to ASEAN's Engagement Policy', *Issues and Studies* vol. 34, no. 9, pp. 95–123.

22 See Haas, Peter M. (1998): 'Prospects for Effective Marine Governance in the Northwest Pacific Region', commissioned for the ESENA workshop: Energy-Related Marine Issues in the Sea of Japan, Tokyo, Japan 11–12 July 1998; Utrikesdepartementet (1998): *Framtid med Asien: Förslag till en Svensk Asienstrategi*, pp. 81–82, Stockholm: Utrikesdepartementet.

23 See ASEAN (1994): *ASEAN Strategic Plan of Action on the Environment*. Jakarta: ASEAN Secretariat; and ASEAN (1998): The First ASEAN State of the Environment Report. Jakarta: ASEAN Secretariat.

24 Chou Loke Ming and Hong Woo Khoo (1993): 'Marine Science Training, Networking and Information in the South China Sea Region'. Paper presented to the First Working Group Meeting on Marine Scientific Research in the South China Sea, Manila, Philippines, 30 May–3 June 1993.

5

THE ECONOMIC DIMENSION: NATURAL RESOURCES AND SEA LANES

Stein Tønnesson

This chapter focuses on the economic potential and importance of the South China Sea. While in the narrowest sense the question concerns only the natural resources, a wider analysis must consider too that the South China Sea is an essential waterway for ships sailing between the Indian and the Pacific Ocean, and for trade between Australia and a significant part of the Asian continent.

Stakes are high in the South China Sea. Further environmental degradation could impede the provision of animal protein to huge coastal populations. There is still a chance that the disputed areas could contain huge quantities of oil and gas, although expectations have been much reduced. A war, or further lawlessness and piracy, could disrupt some of the most frequented transport routes in the world.

We shall now briefly present the South China Sea's main economic assets. While there may be exploitable minerals under the sea-bed of the South China Sea,[1] it is fair to say that the current economic potential of the area is mainly based on its fish, oil and waterways.

FISH

The environmental aspects of fisheries have bee discussed in Chapter 4. Suffice it to say here that the South China Sea is one of the richest fishing areas in the world, and that the disputed coral reefs are vital breeding grounds for the fish stocks. Fisheries have a long historical tradition, but in some societies fishermen have traditionally belonged to the poorest classes, with a low social status. Thus we have much less knowledge about the history and sociology of the fishing communities than of agricultural villages and industrial towns. Important coastal populations depend on fishing for their livelihood, and many more people depend on the protein that they get from fish and other seafood caught in the South China Sea. In areas protected from monsoons there may be a bright future for aquaculture.

At any rate there is an urgent need for an internationally recognised fishery regime, with a regional authority that has the power to enforce regulations, in order to protect the coral reefs and preserve the basic fish stocks. This will require port controls as well as a major fleet of patrol boats, and close cooperation between the governments concerned.

OIL AND GAS

The area north of Borneo has been an important offshore oil province since the 1960s, but in other parts of the South China Sea exploration has yielded disappointing results relative to the expectations of the industry in the 1970s. Apart from the now mature oil province on the continental shelf of Brunei and East Malaysia, there are two important oilfields on the continental shelf of southern Vietnam, and smaller oilfields on the shelf of the Philippines and the PRC. The huge Yacheng gasfield south of Hainan Island provides gas through a pipeline to the energy market in Hong Kong and Guangzhou. Important quantities of gas have also been found in neighbouring blocks, and the Sino–Vietnamese treaty on maritime delimitation in the Gulf of Tonkin (signed in December 2000) may pave the way for joint exploitation of gas in the Gulf. The Malampaya gasfield northwest of Palawan started producing gas for the Philippines early 2002, and the enormous Indonesian Natuna gasfield, which is operated by Exxon, plans to serve Singapore through a pipeline.

The race for oil started in 1969–70, when an international report held out the prospect of finding huge reserves of oil and gas in the South China Sea. The oil that has since been discovered is mainly on the slopes near the coasts. Both foreign and regional companies are operating in the South China Sea, often through joint ventures. Most of the oil production is taking place in areas that are not contested, but commercial discoveries of gas have been made within the outer limits of the Chinese U-shaped line by companies operating under concessions from other governments:

- The Malaysian, already producing, Central Luconia gasfields off the coast of Sarawak.
- The Philippine fields Camago and Malampaya, northwest of Palawan.
- The Indonesian Natuna gasfield, with its planned pipeline to Singapore.
- The Vietnamese Lan Tay and Lan Do gasfields, which are being operated by BP, in a joint venture with the Indian oil company

ONGC and PetroVietnam. The investment contract with the Vietnamese government was signed in December 2000, and the plan is now to build a pipeline to the coast of Vietnam, where the gas will be used to produce electricity for the Vietnamese home market.

This means that pipelines are being built from within the outer perimeter of the Chinese U-shaped line to markets in the Philippines, Singapore and Vietnam. If gas discoveries are made in the future not only in the vicinity of the coasts, but also in the central part of the South China Sea, one could imagine the construction of a huge network of pipelines.

Some controversial concessions for oil and gas exploration have been granted in the disputed Spratly zone, although not in the central area (the Nanshan Basin), only in the eastern area (Reed Bank) and the western area (Vanguard Bank):

- *Kirkland and Alcorn:* In 1974, the Philippines authorised a consortium of companies to conduct surveys in the Reed Bank area of the eastern Spratlys. The first results seemed promising, but subsequent drilling by several different companies produced meagre results. Kirkland Oil received a contract for exploration in a huge area in the late 1980s, and Alcorn, the Philippine subsidiary of the American Vaalco Energy company, received a permit to conduct a desk-study of the Reed Bank area in 1994. Apparently, four holes have been drilled over the years, three of which were dry and the fourth indicating a sub-commercial deposit. Probably in part because of Chinese and Vietnamese protests against the Philippine concessions, it has been difficult for the Philippine companies to finance their operations.

- *Crestone and Conoco:* On 8 May 1992, the PRC awarded a 25,155 sq km zone in the western part of the Spratlys (the Vanguard Bank or *Wan'an Bei*) to the small US Crestone Energy Corporation. The concession was carefully designed to avoid areas claimed by Malaysia, Indonesia or the Philippines, while encompassing a major part of the territory disputed between the PRC and Vietnam. Vietnam issued a strongly worded protest, awarded an adjacent bloc to Mobil, and for some time tried to attract Russian interest. This led to Chinese protests and to brief naval episodes when Mobil and Crestone sent exploration vessels to the area. In 1996, Vietnam was able to persuade the US oil giant Conoco to accept a concession in much of the same area that Crestone had obtained from the PRC. Since then there have been no reports that either Crestone or Conoco have conducted any drilling, and the Crestone concession, which originally was a seven-year contract, has been transferred to another small US company, Benton Oil.

There has been much speculation about the prospects of finding oil and gas in the Spratly area, and in the press it is frequently referred to as 'oil-rich'. Chinese sources provide highly exaggerated figures. Research institutes and news organs based in the PRC have often voiced expectations for major oil finds or published overall figures that include all the proven reservoirs along the coasts of Vietnam, Malaysia, Brunei and the Philippines. Foreign oil companies are taking the Chinese estimates with a good pinch of salt, and independent consultants have made less sanguine assessments of the potential. The United States Energy Information Administration claims that even if the extremely optimistic Chinese estimates of 105 billion barrels of oil under the Spratlys should prove to be correct, a 'rule-of-thumb' whereby normally only about 10% of potential resources can be economically recovered in 'such frontier areas', implies a potential production of only some 1.9 million barrels/day. This is one and a half times today's total production from the South China Sea (1.37 million in 1996/97) and well over half of the PRC's total production (3.2 million in 1998), but only one-tenth of the production from the Persian Gulf region, and less than one-sixth of the production in the North Sea.[2]

The Norwegian firm TGS Nopec, which carried out a survey in 1997 with the permission of the Indonesian, Malaysian and Vietnamese governments, failed to substantiate the Chinese forecast. It shot seismic lines in an area west of the Spratlys and gained access to data obtained by an earlier Russian survey into the Spratly area itself. On this basis the company concluded that there existed huge structures that might contain large reserves of hydrocarbons. However, it also found some geological risk factors, notably uncertainty as to the presence of proper source rocks. The conclusion was that the question of whether or not the structures contain oil and gas, could be answered only by drilling.[3] Very little drilling has been done so far, partly because of the sovereignty dispute. One hole drilled in the Vanguard Bank area, by Russian experts working with the Vietnamese, proved to be dry. No drilling or seismic exploration seems to have been undertaken in the central part of the Spratly area.

If a major find were to be made in the disputed Spratly area, the conflict would most likely escalate. The problem is that major oil companies are reluctant to drill for oil while the jurisdictional dispute remains unresolved and while the expectation of actually finding oil is low. The sum of the political and economic risks is too great. In the second part of the 1990s, the reluctance of the oil companies was reinforced by the fact that so much oil and gas had been discovered in other parts of the world; this was exacerbated by the drop in the world oil price in 1998. With the resurgence in the oil price in 2000, the likelihood increased again that oil companies coould be induced to search for oil in disputed areas.

If the disputes remain unsettled, one option for the states around the South China Sea would be to establish joint development zones (JDZs). Models can be found in the Timor Gap treaty (between Indonesia [now between East Timor] and Australia) and in the joint development zones between Malaysia and Thailand and between Malaysia and Vietnam in the Gulf of Thailand. Since 1990, the PRC has been in favour of the principle of joint cooperation. It does seem difficult, however, to establish an equitable joint development regime in a zone where not two, but many states have overlapping claims.

THE WATERWAYS

Brunei, Indonesia, Malaysia and Vietnam are oil-producing nations with surplus production, but it is most unlikely that the energy needs of the other countries surrounding the South China Sea can be met through domestic production, including offshore fields. Taiwan and the Philippines are likely to continue to depend on importing oil. The same is now the case for southern China. The PRC energy imports will focus attention on the need for secure sea-lanes through the South China Sea.

Some of the world's busiest sea-lanes run through the South China Sea. Their importance for the local economies cannot be exaggerated. The region is maritime; it has few roads and railroads, but thousands of small harbours and three major ports: Singapore, Hong Kong and Kaohsiung. Internal trade between the countries surrounding the South China Sea depends on open sea-lanes. The South China Sea is also a major thoroughfare for globally operating merchant marines, who rely on the freedom of navigation. A basic principle in the Law of the Sea is the freedom of navigation not only on the High Seas, but also in the Exclusive Economic Zones (EEZs) and the territorial waters of states. There are three regimes that ensure the freedom of navigation in territorial and archipelagic waters: innocent passage in territorial seas, transit passage, and archipelagic sea-lanes passage. The latter applies to the straits within the archipelagic waters of Indonesia and the Philippines.

Generally, oil and minerals are transported northwards through the South China Sea, while food and manufactured goods are taken southwards. Tankers and other ships approaching from the south and west can choose from three main passageways: the Malacca, Sunda and Lombok-Macassar Straits.[4] The Malacca Strait is the second busiest strait in the world after the English Channel. The Sunda Strait is much used by vessels coming from or going to Africa. Ships passing northwards through the Lombok and Macassar Straits, a route that is primarily used by Australian north–south trade, can either go into the South China Sea west of Palawan, or move into the Pacific south of Mindanao. The most utilised route through the South China Sea enters through the Malacca

Strait, traverses the sea between Vietnam and the Spratlys, and exits through the Luzon or Taiwan Strait.

These sea-lanes are of vital importance to the Philippines, South Korea and Japan. The three countries receive 85%, 74% and 67% respectively of their oil from tankers passing through the South China Sea.[5] About 40% of Japan's total imports and exports traverse that sea.[6] Since 1993, the PRC has also been a net importer of crude oil, and the PRC is now starting to import liquefied natural gas (LNG) into the Guangzhou area. The regional dependence on energy imports is likely to grow significantly in the years to come, although the Asian crisis somewhat reduced the pace of growth in energy consumption. By contrast, the United States receives only 12% of its oil consumption from the Middle East, and can easily channel provisions to its west coast through the Lombok Strait or south of Australia.[7] Thus, the South China Sea is not of vital importance to the United States itself. It is out of concern for the stability of the East Asian region, for its allies Japan and South Korea, and for the overall principle of the freedom of navigation, that the US considers it imperative to secure the sea-lanes.

Washington has been worried by the Chinese Law on the Territorial Sea and the Contiguous Zone of 1992, which empowers the Chinese Navy to evict trespassing nations in the South China Sea by force if need be.[8] On 10 May 1995, the US foreign minister warned local governments against moves that could endanger the security of sea-lanes. The US naval reaction to the PRC's missile tests in the Taiwan Strait in 1996 was not just meant to bolster Taiwan's democracy, but to demonstrate Washington's resolve to protect the freedom of navigation, as a prerequisite to global free trade. The PRC has since been eager to affirm that it also intends to uphold and safeguard the freedom of navigation.[9]

In 1997, a working group under the ASEAN Regional Forum even discussed the possibility of issuing a Declaration on Navigational Rights.[10]

PIRACY

It is not only states that can hamper the freedom of trade. The South China Sea has always been a haven for pirates. Piracy thrives in waters where no state has an internationally recognised authority, and where it is possible to pay off local police. Piracy and armed robbery, which led to the loss of so many Vietnamese refugees' lives in the 1970s, were less frequent in the 1980s, when there was a strong US and Soviet naval presence, but surged again in the 1990s. In 1997, 105 of the 229 shipboard attacks reported worldwide took place in the South China Sea.[11]

Because of reduced state capacity after the Asian crisis, particularly in Indonesia, the piracy problem continued to increase during 1998–2001. Before the Asian crisis, cooperation between Indonesia, Malaysia and Singapore had reduced the number of piracy incidents in the Straits of Malacca and Singapore.[12] After the crisis, notably because of the erosion of government authority in Indonesia, the problem has again become more serious. One of the motives behind attempts to foster contact and confidence between representatives of the several navies and coastguards in the region has been to enhance cooperation in suppressing piracy. Japan has expressed strong interest in the issue, and may take part in anti-piracy operations in the Strait of Malacca.

The piracy issue has already become a bone of contention between the countries in the region, since the need to suppress piracy may serve as an excuse for naval build-ups and naval deployments that can create suspicion and distrust in other countries. The PRC has for a number of years been building up its navy, which now seeks a role in securing the sea-lanes that ensure the provision of energy to the PRC. Beijing has therefore been worried by the recent agreements on naval cooperation between India and Vietnam, and will be even more worried if there is a Japanese naval presence in the South China Sea.

CONCLUSION

The 1990s witnessed two main changes. One was a reduction in the expectation of making major oil and gas finds. This has increased the PRC dependency on energy imports, a fact that is bound to have an effect on the PRC's South China Sea policy. For the PRC it will be even less tempting than in the past to engage in a conflict with other regional states over the access to offshore natural resources. On the other hand it will be increasingly important to secure sea-lanes. The PRC may seek to do this either through a radical naval build-up, which could lead to a regional arms race, or by modifying its maritime policy and adopting a stance much closer to that of Japan and the United States. This means defending navigational rights within the International Maritime Organisation (IMO).

The other main change during the past decade is the growing danger that fish stocks may be depleted. In the short run this is likely to lead to intensified competition for catching the fish that is still left. Thus the problem will be further aggravated. Hopefully, however, the regional states will be able to establish a regulatory regime before it is too late.

NOTES

1   In the future it may also be possible to produce energy from waves or from the pressure differences between the enormously varying depths.

2   See: http://www.eia.doe.gov/emeu/cabs/schina.html. A reasonably updated study of energy in Asia can be found in Robert A. Manning, *The Asian Energy Factor*. New York: Palgrave, 2000.

3   Personal communication from Mr Kjell Bugge Johansen, PGS, 19 February 1999 and 31 January 2000. Two reports on the hydrocarbon potential are available on commercial terms: *South East Asia Super Tie-95* (SEAS-95), and IEDS: *A Review of the Hydrocarbon Potential of the South West China Sea.*

4   An American study reports that 8,842 vessels larger than 1,000 deadweight (US) tons passed through one of the three straits, or sailed past the Spratlys on international voyages in 1993. J.H. Noer, *Chokepoints...*, p. 9.

5   http://www.cpf.navy.mil/pages/factfile/cmdbrief/cb1210/sld001.htm (slide 8).

6   J.H. Noer, *Chokepoints,* p. 24.

7   3.3% of US total exports and 4.5% of its imports transit the South China Sea. J.H. Noer, *Chokepoints,* p. 25.

8   F. A. Magno, 'Environmental Security in the South China Sea', *Orbis,* vol. 28, no. 1 (1996), p. 101.

9   'Any country shall enjoy the freedom of navigation in and of overflight over the exclusive economic zone of the People's Republic of China ...' Article 11 of the 'Law of the People's Republic of China on the Exclusive Economic Zone and the Continental Shelf' (adopted at the Third Session of the Standing Committee of the Ninth National People's Congress of the PRC on 26 June 1998). Unofficial translation in MIMA Bulletin, vol. 7, no 1/ 99, pp. 27–29.

10 Ramses Amer, 'Towards a Declaration on "Navigational Rights" in the Sea-lanes of the Asia-Pacific'. *Contemporary Southeast Asia,* vol. 20, no. 1 (April 1998), pp. 88–102.

11 Tracy Dahlby, 'Crossroads of Asia: South China Sea', *National Geographic,* vol. 194, no. 6, December 1998, p. 23.

12 Ramses Amer, 'Towards a Declaration ...'.

6

THE MILITARY ASPECTS OF THE DISPUTES

Bjørn Møller

The security complex of East Asia clearly comes closer to the paradigm of a conflict formation than to that of a security community[1] The fact that great powers such as the People's Republic of China (PRC) and, less directly, the United States, Japan and India are involved makes territorial disputes such as that over the Spratly Islands potentially dangerous – especially since arms acquisitions and evolving military doctrines may place the parties to the conflict on a collision course. The situation is even more unstable because of the near absence of suitable institutional or arms control settings to handle disputes.

- The People's Republic of China has recently adopted a new military doctrine, placing the main emphasis on the ability to fight minor wars in the PRC's immediate vicinity. It has been striving moreover for some time to build a genuine ocean-going ('blue-water') navy. Upon completion of this project, the PRC may be in a position to exercise 'sea control' in the South China Sea and even possess a significant power projection capability. This would not only constitute a threat to Taiwan, but might also lead to naval rivalry with Japan.

- Several member states of the Association of South East Asian Nations (ASEAN), especially Malaysia, already possess significant 'green-water' naval capabilities as well as embryonic blue-water capabilities. Most of them have also been investing heavily in major warships as well as maritime aircraft – the primary rationale being the need to patrol expanded territorial waters and Exclusive Economic Zones (EEZs).

- Under pressure from the United States, Japan has accepted greater responsibility for the defence of its own sea lanes of communications (SLOCs), some of which run through waters also claimed as vital by the PRC.

- India has for some time been building a primitive blue-water capability, including aircraft carriers, and it has exhibited interest in extending its naval reach into the South China Sea, if only to contest the PRC hegemony.
- The United States continues to regard the South China Sea as important and will, with the world's largest and most capable navy, remain determined to safeguard the freedom of the high seas.[2]

This chapter is a review of the military hardware, doctrines and interests of the conflicting nations and about the existing military mechanisms of crisis stability and confidence-building among the disputants.

THE SPRATLY DISPUTE

The main players in the dispute over the Spratly Islands are the 'two Chinas', i.e. the PRC and Taiwan (official name: Republic of China, ROC) and three members of ASEAN (Vietnam, the Philippines and Malaysia) as well as, indirectly, the organization as such.

All five states have not only raised claims to, but actually occupied and garrisoned some of the islands, as summarized in Table 6.1. Brunei has also laid claim to some of the islands, but so far taken no military steps to enforce these claims, something for which it would also lack the capacity.

There have even been a few military clashes over the islands, e.g. between the PRC and Vietnam and the Philippines. While most have been fairly minor, e.g. the sinking of Chinese fishing boats by the Philippine Navy in 1999,[3] others (such as those between the two countries over the Mischief Reef in 1995 and 1998) have been more serious, as were those between the PRC and Vietnam over the Fiery Cross Reef in 1988.[4] Moreover, all of them certainly have the potential of escalating. While ASEAN has attempted to present a united front against China, e.g. with the ASEAN Declaration on the South China Sea (Manila, 22 July 1992, see below),[5] there are also disputes among its member states, e.g. between the Philippines, Malaysia and Vietnam.[6]

In the following no attempt shall be made to assess the validity of the competing claims,[7] but the focus shall instead be placed on the military potentials which might be brought into play, should the conflict escalate. The main emphasis is placed on the main players, i.e. the PRC, Taiwan, Malaysia, Vietnam and the Philippines. In recognition of the importance of external players, however, short sections are also included on Indonesia (an indirect party to the dispute as an ASEAN member), Japan, Russia, Australia, India and the United States, all of whom have stakes in the conflict as well as the means to influence developments.

Table 6.1 Military installations in the Spratly Islands

State	Total islands claimed/ Major garrisoned islands	Year occupied	Troops/ Installations
PRC	7 Yongshu Jiao	1988	260 helicopter pads
Taiwan	1 Taiping	1956	100 1 helicopter pad
Philippines	9 Pagasa	1971	480 1300-m runway
Vietnam	24 Truong Sa Dong, Nanwei Dao	1974	600 600-m runway
Malaysia	3 Terumbu Layang Layang	1983	70 600-m runway

Source: Adapted from Cossa, Ralph A.: *Security Implications of Conflict in the South China Sea: Exploring Potential Triggers of Conflict.* A Pacific Forum CSIS Special Report (Washington, DC: Center for Strategic and International Studies, 1998), p. B–3.

THE PEOPLE'S REPUBLIC OF CHINA

The PRC remains something of an enigma, both to the West and to its neighbours, *inter alia* because of the closed nature of the PRC political culture and the lack of reliable data on military expenditure, arms production, military planning, etc. Interpretations of prevailing trends therefore differ widely, in several respects.

Leaving aside as implausible the hypothesis that the PRC should be seeking genuine superpower status, many observers believe that it is aiming for a future role as a regional hegemonic power.[8] This would explain Beijing's quest for the acquisition of power projection capabilities such as aircraft carriers, long-range aircraft and ballistic missiles. It would also explain its forging of ties with a Myanmar that might serve as a possible bridgehead at the meeting point of South and Southeast Asia,[9] hence useful for an encounter with either India or the rest of ASEAN states, or both.

Such ambitions may not merely be understandable for what is, after all, the world's largest nation-state. They may also be, at least partly, defensively motivated, e.g. by fears of a resurgent Japanese imperialism,[10] or apprehensions over US hegemonic ambitions, or both in combination.[11] Moreover, the perception of the 1991 Gulf War as a defeat for Soviet-type weaponry (very similar, indeed superior to, what the PRC has in its inventory) may have created a sense of greater urgency about this military modernization.[12]

The requirements of Deng Xiao-ping's economic reforms also have implications for foreign policy, *inter alia* by making the PRC a major energy consumer. This means that the PRC must either exploit (what it regards as) indigenous oil deposits (e.g. in the South China Sea), or import oil, in turn calling for the capability to defend sea lanes (i.e. SLOCs) – both of which have implications for military strategy.[13]

The accompanying dismantlement of communism as national ideology has, furthermore, led to a quest for alternative sources of regime legitimation, for which purpose nationalism is the most obvious candidate. This might explain at least some of Chinese territorial claims, e.g. for the Spratly Islands and other off-shore territories claimed to belong historically to China, such as the Diaoyu Islands.[14]

It is impossible to determine with any certainty whether the offensive/assertive or the defensive/reactive interpretation of the PRC policy, including defence policy, or any combination thereof, is correct. Indeed, we do not even know what the leadership in Beijing spends on whatever military plans it may have. Noting the unreliability of official PRC military expenditure (MILEX) data, some observers systematically prefer the highest estimates, while others opt for the lowest. The most 'responsible' analysts tend to assume the truth to lie somewhere in-between. However, the only thing that can be said with any degree of certainty and scholarly rigour is that nobody knows, as the price structure may simply be so artificial that real military expenditures are incommensurable both with themselves over time and with those of other countries. A rather safe, but vague, bet may thus be that the PRC's MILEX are rising (which nobody seems to dispute), yet from an unknown baseline and at an unknown rate.[15]

The PRC acquisitions of major weapons systems from abroad (especially from Russia) are, however, known with some certainty from various sources, despite gaps in the reporting to the UN conventional arms transfer register.[16] Acquisitions from domestic sources are more uncertain, yet it appears implausible that any major changes would go undetected. Combining these data with the above-mentioned changes in (declared) national policies may yield some insights into the PRC military doctrine and strategy.[17]

For all its vagueness, the emerging picture is that of a PRC which has abandoned the Maoist 'people's war doctrine'. This doctrine called for, among other things, a PLA (People's Liberation Army) comprising large numbers of mobilizable troops of a fairly primitive and 'rugged' nature, outfitted with rather basic equipment and weaponry. Such were the PRC perceived needs in the event of a major war (e.g. a world war between socialism and either capitalism or 'social imperialism'), in which it was envisioned to withdraw the bulk of the defence forces into the depth of the country and fight a protracted war of resistance (as was the strategy of the communist guerrillas during the war against the Japanese invaders in the 1930s).[18] Neither the PLA Navy (PLAN) nor the PLA Air Force (PLAAF) had much of a role to play under this strategy.

The nuclear weapons acquired by the PRC since the 1960s constituted a perfect fit for this 'grand strategy', providing an 'existential' guarantee that might ensure the very survival of the PRC in the same contingency, i.e. that of a world war. Gradually, of course, the PRC improved these nuclear capabilities, not merely in the sense of ensuring their survivability (i.e. the PRC second-strike capability), but also to the point where the nuclear weapons might conceivably also be used for intimidation and 'compellence', albeit not really for invasion or other forms of attack.[19]

The subsequent reassessment of the threat and the resultant abandonment (or major revision) of this people's war doctrine helps to explain why in the 1980s the PRC undertook a large-scale demobilization of more than one million troops and embarked on a programme of conversion of large parts of its arms industry.[20]

What has replaced the former doctrine, however, remains somewhat obscure. New terms have been put forward such as 'active defence' or 'people's war under modern conditions',[21] both of which would require medium-range power projection capabilities, mainly for limited, short contingencies in the PRC's regional neighbourhood, and in which technological sophistication would play a role.[22] Hence the quest for such weapons platforms as longer-range aircraft, air refuelling capacities, medium-range ballistic missiles to ensure some 'stand-off striking capacity' as well as for major surface combatants as elements of what may eventually become (but is not yet) a blue-water navy.[23]

These doctrinal and strategic developments have influenced both naval strategy and procurement. The emerging picture is one of a green-water navy under expansion, the target apparently being a truly ocean-going, i.e. blue-water, navy a decade or so hence. For the details, see Table 6.2.

The present transition period has, moreover, seen some innovative attempts at utilizing 'green-water capacities' for 'blue-water missions', but none that is really convincing.[24] The main deficits remain on-board airpower, i.e. the lack of a genuine aircraft carrier. While there have been efforts both to purchase one (from Russia/Ukraine) and at indigenous construction, the prospects remain uncertain, also because the PRC lacks such carrier-capable aircraft as would be indispensable for it to function properly. An interim solution may be a helicopter ship or a VSTOL (Vertical/Short Take-off Landing) 'carrier', which would possess some offensive capabilities vis-à-vis clearly inferior opponents such as Vietnam, but none that could stand up to navies such as those of the United States or Japan.

Table 6.2: PLA naval facilities

TYPE	CLASS	DISPL	1985	2000	2010
Aircraft Carriers			0	0	1
n.a.	NEWCON CV	> 45,000	0	0	1
Destroyers			15	21	20
Type 956	Sovremenny	8,480	-	1	2
Type 054	Luhai	6,600	-	1	5
Type 052	Luhu	5,700	-	2	2
Type 051	Luda	3,960	11	17	~ 11
Type 07	Anshan	2,040	4	-	-
Frigates			31	36	39
Type 059	Jiangwei III	3,000	-	-	3
Type 057	Jiangwei II	2,250	-	2	6
Type 055	Jiangwei	2,250	-	5	5
Type 053	Jianghu	1,925	20	28	~ 25
Type 053K	Jiangdong	1,925	2	1	-
Type 065	Jiangnan	1,400	5	-	-
Type 01	Chengdu	1,510	4	-	-
Guided Missile Boats			100	83	55
Type 520T	Houjian	520	-	4	4
Type 343M	Houxin	478	-	14	~36
Type 021	Huangfeng	205	100	65	~25
Submarines			117	66	62
Type 094	NEWCON SSBN	8,000	-	-	8*
Type 092	Xia SSBN	6,500	1	1	-
Type 093	NEWCON SSN	6,500	-	-	4

TYPE	CLASS	DISPL.	1985	2000	2010
Type 091	Han SSN	5,500	3	5	5
n.a.	Kilo	2,325	-	2	4
Type 039	Song	2,250	-	2	5
Type 035	Ming	2,100	2	16	20
Type 033	Romeo	1,710	90	38	15
Type 03	Whiskey	1,350	20	-	-
Type 031	Golf SSB	2,700	1	1	-
n.a.	Wuhan	2,100	-	1	1
Amphibious Warfare			4	15	29
Type 074	Yuting	4,800	-	6	20
Type 072	Yukan	4,170	3	7	7
	Yudeng	1,850	-	1	1
Type 073	Yudao	1,460	1	1	1
Naval Aviation			780	765	730
Type	Mission				
B-6	Bomber	50	30	30	
B-5	Bomber	130	80	25	
Q-5	Attack	0	75	> 75	
FH-7	Attack	0	> 25	> 100	
F-4, F-5, F-6, F-7	Fighters	600	580	600	

*uncertain estimate

Source: Federation of American Scientists: 'People's Liberation Army Navy', at http://www.fas.org/man/dod–101/ sys/ship/row/plan/index.html

TAIWAN

While Taiwan has longstanding claims to the Spratly Islands (see above), it has so far done little to enforce them.

Until recently, Taiwan had the declared ambition to 'liberate' the mainland, a mission which obviously called for an offensive military strategy and posture. These offensive capabilities acquired for the envisioned invasion of the PRC would then, of course, also be available for other purposes than the (much less demanding) occupation of a small island in the South China Sea, as happened in 1956. There is little doubt that Taiwan would have the means to occupy and garrison additional islands, should it choose to do so – as it seemed to be doing in 1999.[25]

However, in parallel with the gradual introduction of democracy, the former offensive strategy has been replaced with an explicitly non-nuclear and defensive strategy. The shift was *expressis verba* with reference to the security dilemma, and actually used the label 'defensive defence', [26] for instance in the *1993–94 Defence Report*:

> The main objective of national defense is to protect the national security from being violated and threatened. In the process of pursuing [security], it is impossible for any given country to obtain absolute safety, because as soon as one country obtains absolute safety, other neighbouring countries around it would conversely have a feeling of absolute unsafety … the concept of our armed forces build-up has been transformed from the strategy of 'offensive defensive' to 'defensive defense'.[27]

The missions of all four branches of the armed forces have likewise become more defensive, reflected in a predominantly defensive military posture.[28] Among its distinguishing features are a high percentage of reserves to active armed forces (combining enhanced defensive strength with reduced offensive power); a clear emphasis on anti-invasion and counter-mobility force elements such as fighter aircraft and ground-based air defence, coastal artillery, mine warfare vessels and anti-tank weapons; and a low priority given to offensive (or counter-offensive) force elements such as long-range strike aircraft (fighter-bombers, for instance), surface-to-surface ballistic missiles, and amphibious forces. To this should be added the explicit abandonment of the apparent former (quite understandable) quest for a nuclear deterrent, manifested in a declaration of intent to observe the norms of the NPT (Non-Proliferation Treaty), even though Taiwan, as a 'non-state', cannot actu-ally sign the treaty.[29]

The above formulations were amended slightly in the *2000 Defense Report*, yet seemingly without much change of substance. While pointing out that the 'strategic guidance' had been adjusted from 'strong defense posture and effective deterrence' to 'effective deterrence and strong defense posture' (the difference between which escapes the present author), it still emphasized that 'the defense preparations and defense readiness of ROC are purely for self-defense and peace-keeping'.[30] While it may be hard to fathom what peace Taiwan would be asked to help keep (not being a member of the United Nations), the self-defence task would seem to be quite achievable given the rather favourable balance-of-power between the two sides of the Taiwan Strait, at least until the PRC has completed the aforementioned transition.[31]

As far as the navy is concerned, its primary mission is defined as 'to safeguard the security of the Taiwan Strait and smooth marine transportation'. The peacetime tasks of the navy are defined as 'marine reconnaissance and patrolling, supply of offshore islands and escort of ships', whereas its wartime missions are stipulated as being 'to carry out counter-sea blockades and surface interception operations to ensure command of the sea'.[32] This somewhat unfortunate formulation notwithstanding, the real ambition does not appear to be any 'Mahanian' command of the sea (which would in any case be quite beyond Taiwan's means), but rather some form of 'defensive sea control', entailing no ambitions to be able to threaten the SLOCs of other countries.[33]

ASEAN

Because of the relative openness in military matters, which characterizes most of the ASEAN countries (with the notable exception of Myanmar and to some extent Vietnam), it is possible to get a rather clear and reliable picture of the region's arms acquisitions and holdings as well as military expenditures.[34]

Until the economic crisis struck in 1997/98, from which the ASEAN nations have only partially recovered, the emerging picture was one of quite steeply rising military spending and fairly massive arms purchases.[35] In particular, the navies were set to be expanded as well as modernized, as were at least those parts of the air forces that were tasked with maritime surveillance and defence.[36] While the implementation of some of these plans was suspended because of the economic crisis, most are set to proceed, once the financial situation permits it.

This would in normal circumstances be a cause for some alarm. What might appear even more worrisome is the fact that a substantial part of the planned outlays are for major conventional weapons systems (warships and aircraft) which will provide states with enhanced power projection capabilities, pointing towards a situation where they may pose offensive threats to each other.[37] Because transparency does not extend to the intentions underlying this arms build-up, there is room for different interpretations.[38]

- There is little doubt that the China factor looms large for all ASEAN member states.[39]

- Some might therefore interpret the ASEAN arms build-up as an arms race with the PRC, i.e. as a defensive response to the above-mentioned PRC military build-up.

- Others might see the regional states as being entrapped in a traditional arms race with each other, each responding to perceived potential threats created by the arms acquisitions of the others. If Greece and Turkey can engage in an arms race with each other within a closely knit alliance such as NATO, it is surely conceivable that members of a much looser structure such as ASEAN might do the same.

- Alternatively, one might see it as a special (almost 'virtual') arms race, where it is not actual military capabilities that matter as much as the projected image of great power status. Large warships, for instance, are not merely useful for extending one's maritime perimeter, but also for impressing one's neighbours, even if they are only used for friendly port calls. By implication, if what is happening in Southeast Asia is an arms race at all, it may not be a 'serious' one, but one of posturing and make-believe.

- Even if one takes the arms build-up seriously, it is possible to interpret most arms purchases as reflecting perfectly 'innocent' amendments of military doctrine. The armed forces were formerly used mainly for counter-insurgency warfare, but most of these insurgencies have been 'put to rest' (one way or the other) over the last decade. As a result, governments have been in a position to reassign the armed forces to their 'real' mission, namely national defence.[40] For obvious reasons, this necessitates certain arms acquisitions, the more so as it happens to coincide with new developments in the law of the sea (especially the UN Convention of the Law of the Sea, UNCLOS II) which require states to patrol expanded EEZs.[41]

- A final, and related, interpretation is that the arms build-up represents nothing but business-as-usual, i.e. that it simply reflects the growing purchasing power produced by an extended period of high economic growth.

Even if the 'innocent' interpretations hold true (as seems likely), there may still be grounds for concern. Even in those cases where the original impetus for the build-up may have had little or nothing to do with an arms race, states may gradually come to regard their neighbours' growing military strength as a threat calling for counteracting steps. It is also conceivable that some of the ASEAN states may gradually develop ambitions that go beyond their (likely) present one of national defence. The appetite may simply grow with the eating, and states may develop ambitions commensurate with their growing military strength, rather than the other way around.

The well-known 'security dilemma' may thus become activated, leading states to pursue their quest for security at the expense of their respective neighbours.[42] One might even envision a territorial manifestation thereof in the form of 'pre-emptive island grabs', where states table claims for some of the Spratly Islands in order to pre-empt others from doing so first, and where they feel compelled to actually occupy and garrison the claimed islands. Military clashes might well result from this, which might in turn escalate out of control. Of particular interest in this context are the three ASEAN contenders for the Spratly Islands, i.e. Vietnam, the Philippines and Malaysia, as well as the regional great power, Indonesia.

Vietnam has been reducing militarily, since around 1986, under the *Doi Moi* ('renovation') strategy, which entailed, *inter alia*, a withdrawal of forces from abroad. The opportunity for this was created by the disappearance of the most important threats to Vietnamese national security (e.g. the signing of an accord with the PRC), while the need for adjustment was brought about by the collapse of the socialist bloc that had previously supported the country.[43] There is no reason to expect this to change in the foreseeable future. Therefore Vietnam's ability to enforce its claims to the Spratly Islands, or even to defend what it presently has laid hands on, will remain very limited.[44] As a consequence, it is reasonable to expect Hanoi to want to enlist the (political and perhaps even military) support of the rest of ASEAN for its claims.

The Philippines presents a similar situation, as its armed forces in general, and not least its navy, are in a rather dismal shape. Despite a modernisation programme launched about decade ago, and a subsequent parliamentary decision (following the Mischief Reef incident) to allocate further resources to an upgrade of the armed forces, very little progress has been made because of a shortage of funds.[45] Manila lacks both an ocean-going fleet worthy of that name and any long-range maritime aircraft that might allow it to lay hands on additional islands. It would probably therefore be incapable of defending its present possessions in the face of a determined assault on them. Its warships are both few and small as well as so utterly obsolete (mostly vintage 1945) that they would not be much of a match for even the PLAN of today, much less for the same navy a decade hence. Moreover, since the departure of the last US forces from the Philippines in 1992, the United States has shown little willingness to support its former colony and ally.

Malaysia is in an altogether different league. Its navy is both quite large and entirely seaworthy, with a small(ish) aircraft carrier as the capital ship. While military expenditures were reduced as a result of the 1997/98 economic crisis, the reductions took place from a rather high level, and a renewed upward turn has already become clearly visible. Not only is the army being upgraded with tanks and armoured personnel carriers, and the air force being modernized, but the navy is also undergoing a more significant expansion-*cum*-modernization. In addition to the six major surface warships delivered in recent years, four new ones are being built, all of which are outfitted with anti-ship missiles and adequate on-board air defence, some with helicopter pads. There are even plans to acquire submarines, ostensibly for SLOC-protection, but with an inherent capability of threatening the SLOCs of other states.[46]

Indonesia is strictly speaking an 'external player' as far as the Spratly dispute is concerned, as it has no claims to any of the islands. As a leading member of ASEAN, however, it is an indirect, rather than external, player. Moreover, should Indonesia at some stage decide that it wants to claim its 'share' of the Spratly Islands, it would certainly possess the means to enforce such claims, making it a direct player of some significance. Its navy is quite large, comprising 42,000 personnel (planned rise to 47,000), 13 frigates, 16 corvettes, 2 submarines, 12 patrol boats and 13 mine-clearing vessels, 2 marine brigades and 28 landing ships.[47] Because of the archipelagic nature of the country, however, most of this capacity is probably intended for internal use, as well as for the protection of shipping against the growing problem of piracy.[48] At least some of this potential would, however, also be available for other use, should the Indonesian government so decide.

The importance of the military strength of individual ASEAN member states depends, of course, on the likelihood that they would stand united in the face of a threat. This will probably remain a matter of guesswork.

For nearly all of ASEAN the China factor is of decisive importance for future developments. The moment of truth would come, for example, if the PRC should seek to extend its reach to the Spratlys once again, and/ or if the PRC should try to 'teach lessons' to any of the ASEAN states (as happened with Vietnam in the past).[49] In such an eventuality, at least three different scenarios are conceivable:

1. The nations of Southeast Asia might close ranks against the PRC, say by transforming the organization into a military alliance or a regional collective security system, providing military assistance by all to any member state under attack.[50]

2. They might invite a countervailing great power into the region, which would most likely be the United States, but which might conceivably be Japan or India. In either case, this would be tantamount to an abrogation of the ZOPFAN treaty (establishing the Zone of Prosperity, Freedom and Neutrality, 1971). Because of the saliency of this treaty, and the underlying norm of national and regional self-reliance and resilience, this would bode ill for the future of ASEAN as we know it.

3. Finally, ASEAN might disintegrate under the strains of conflicting pressures, say if one or more states (Singapore or Burma, for instance) should choose to 'bandwagon' with the PRC rather than adopt a counter-balancing stance against it.[51] Indeed, even Indonesia seems recently to have tilted towards the PRC.[52]

EXTERNAL PLAYERS

If only because of its maritime nature, the region around the South China Sea is inevitably an open one, where external actors are able to exert significant influence. While other states (e.g. Australia) and organizations (the European Union or APEC, for instance)[53] might arguably be significant, I shall limit the following account to three states, which virtually every analyst would agree form part of the picture: Japan, India and the United States. This is followed by a very brief account of the roles of Russia and Australia.

Japan remains a constrained military power, partly as a result of its 'peace constitution' and the 'one per cent rule'. The former prohibits Japan from fielding armed forces (yet permits self-defence, hence the label JSDF: Japanese Self-Defence Forces), while the latter is based on a political consensus to limit military expenditures to 1 per cent of gross national product (GDP).[54] However, 1 per cent of a huge and, until recently, rapidly rising GDP can buy a country very formidable 'self-defence forces'. Depending on the PRC estimate (see above), Japan is thus either the world's third or fourth largest military spender. Furthermore, its unique type of dispersed and diversified arms industry provides it with a particularly formidable force generation potential. Should a decision to mobilize the nation for war be taken, the government could put Japan on a war footing faster than most other countries would be able to.[55]

Opinions differ when it comes to the future. Some analysts regard the above constraints as purely externally imposed, hence widely resented by the population of Japan and, as a result, fragile and unlikely to last. According to this interpretation, as soon as the opportunity arises, Japan is bound to re-emerge as what it has secretly been all along, namely an inherently expansionist, aggressive and militaristic state.[56] Others (including the present author) regard the constraints as quite firmly internalized, and see Japan as a 'post-militaristic' (or even 'post-military') nation which has come to understand both the horrors and the futility of war, which has discovered the advantages of low military spending, and which has maintained strong civilian control over the military as an additional safeguard against militarization.[57]

The two different basic views just presented are reflected in diverging interpretations of concrete phenomena such as the (very modest) reinterpretations in recent years of the constitution to allow Japan to participate in UN operations. While those taking the former view are alarmed by this, viewing it as the first step in the direction of renewed military assertiveness, the latter group welcome it as reflecting a laudable cosmopolitan attitude, i.e. as personifying 'the Japan that wants to be liked'.[58]

Both interpretations are able to account for more recent developments such as Tokyo's response to repeated US admonitions that Japan ought to assume a greater part of the burden of upholding the world order from which it benefits so much, as well as make more of an effort with regard to its own national security, thereby producing a more equitable burden-sharing.[59] The revised 1997 US–Japan defence pact thus envisaged Japan assuming an expanded role in support of US operations in East Asia, seemingly including the Taiwan Strait – a plan to which the PRC did not respond favourably at all.[60] Moreover, pursuant to the agreement with the US, Japan is assuming greater responsibility for the defence of its own SLOCs, which is also reflected in naval procurement programmes and activities,[61] in turn extending Japan's defence perimeter to where it partly overlaps with that of the PRC.

While what Japan is presently doing may well be entirely defensively motivated, it also operates under the auspices of the security dilemma, hence its defensive steps may be regarded by others as threatening. As far as the South China Sea disputes are concerned, Japan has (fortunately) no territorial aspirations that would place it on a direct collision course with the PRC. On the other hand, it is so dependent on the free passage through the area that it would surely be forced to react to any further Chinese 'island grabs' which might place its SLOCs in jeopardy. In that eventuality, the stage would be set for a naval arms race between the two regional giants that would bode very ill for regional stability.

India does not yet play any significant role in the South China Sea. Indeed, the very direction of its security and defence policy remains disputed, notwithstanding the almost complete transparency that characterizes military planning in this the world's largest democracy, where the military remains under firm civilian control.[62]

Some analysts view India as aiming for a role as a regional hegemon in the Indian Ocean region,[63] an interpretation that is at least compatible with recent arms programmes. These will, in due course, provide India with a true blue-water navy as well as with longer striking range by means of missiles and aircraft.[64] In view of its long-standing rivalry with the PRC, India might feel compelled to respond, if only defensively, to its perception of a growing Chinese reach into the South China Sea as well as Indochina (especially Myanmar, almost on its own doorstep).

Such defensive steps as a more substantial peacetime presence in the area might, in the fullness of time, make India a significant player in the

South China Sea, as would an expansion of its incipient military collaboration with Vietnam, the future direction of which is difficult to predict.[65] On the other hand, it is also conceivable that India will remain so preoccupied with both the conflict with Pakistan and its domestic problems that it will (prudently) refrain from such a geopolitical contest with the PRC, remaining content with its recent acquisition of nuclear status.[66]

The United States remains not only a global, but also very much a regional player impacting on the South China Sea. It maintains bases in Hawaii, Japan and the Republic of Korea (ROK), and previously also in the Philippines, plus access rights in Thailand (U Tapao), Malaysia (Lumut), Indonesia (Surabaya) and Australia.[67] These are not merely designed for the defence of Hawaii and CONUS (Continental United States), but also for the defence of US allies, i.e. the ANZUS treaty members Australia and New Zealand and countries enjoying bilateral US security guarantees, i.e. Japan and the ROK and, more ambiguously, Taiwan, to the defence of which the US retains some commitment, as evidenced by its behaviour during the 1996 Taiwan Straits crisis.[68]

While the Pacific Fleet has shrunk somewhat (as has the US Navy in general), it remains by far the most formidable naval force. By July 1998 it counted 193 ships (down from 283 in 1986), including six aircraft carriers (all much larger than any other state's), 14 cruisers, 24 destroyers, 18 frigates, 30 submarines (nuclear ones, i.e. SSBNs, not included), plus no less than 1,432 aircraft (all very capable) and a very strong marine corps.[69] Not only does the United States thus dwarf all other players with regard to capabilities, it has also traditionally behaved very 'assertively', showing extreme reluctance to accept any constraints on its freedom of movement and action.

By virtue of this strength and reputation, the United States would be in a unique position to play the traditional role of an 'external balancer', providing security guarantees to whatever state might be attacked by another, and thereby making regional balances-of-power much less significant. Unfortunately for regional stability, however, this does not appear to be the role that the US wants to play, apparently preferring that of the 'lone ranger' in pursuit of 'bad states', rather arbitrarily defined as such.

Russia is no longer a major player in the South China Sea, its recent attempts at regaining rights at the Cam Ranh base in Vietnam notwithstanding.[70] Because of the simultaneous absence of strong political interests in the region and the requisite military capabilities to exert any influence, it can safely be disregarded.

• First of all, in conformity with its new focus on the 'near abroad', Russia retains an interest in Northeast Asia,[71] but both Southeast

Asia and the South China Sea fall beyond its perimeters. While Russia thus regularly attends ARF meetings, it has exhibited little real interest in the region.

- Second, its Pacific Fleet has shrunk dramatically since the end of the Cold War,[72] from 41 major surface combatants in 1990 (16 cruisers, 14 destroyers, 11 frigates) to a mere 18 in 1998 (4 cruisers, 11 destroyers and 3 frigates); and from 101 submarines (SSBNs not included) in 1990 to a mere 22 in 1998.[73]

Australia is arguably a potential relevant player in the South China Sea, if only because of its historical ties and remaining geopolitical links to Southeast Asia.[74] However, while Canberra is thus very much politically involved (albeit on the sidelines), e.g. in both the ARF and APEC as well as with unilateral initiatives, there are no indications that it will come to play any military role in the foreseeable future. Hence I have chosen to disregard it in the present context.

CONCLUSION

What may be of concern is not so much the balance of naval forces as such, but the sheer magnitude of the opposing contestants. The balance sheet in Table 6.3 does not reveal any imbalances that could lead any state (e.g. the PRC) to expect an easy victory over likely combinations of the others – especially if the United States is brought into the equation, in the aforementioned role of external balancer.

What has disturbed some authors (e.g. Barry Buzan and the late Gerald Segal) has been the almost complete lack of institutions or other mechanisms for conflict management. According to such analyses, East Asia comes close to the paradigm of a 'raw anarchy', where there are few inhibitions against war.[75] If this is true, the combination of conflicting territorial claims with a fairly high level of armaments described above bodes very ill for stability and peace in the region.

Fortunately, however, a certain institutional framework for collaboration does exist, even though its non-European nature may make it difficult to be recognized as such. In the 1990s, the cooperation among ASEAN member states was extended to the security field with the declaration of a nuclear weapons free zone,[76] and with an institutionalization of, first, the ASEAN Post-Ministerial Conferences (PMC) and subsequently the ASEAN Regional Forum (ARF). In both forums, security-political matters are discussed in a highly formalized setting, even though the participating states guard their sovereignty by avoiding binding decisions and by refraining from any semblance of supranationalism. Nevertheless, most observers agree in viewing especially the ARF as a very significant conflict prevention and management mechanism *sui generis*.[77]

Table 6.3 The naval military balance in the South China Sea

State	S	C	D	F	MP	OP	M	A
PRC	57	0	18	35	163	228	119	73
Vietnam	2	0	0	7	10	34	11	6
Thailand	0	1	0	19	6	76	5	9
Singapore	1	0	0	6	18	0	4	3
Philippines	0	0	0	1	0	67	0	9
Myanmar	0	0	0	2	6	28	0	15
Malaysia	0	0	0	8	8	29	5	3
Laos	0	0	0	0	0	0	0	
Indonesia	2	0	0	33	4	37	13	26
Cambodia	0	0	0	0	0	6	0	0
Japan	16	0	9	48	3	3	32	6
Taiwan	4	0	18	21	53	45	12	19
India	19	1	6	37	8	22	20	10
Australia	4	0	3	8	0	15	7	7
PRC/ ASEAN	1140	-	-	46	313	82	313	103
PRC/ ASEAN+ Others	119	-	50	18	141	63	109	65

Key: S: Submarines; C: Carriers; D: Destroyers; F: Frigates; MP: Missile Patrol Ships; OP: Other Patrol Ships; M: Mine Warfare Ships; A: Amphibious Ships

Source: Figures from Cordesman, Anthony H.: *The Asian and Chinese Military Balance. A Comparative Summary of Military Expenditures; Manpower; Land, Air, Naval, and Nuclear Forces; and Arms Sales* (Washington, D.C.: Center for Strategic and International Studies, January 2000), p. 28.

In addition to thus promoting transparency and confidence-building through dialogue, both ASEAN and the ARF have also contributed to conflict prevention by significant inroads into the field of both 'traditional' and maritime confidence-building measures (CBMs),[78] as well through their ongoing consultations with the PRC, e.g. about the South China Sea disputes. In this connection the ASEAN nations have wisely presented a united front, not in the form of identical positions on the conflicting claims, but by standing firm on procedural matters, maintaining that disputes should be solved without recourse to military force, preferably through international and binding legal adjudication.[79]

NOTES

1   On security complexes, see Buzan, Barry: 'A Framework for Regional Security Analysis', in B. Buzan, Rother Rizwi *et al.*: *South Asian Insecurity and the Great Powers* (London: Macmillan, 1986), pp. 3–33; Lake, David A. and Patrick M. Morgan (eds): *Regional Orders. Building Security in a New World* (University Park, PA: Pennsylvania State University Press, 1997). On conflict formations, see Väyrynen, Raimo: 'Regional Conflict Formations: An Intractable Problem of International Relations', *Journal of Peace Research*, vol. 21, no. 4 (1984), pp. 337–359. On security communities see Deutsch, Karl W. *et al.*: *Political Community and the North Atlantic Area. International Organization in the Light of Historical Experience* (Princeton, NJ: Princeton University Press, 1957).

2   The chapter is partly based on Møller, Bjørn: 'Introduction: Defence Restructuring in Asia', in B. Møller (ed.): *Security, Arms Control and Defence Restructuring in Asia* (Aldershot: Ashgate, 1998), pp. 1–36.

3   'In Brief. Philippines Sink Chinese Fishing Boat', *Jane's Defence Weekly*, vol. 32, no. 4 (28 July 1999). On the background, see 'China Stirs up Tension on Mischief Reef', ibid., vol. 30, no. 20 (18 November 1998); Hollingsbee, Trevor: 'China Moves in on Mischief Reef', *Jane's Intelligence Review*, vol. 11, no. 1 (1 January 1999), p. 5.

4   Valencia, Mark J.: 'China and the South China Sea Disputes', *Adelphi Paper*, no. 298, pp. 30–39 (on Vietnam) and pp. 44–48 (on the Philippines).

5   Available at http://www.aseansec.org. 'See also Statement by the ASEAN Foreign Ministers on the Recent Development in the South China Sea, 18 March 1995, available on same website.

6   Hollingsbee, Trevor: 'Spratlys Rivalry as Philippines Faces Malaysia', *Jane's Intelligence Review*, vol. 11, no. 10 (1 December 1999); Bristow, Damon: 'Between the Devil and the Deep Blue Sea: Maritime Disputes between Association of South East Asian Nations (ASEAN) Member States', *RUSI Journal*, vol. 141, no. 4 (August 1996), pp. 31–37.

7   A good analysis is Dyke, Jon M. Van and Mark J. Valencia: 'How Valid Are the South China Sea Claims under the Law of the Sea Convention?', *Southeast Asian Affairs 2000* (Singapore: Institute of Southeast Asian Affairs, 2000), pp. 47–63.

8   A systematic analysis, based on history, is Swaine, Michael D. and Ashley J. Tellis: *Interpreting China's Grand Strategy. Past, Present, and Future* (Santa Monica, CA: RAND, 2000).

9   On ties between Myanmar and China, see (for Indian perspectives) Singh, Udai Bhanu: 'Recent Trends in Relations between Myanmar and China', *Strategic Analysis*, vol. 18, no. 1 (April 1995), pp. 61–72; Singh, Swaran: 'Sino–

Myanmar Military Ties: Implications for India's Security', *U.S.I. Journal*, vol. 125, no. 521 (July–September 1995), pp. 348–357.

10 Whiting, Allen S. and Xin Jianfei: 'Sino-Japanese Relations. Pragmatism and Passion', *World Policy Journal*, vol. 8, no. 1 (Winter 1990–91), pp. 107–136; Segal, Gerald: 'The Coming Confrontation between China and Japan?', *World Policy Journal*, vol. 10, no. 2 (Summer 1993), pp. 27–32; Li, Rex: 'Partners or Rivals? Chinese Perceptions of Japan's Security Strategy', *Journal of Strategic Studies*, vol. 22, no. 4 (December 1999), pp. 1–25.

11 Shambaugh, David: ' China's Military Views the World: Ambivalent Security', *International Security*, vol. 24, no. 3 (Winter 1999/2000), pp. 52–79; Whiting, Allen S.: 'The PLA and China's Threat Perceptions', in David Shambaugh and Richard H. Yang (eds): *China's Military in Transition* (Oxford: Oxford University Press, 1997), pp. 332–352; Li, Rex: 'Unipolar Aspirations in a Multipolar Reality: China's Perceptions of US Ambitions and Capabilities in the Post-Cold War World', *Pacifica Review*, vol. 11, no. 2 (June 1999), pp. 115–149; Munro, Ross H.: 'Eavesdropping on the Chinese Military: Where It Expects War – Where It Doesn't', *Orbis*, vol. 38, no. 3 (Summer 1994), pp. 355–372. See also Nathan, Andrew J. and Robert S. Ross: *The Great Wall and the Empty Fortress: China's Search for Security* (New York: W.W. Norton & Co., 1997).

12 Chong-Pin Lin: 'Chinese Military Modernization: Perceptions, Progress, and Prospects', *Security Studies*, vol. 3, no. 4 (Summer 1994), pp. 718–753.

13 Leifer, Michael: 'Chinese Economic Reform and Security Policy: The South China Sea Connection', *Survival*, vol. 37, no. 2 (Summer 1995), pp. 44–59; Salameh, Mamdouh G.: 'China, Oil and the Risk of Regional Conflict', *Survival*, vol. 37, no. 4 (Winter 1995–96), pp. 133–146; Singh, Swaran: ' China's Energy Policy for the 21st Century', *Strategic Analysis*, vol. 22, no. 12 (Delhi: IDSA, March 1999), pp. 1871–1885; Feigenbaum, Evan A.: ' China's Military Posture and the New Economic Geopolitics', *Survival*, vol. 41, no. 2 (Summer 1999), pp. 71–88.

14 Downs, Erica and Philip Saunders: 'Legitimacy and the Limits of Nationalism. China and the Diaoyu Islands', *International Security*, vol. 23, no. 3 (Winter 1998/99), pp. 114–146; Paal, Douglas H.: 'The Regional Security Implications of China's Economic Expansion, Military Modernization, and the Rise of Nationalism', in Hung-mao Tien and Tun-jen Cheng (eds): *The Security Environment in the Asia-Pacific* (Armonk, NY: M.E. Sharpe, 2000), pp. 79–91.

15 For an overview of the methodological problems see IISS: *The Military Balance 1995/96*, pp. 270–275; or Wang, Shaoguang: 'The Military Expenditure of China, 1989–98', *SIPRI Yearbook 1999*, pp. 334–350.

16 Gill, Bates and Taeho Kim: 'China's Arms Acquisitions from Abroad: A Quest for "Superb and Secret Weapons"'. *SIPRI Research Report*, no. 11 (Oxford: Oxford University Press, 1995); Kondapalli, Srikanth: ' China's Naval Equipment Acquisition', *Strategic Analysis*, vol. 23, no. 9 (New Delhi: IDSA, December 1999), pp. 1509–1530.

17 For excellent analyses of Soviet strategy based on this methodology, see McGwire, Michael: *Military Objectives in Soviet Foreign Policy* (Washington, DC:

The Brookings Institution, 1987). Similar interpretations of Chinese arms acquisitions include Hua, Di: 'Threat Perception and Military Planning in China: Domestic Instability and the Importance of Prestige', in Eric Arnett (ed.): *Military Capacity and the Risk of War. China, India, Pakistan and Iran* (Oxford: Oxford University Press, 1997), pp. 25–38; Godwin, Paul H.B.: 'Military Technology and Doctrine in Chinese Military Planning: Compensating for Obsolescence', in ibid., pp. 39–60.

18 Lin Piao (1965): 'Long Live the Victory in the People's War', in Walter Lacqueur (ed.): *The Guerrilla Reader. A Historical Anthology* (London: Wildwood House, 1978), pp. 197–202. It is based on the writings of Mao Zedong from the 1930s.

19 Pollack, Jonathan D.: 'The Future of China's Nuclear Weapons Policy', in John C. Hopkins and Weixing Hu (eds): *Strategic Views from the Second Tier. The Nuclear Weapons Policies of France, Britain and China* (New Brunswick: Transaction Publishers, 1996), pp. 157–166; Lewis, John Wilson and Xue Litai: *China's Strategic Seapower. The Politics of Force Modernization in the Nuclear Age* (Stanford: Stanford University Press, 1994). On the logic of second-strike capabilities, see Wohlstetter, Albert: 'The Delicate Balance of Terror', in Henry M. Kissinger (ed.): *Problems of National Strategy* (New York: Praeger, 1965), pp. 34–58. On the (questionable) use of strategic nuclear weapons for 'compellence', see Schelling, Thomas: *The Strategy of Conflict* (Cambridge, MA: Harvard University Press, 1960), pp. 230–255; Betts, Richard K.: *Nuclear Blackmail and Nuclear Balance* (Washington DC: The Brookings Institution, 1987).

20 Brömmelhörster, Jörn and John Frankenstein (eds): *Mixed Motives, Uncertain Outcomes. Defense Conversion in China* (Boulder, CO: Lynne Rienner, 1997); Shichor, Yitzhak: 'Demobilization: The Dialectics of PLA Troop Reduction', in Brömmelhörster and Frankenstein, *op. cit.*, pp. 336–359; Shichor, Yitzhak: 'Defence Conversion and Conservation: China's Ambivalent Military Reform', in Møller: *op. cit.* (note 2), pp. 137–156; Singh, Swaran: ' China's Military Modernization', *Asian Strategic Review 1993–94* (New Delhi: IDSA, 1994), pp. 274–305.

21 Ma Ping: 'The Strategic Thinking of Active Defence and China's Military Strategic Principle', *International Strategic Studies*, no. 1 (Beijing: China Institute for International Strategic Studies, March 1994), pp. 1–6; Xu Xin: ' China's Defence Strategy under New Circumstances', in *International Strategic Studies*, no. 3 (September 1993), pp. 1–6; Nan Li: 'The PLA's Evolving Warfighting Doctrine, Strategy and Tactics, 1985–95: a Chinese Perspective', *The China Quarterly*, no. 146 (June 1996), pp. 443–464.

22 Shulong Chu: 'The PRC Girds for Limited, High-Tech War', *Orbis*, vol. 38, no. 2 (Spring 1994), pp. 177–191; Lin, Chong-Pin: 'Chinese Military Modernization: Perceptions, Progress, and Prospects', *Security Studies*, vol. 3, no. 4 (Summer 1994), pp. 718–753; Kayahara, Ikuo: 'China as a Military Power in the Twenty-first Century', *Japan Review of International Affairs*, vol. 12, no. 1 (Spring 1998), pp. 49–68; Kondapalli, Srikanth: *China's Military. The PLA in Transition* (New Delhi: Knowledge World and Institute for Defense Studies and Analyses, 1999).

23 Zhan, Jun: 'China Goes to the Blue Waters: The Navy, Seapower Mentality and the South China Sea', *The Journal of Strategic Studies*, vol. 17, no. 3 (September 1994), pp. 180–208; Till, Geoffrey: 'China, Its Navy and the South China Sea', *The RUSI Journal*, vol. 141, no. 2 (April 1996), pp. 45–51.

24 Ji, You: *The Armed Forces of China* (London: I.B. Tauris, 1999), pp. 160–200; Zhan, Jun: 'China Goes to the Blue Waters: The Navy, Seapower Mentality and the South China Sea', *The Journal of Strategic Studies*, vol. 17, no. 3 (September 1994), pp. 180–208.

25 On Taiwanese moves to garrison Taiping, see Hollingsbee, Trevor: 'Taiwan Copies China's Tactics', *Jane's Intelligence Review*, vol. 11, no. 6 (1 June 1999).

26 On defensive (or better: non-offensive) defence, see Møller, Bjørn: *Resolving the Security Dilemma in Europe. The German Debate on Non-Offensive Defence* (London: Brassey's Defence Publishers, 1991); Møller, Bjørn: *Common Security and Nonoffensive Defense. A Neorealist Perspective* (Boulder, CO: Lynne Rienner/London: UCL Press, 1992); *Dictionary of Alternative Defense* (Boulder, CO: Lynne Rienner/London: Adamantine Press, 1995).

27 *National Defence Report 1993–94* (Taipei: Ministry of National Defence, 1994), pp. 83, 101.

28 Ibid., pp. 200–201 (on the army), 204–205 (navy), 208–209 (air force), 212 (coast guard). See also Yang, Andrew N.D.: 'Threats across the Taiwan Strait: Reaching out for the Unreachable', *The RUSI Journal*, vol. 141, no. 2 (April 1996), pp. 52–56; 'The Jane's Interview' with Taiwanese General Tang Fei, *Jane's Defence Weekly*, vol. 30, no. 1 (8 July 1998).

29 Albright, David and Corey Gay: 'Taiwan: Nuclear Nightmare Averted', *Bulletin of the Atomic Scientists*, vol. 64, no. 1 (January 1998), pp. 54–60.

30 *2000 National Defense Report*, chapter 2.2, at http://www.mnd.gov.tw/report/830/html/2-2.html.

31 Lin, Chong-pin: 'The Military Balance in the Taiwan Straits', in Shambaugh and Yang: *op. cit.* (note 12), pp. 313–331; Møller, Bjørn: 'Unification of Divided States in East Asia', in ibid., pp. 161–201.

32 Ibid., at http://www.mnd.gov.tw/report/830/html/4-1.html.

33 On sea command see Mahan, Alfred T.: *The Influence of Sea Power upon History 1660–1783* (1894 [Reprint: New York: Dover Publications, 1987]). On defensive sea control see Mearsheimer, John J.: 'A Strategic Misstep: The Maritime Strategy and Deterrence in Europe', *International Security*, vol. 11, no. 2 (Fall 1986), pp. 3–57; Møller, Bjørn: 'Restructuring the Naval Forces towards Non-Offensive Defence', in Marlies ter Borg and Wim Smit (eds): *Non-provocative Defence as a Principle of Arms Control and its Implications for Assessing Defence Technologies* (Amsterdam: Free University Press, 1989), pp. 189–206.

34 Chalmers, Malcolm: *Confidence Building in South-East Asia* (Boulder, CO: Westview, 1996), pp. 61–119; Nayan, Md Hussin: 'Openness and Transparency in the ASEAN Countries', *Disarmament*, vol. 18, no. 2 (1995), pp. 135–144.

35 Setboonsargn, Suthad: 'ASEAN Economic Cooperation: Adjusting to the Crisis', *Southeast Asia Affairs 1998* (Singapore: Institute of Southeast Asian

Affairs, 1998), pp. 18–36. On the previous growth see Campos, Jose Edgardo and Hilton L. Root: *The Key to the Asian Miracle. Making Shared Growth Credible* (Washington, DC: Brookings, 1996). On the gradual recovery from the crisis see Booth, Anne: 'Southeast Asia: Towards a Sustained Recovery?', *Southeast Asia Affairs 2000* (Singapore: Institute of Southeast Asian Affairs, 2000), pp. 25–46.

36 Bateman, Sam: 'ASEAN's Tiger Navies Catching Up or Building Up?', *Jane's Navy International*, vol. 102, no. 3 (1 April 1997), p. 18.

37 Singh, Udai Bhanu: 'Growth of Military Power in South-East Asia', *Asian Strategic Review 1994–95* (New Delhi: IDSA, 1995), pp. 311–351.

38 For an excellent analysis, see Acharya, Amitav: *An Arms Race in Post-Cold War South-East Asia: Prospects for Control* (Singapore: Institute of Southeast Asian Studies, 1994); and Chalmers: *op. cit.* (note 36), pp. 61–119. On arms race theory in general, see also Møller, Bjørn: 'From Arms to Disarmament Races: Disarmament Dynamics after the Cold War', in Ho-Won Jeong (ed.): *The New Agenda for Peace Research* (Aldershot: Ashgate, 1999), pp. 83–104.

39 Carey, Merrick: 'Promise and Peril on the Pacific Rim', *The 2000 Almanac of Seapower Seapower*, January 2000, pp. 59–65, at http://www.navyleague.org /seapower/ promise_and_peril.htm.

40 Cunha, Derek da: 'The Need for Weapons Upgrading in Southeast Asia: Present and Future', *ISEAS Working Papers*, no. 1/96 (Singapore: Institute of Southeast Asian Studies, 1996); Mak, J.N. and B.A. Hamzah: 'The External Maritime Dimension of ASEAN Security', in Desmond Ball (ed.): *The Transformation of Security in the Asia/Pacific Region* (London: Frank Cass, 1996), pp. 123–146; Desmond Ball: 'International Cooperation in Regional Security: 'Non-Interference' and ASEAN Arms Modernization', in Møller (ed.): *op. cit.* (note 2), pp. 77–92. On the resolution of domestic conflicts, see Findlay, Trevor: 'Turning the Corner in Southeast Asia', in Michael E. Brown (ed.): *The International Dimensions of Internal Conflict* (Cambridge, MA: MIT Press, 1996), pp. 173–204.

41 Janssen, Joris: 'ASEAN Navies Extend their Maritime Reach', *Jane's Defence Weekly*, vol. 26, no. 22 (27 Nov 1996), p. 25. On the UN Convention on the Law of the Sea, which finally entered into force in November 1994, see Oxman, Bernhard H.: 'Law of the Sea', in Oscar Schachter and Christopher C. Joyner (eds): *United Nations Legal Order*, vols 1–2 (Cambridge: Grotius Publications/Cambridge University Press, 1995), vol. 2, pp. 671–714. On the background, see Shaw, Malcolm N.: *International Law*. Third Edition (Cambridge: Grotius Publications, 1991), pp. 337–392; Jenisch, Uwe: 'The Future of the UN Law of the Sea Convention', *Aussenpolitik*, no. 1 (1988), pp. 46–60.

42 Security dilemma refers to a situation where one nation's pursuit of security causes a reduction in security for other nations. On the security dilemma, see Herz, John M.: *Political Realism and Political Idealism. A Study in Theories and Realities* (Chicago: Chicago University Press, 1951), *passim*; Herz, John M.: 'Idealist Internationalism and the Security Dilemma', *World Politics*, no. 2, 1950, pp. 157–180.

43 Thayer, Carlyle A.: *The Vietnam People's Army under Doi Moi* (Singapore: Institute of Southeast Asian Studies, 1994); Thayer, C.A. and Ramses Amer

(eds): *Vietnamese Foreign Policy in Transition* (Singapore: Institute of Southeast Asian Studies, 1999), *passim*.

44 Singh, Udai Bhanu: 'Vietnam's Security Perspectives', *Strategic Analysis*, vol. 23, no. 9 (December 1999), pp. 1489–1491.

45 Karniol, Robert: 'Briefing: Military Modernisation in Asia', *Jane's Defence Weekly*, vol. 32, no. 21 (24 November 1999). In 1995, the navy thus numbered merely 1 frigate, 9 patrol ships and 8 amphibious ships.

46 Nathan, K.S.: 'Malaysia: Reinventing the Nation', in Alagappa: *op. cit.* (note 46), pp. 513–548. On the military build-up, see 'Country Briefing – Malaysia', *Jane's Defence Weekly*, vol. 33, no. 13 (29 March 2000).

47 Lowry, Robert: *The Armed Forces of Indonesia* (London: Allen & Unwin, 1996), pp. 233–234.

48 Lowry: *op. cit.* (note 49), pp. 25–38 and 147–181. See also Renwick, Neil and Jason Abbott: 'Piratical Violence and Maritime Security in Southeast Asia', *Security Dialogue*, vol. 30, no. 2 (June 1999), pp. 183–196.

49 Storey, Ian James: 'Living with the Colossus: How Southeast Asian Countries Cope with China', *Parameters. US Army War College Quarterly*, Winter 1999–2000, pp. 111–125; Leifer, Michael: 'Indonesia's Encounters with China and the Dilemmas of Engagement', in Alastair Johnston and Robert S. Ross (eds.): *Engaging China. The Management of an Emerging Power* (London: Routledge, 1999), pp. 87–108.

50 Bandoro, Bantarto: 'The Prospects of ASEAN Military Cooperation', in Tien and Cheng: *op. cit.*, (note 15), pp. 189–201.

51 On ZOPFAN, see Hänggi, Heiner: *Neutralität in Südostasien. Das Project einer Zone des Friedens, der Freiheit und der Neutralität* (Bern: Verlag Paul Haupt, 1993). On Singapore's ambivalent attitute to China, see Leifer, Michael: *Singapore's Foreign Policy. Coping with Vulnerability* (London: Routledge, 2000), pp. 108–124. On the balance-or-bandwagon dilemma, see Walt, Stephen M.: *The Origins of Alliances* (Ithaca, NY: Cornell University Press, 1979), pp. 27–33.

52 Haseman, John: 'Indonesia, China Expand Co-operation', *Jane's Defence Weekly*, vol. 33, no. 21 (24 May 2000).

53 On APEC, see Aggarwal, Vinod and Charles E. Morrison (eds.): *Asia-Pacific Crossroads. Regime Creation and the Future of APEC* (New York: St Martin's Press, 1998), *passim*.

54 Cronin, Richard P.: 'Japan', in Richard Dean Burns (ed.): *Encyclopedia of Arms Control and Disarmament* (New York: Charles Scribner's Sons, 1993), vol. I, pp. 129–147. The most recent official formulation of Japan's defence policy is the *White Paper Defense of Japan 1996*, available at http://www.jda.go.jp/pab/8aramasi/defcont.htm.

55 Samuels, Richard J.: *'Rich Nation, Strong Army'. National Security and the Technological Transformation of Japan* (Ithaca, NY: Cornell University Press, 1994); Huber, Thomas M.: *Strategic Economy in Japan* (Boulder, CO: Westview Press, 1994).

56 See, for instance, Ienaga, Saburo: 'The Glorification of War in Japanese Education', *International Security*, vol. 18, no. 3 (Winter 1993–94), pp. 113–

133; Mochizuki, Michael M.: 'Review Essay: The Past in Japan's Future. Will the Japanese Change?', *Foreign Affairs*, vol. 73, no. 5 (Sept–Oct 1994), pp. 126–134.

57 Barnett, Robert W.: *Beyond War. Japan's Concept of Comprehensive National Security* (Washington: Brassey's, 1984).

58 Tamamoto, Masaru: 'The Japan that Wants to Be Liked: Society and International Participation', in Danny Unger and Paul Blackburn (eds.): *Japan's Emerging Global Role* (Boulder, CO: Lynne Rienner, 1993), pp. 37–54.

59 Sasae, Kenichiro: 'Rethinking Japan–US Relations', *Adelphi Paper*, no. 292 (1994); Curtis, Gerald L. (ed.): *The United States, Japan, and Asia. Challenges for U.S. Policy* (New York: W.W. Norton & Co., 1994).

60 *The Times*, 25 September 1997.

61 Downing, John: 'A Japanese Navy in All but Name', *Jane's Navy International*, vol. 104, no. 3 (1 April 1999).

62 On the role of the military see Rosen, Stephen Peter: *Societies and Military Power: India and Its Armies* (Ithaca, NY: Cornell University Press, 1996).

63 Gill, Veena: 'India as a Regional Great Power: in Pursuit of Shakti', in Iver B. Neumann (ed.): *Regional Great Powers in International Politics* (New York: St Martin's Press, 1992), pp. 49–69.

64 Smith, Chris: *India's ad hoc Arsenal. Directions or Drift in Defence Policy?* (Oxford: Oxford University Press/SIPRI, 1994).

65 Bedi, Rahul: 'India, Vietnam in Co-operation Pact', *Jane's Defence Weekly*, vol. 33, no. 14 (5 April 2000).

66 Singh, Jasjit: 'Future Directions of India's Defence Policy', *Strategic Digest* (New Delhi: Institute for Defence Studies and Analyses), vol. 26, no. 5 (May 1996), pp. 605–612.

67 Weeks, Stanley B. and Charles A. Meconis: *The Armed Forces of the USA in the Asia-Pacific Region* (London: I.B. Tauris, 1999), pp. 82–98.

68 *Ibid.*, pp. 30–64.

69 Weeks and Meconis: *op. cit.* (note 69), pp. 134–156.

70 Robert Karniol: 'Deadlock over Naval Base Future', *Jane's Defence Weekly*, vol. 31, no. 16 (21 April 1999).

71 Austin, Greg and Alexey D. Muraviev: *The Armed Forces of the Russia in Asia* (London: I.B. Tauris, 2000), pp. 96–129.

72 Asada, Mashiko: 'Revived Soviet Interest in Asia: a New Approach', in Frank C. Langdon and Douglas A Ross (eds.): *Superpower Maritime Strategy in the Pacific* (London: Routledge, 1990), pp. 35–71.

73 Austin and Muraviev: *op. cit.* (note 73), pp. 204–233. Figures from tables 7.1 and 7.2 on pages 208 and 218, respectively.

74 On Australia's military involvement in the region, see Grey, Jeffrey: *A Military History of Australia* (Cambridge: Cambridge University Press, 1999), *passim*.

75 Buzan, Barry and Gerald Segal: 'Rethinking East Asian Security', *Survival*, vol. 36, no. 2 (Summer 1994), pp. 3–21.

76 'Treaty on the Southeast Asia Nuclear-Weapon-Free Zone', *Strategic Digest*, vol. 26, no. 3 (New Delhi: IDSA, 1996), pp. 320–328.

77 On ARF, see Findlay, Trevor: 'South-East Asia and the New Asia-Pacific Security Dialogue', in *SIPRI Yearbook 1994*, pp. 125–148.

78 Chung, Chien: 'Confidence-Building Measures in the South China Sea', in Tien and Cheng (eds.): *op. cit.* (note 15), pp. 259–305; Chalmers: *op. cit.* (note 36), pp. 221–242.

79 Rappai, M.V.: 'South China Sea: Conflict and Cooperation', *Asian Strategic Review* 1996–97 (New Delhi: IDSA, 1997), pp. 276–294.

7

THE POLITICAL DIMENSION: SOURCES OF CONFLICT AND STABILITY

Ramses Amer and Timo Kivimäki[1]

INTRODUCTION

The special problem in the territorial claims of the South China Sea and in all relatively remote areas is that there are no objective aspects to refer to in support of claims. This is why only practices can articulate the 'naturality' of one's claim. In remote uninhabited islands, the most natural way to articulate one's claim is to show a military presence and enforce national legislation in the areas. Clearly, if two or more nations choose this way of articulation in the same place, a military confrontation ensues. This is why symbolic argumentation in these disputes soon involves military confrontation. Thus, these disputes have the potential of triggering conflicts especially if there are other, more fundamental sources of tension between nations.

In the case of Vietnam and the People's Republic of China (PRC), as well as between Taiwan and the PRC, this might be the case. Even if the issue of sovereignty of certain seas and islands is not a sufficient dispute to motivate a costly war, it might easily act as a trigger between countries that have other, more fundamental issues that separate them. In this kind of setting it is important to study the 'political crisis stability' of the region.

How good are the nations in avoiding violence, despite their disputes? This will be assessed, first by looking at the political foundations of stability and then by focusing on the mechanisms of dispute management specific to the question of territorial disputes in the South China Sea.

Table 7.1: Disputes since the 1950s (or since independence) among countries with territorial claims in the South China Sea

Country	Disputes	Started after country was a member of	With ASEAN member	With forth-coming ASEAN member
Indonesia	3C, 17D	0C, 6D	0C, 0D	1C, 3D
Malaysia	1C, 10 D	0C, 8D**	0C, 6D*	1C, 3D
Philippines	2C, 12D	0C, 9D	0C, 5D (all with Malaysia)	1C, 5D
Thailand	14C, 46D	6C, 29D	0C, 0D	10C, 38D
Cambodia	22D, 8C	0D, 0C (data dates before Cambodia's own member-ship)	3D, 3C (data dates before Cambodia's own membership)	10D, 3C
China-PRC	96D, 19C	-	3D, 0C	10D, 5C
Taiwan	29D, 5C	-	1D, 0C	1D, 0C
Vietnam, Dem. Rep.	17D, 9C	0D, 0C (data dates before Vietnam's own membership)	4D, 1C (data dates before Vietnam's own membership)	6D, 2C
Vietnam, Rep.	15D, 4C	-	1D, 0C	11D, 3C

Key: D=Dispute without known casualties, C=Conflict with casualties
* Malaysia has had militarized disputes with the Philippines, Indonesia and Singapore, The Philippines has had a militarized dispute with Singapore, and Vietnam with the Philippines, Malaysia and the PRC after the period of the MID-data (ends in 1994). None of these has produced any casualties. Furthermore, Taiwan and the PRC suffered casualties in their bilateral relations after the end of the MID-data period.
** The MID-data dates the Sabah-related dispute between the Philippines and Malaysia in the 1960s–1968 and gives no data on the casualties. Yet the dispute certainly started and became militarized immediately after the independence of Malaysia in 1963, much before 1968.[2]

Source: Correlates of War Projects Militarized Inter-State Disputes Data-base, Jones *et al.* 1996.

Elements of political stability in the South China Sea region

There are a number of unresolved disputes in Southeast Asia. Yet the area does not have a strong inter-state conflict tradition. The 'normative community' of ASEAN seems to have been an important factor in preventing the escalation of disputes into violent conflicts. As Table 7.1 shows, ASEAN countries have not yet fought one another, despite the fact that these countries used to be involved in violent altercations.

If we look at the traditional patterns of fighting in Southeast Asia and in the South China Sea region, we can see that the number of disputes is not necessarily correlated with the number of conflicts in the Southeast Asian inter-state relations. For example, between 1950 and 1992 there was not a single dispute without casualties between the Democratic Republic of Vietnam and the Philippines, but there was a major war between the countries. Yet after the establishment of ASEAN, there have been a large number of disputes between ASEAN countries, but not a single casualty. Figure 7.1 illustrates the conflicts and disputes in Southeast Asia. It reveals that while disputes can occur between practically any two countries sufficiently close to each other, conflicts have not been experienced between countries that are generally seen as belonging to the same 'camp' or 'normative community'.

The conflict patterns in Southeast Asia show, for example, how the PRC's conflict behaviour towards the Philippines changed as the perceptions of world divisions changed. When the West was perceived as the PRC's main opponent, the PRC had conflicts with Taiwan and the Philippines, but as soon as the Soviet Union became the PRC's principal opponent, the PRC started having conflicts with the pro-Soviet Vietnam. Similarly when Indonesia felt that the world was divided between the new emerging forces (communists and nationalists) and the old established forces (colonialists and imperialists), Indonesia fought against Malaysia, which it believed to be an agent of colonial power. When the Indonesian perception changed, and it started viewing ASEAN as one entity, its aggression against Singapore and Malaysia stopped. Malaysia and the Philippines have had some very serious diplomatic disputes, some of which have become militarized, but never a conflict with casualties. Again, these two countries have never perceived each other as in adversarial camps in world affairs. The de-escalation of tension in Indochina also proves the importance of perceptions of common interests, identities and norms in the prevention of conflicts in Southeast Asia.

While one could claim that the patterns of conflict in Southeast Asia prove the importance of geopolitics in the area, one could also interpret Figure 7.1 as evidence of the importance of subjective perceptions of common identity and thus the importance of confidence-building measures, the pertinence of the promotion of common identity, and sense of positive interdependence. The establishment of ASEAN and its security implications show that Southeast Asia is not merely reacting to global geopolitical developments, but itself constructs the social reality of geopolitics in its area. The forces that consolidate soft peace structures in the South China Sea region are related to (a) subjective sense of common interest, (b) the feeling of common identity and (c) a reliance on common procedures of dispute management.

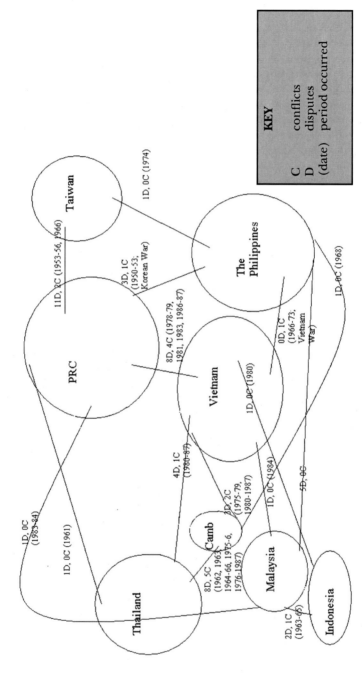

Figure 7.1: Number of inter-state disputes and conflicts among the South China Sea nations (*Source:* Correlates of War Projects Militarized Inter-State Disputes Data-base, Jones et al. 1996)

COMMON INTERESTS

Developmentalism – an ideology which bases the value of a political decision on its economic consequences – has been a major orientation in Southeast Asia in the 1970s, 1980s and 1990s. This orientation has been instrumental in increasing the subjective evaluation of the common economic interests.[3]

The subjective sensitivity towards common economic interests also has its institutional expressions. While most clearly articulated in ASEAN cooperation, the developmentalist sense of interdependence is also strengthening the ties between ASEAN countries and the PRC, as well as the PRC and Taiwan. The first sentence of the Bangkok Declaration, the founding document of ASEAN, emphasizes the importance of the common interests of the ASEAN countries.

In later ASEAN publications, national development achievements are often seen as parts of the collective ASEAN development. Development and stability have been explicitly linked in many ASEAN documents and this link has been seen as one of the rationales of ASEAN cooperation in development.[4] According to former President Fidel Ramos of the Philippines, ASEAN countries 'try to build up something that unites us, and cope with all problems that separate us'.[5] Developmentalism has clearly served the ASEAN strategy of promoting a subjective sense of interdependence:[6] 'The economic integration in the region has brought interdependence and a shared destiny to the region.'[7]

In relations between ASEAN countries and the PRC, economic interdependence is also highlighted by many scholars.[8] When the PRC announced its proposal of shelving the sovereignty issue, and concentrating on the joint exploration of the economic resources in the disputed areas, Deng Xiaoping explicitly used the rationale of economic interdependence as the core motive for accepting his proposal.[9] Economic rationales are also repeatedly emphasized in Chinese official statements of the PRC's policies towards ASEAN.[10]

More generally, it has been suggested that the economic build-up is the prime task of the PRC and that Chinese military strategy is dictated by this priority.[11] Military strategists often maintain that the main reason for the PRC's hesitance in using military force in the South China Sea is its desire to pursue economic cooperation with ASEAN.[12]

The emphasis on development-related interdependence has also led to transnational institution building in Southeast Asia. All these transnational sub-regional cooperative institutions have concentrated their attention on issues of common economic interest rather than on issues where the nations compete or are in conflict.[13] This is also the case in the growth areas, growth triangles and natural economic zones[14] or institutions set up for the resolution of a particular dispute.[15] As a result, disputes have a lesser subjective weight compared to the issues of common interest.

The elite-promotion of the popular perception of positive inter-dependence also means discouraging media exposure on disputes. When in 1994 Indonesia discovered that the PRC had included some sea areas close to its Natuna Islands in its official maps, Jakarta sought a response from Beijing about the matter and demanded an explanation. This diplomatic dispute remained undisclosed for more than a year, simply because according to Indonesia's Foreign Ministry spokesperson, 'We did not want to make a big fuss about it'.[16]

During the Chinese dispute with the Republic of Vietnam in 1974 over the Paracel Islands, the PRC captured an American military observer, along with Vietnamese soldiers, in the Vietnamese military facilities in the disputed islands. Instead of using the US support for the Vietnamese military in her conflict propaganda, the PRC tried to play down the fact in the media and tried to avoid making a fuss about this potentially escalating detail of the Sino–Vietnamese confrontation.[17]

During the initial phase of the dispute over the Sipadan and Ligitan Islands between Indonesia and Malaysia, when the Indonesian military started to investigate 'foreign activities' around the islands, 'both the Malaysian and Indonesian governments tried to play down the incident discouraging press coverage and no clear account of the events was given'.[18] The clear rationale behind secrecy in all these cases was the elite effort to prevent negative popular sentiments. Restrictive publicity on disputes is also rationalized on the grounds of diplomatic prudence: playing down disputes simply means avoiding washing dirty linen in public.[19]

The playing down of disputes and emphasis on common interests has resulted in conciliatory policies in territorial disputes in Southeast Asia. In 1991, the dispute over Ligitan and Sipadan escalated after Indonesia discovered that Malaysia had built tourist facilities there. After protests by Indonesia, the Malaysian government cancelled its programme of upgrading tourist facilities in the area, dropped the area from their list of nature reserve development plans, and rationalized both moves publicly on the grounds of not harming the mutually beneficial relationships between Malaysia and Indonesia.[20]

When mediating in 1987 in a diplomatic dispute between Singapore and Malaysia over policies towards Israel, Suharto emphasized the commonality of economic interests of ASEAN states. In addition to press statements, Suharto demonstrated the link between the destinies of the two countries by driving along the road that physically connects the two countries whenever he needed to move from Malaysia to Singapore.[21]

In another territorial dispute between Singapore and Malaysia (which was further aggravated by Malaysia–Indonesian military exercises) the commonality of interests between the ASEAN nations was again emphasized when Malaysia and Singapore found their first legal formula for the settlement of the issue. Malaysia's prime minister went public by declaring that due to the weight of common economic interests: 'Malaysia and Singapore will not go to war over a piece of white rock.'[22]

While the perceptions of common interest have served as an important rationale for playing down the disputes and preventing their escalation into conflict, one should not view the positive development as given. Even though in the objective sense economic interdependence among ASEAN countries has gradually grown from the latter half of the 1970s, and between the PRC and ASEAN from the latter half of the 1980s, and between ASEAN and Taiwan in the 1990s, a subjective sense of interdependence does not necessarily follow this development.

Especially during the Asian economic crisis, when Asian nations found themselves as competitive destinations of foreign investment, the feeling of positive interdependence was drastically reduced. Furthermore, criticism against globalist developmentalism has grown among some Asian countries and, if this were to continue, the subjective value of economic cooperation might decline again as it did in the belligerent period of the 1960s.[23]

COMMON IDENTITY

A common Asian identity has played a stabilizing role in the politics of the region. Southeast Asian countries have developed common political values which have been the strongest bases of identity within ASEAN, but which occasionally have served as the basis of a broader, Asian or East Asian identity.

The global construction of 'otherness' between East and West penetrated and cut across Southeast Asia in the 1960s. After Indonesia moved from the anti-Western camp into the anti-communist camp, the global construction of an East–West division became an asset rather than a liability vis-à-vis stability in ASEAN, while it became the dividing line between the original ASEAN countries and the Indochinese latecomers of the 1990s.

It has been argued that one of the cornerstones of ASEAN unity has been united opposition to communist values. This has provided the organization with a common enemy and made it impossible for one ASEAN country to legitimize aggression against another.[24] At the same time, the relations between the West and the Chinese and the Soviet communist blocs have played an important identifying role in Southeast Asian geopolitics.

During simple antagonism between East and the West, the PRC opposed most violently the overlapping territorial claims in the South

China Sea by the Western powers. In the 1950s, Philippine policies were seen as reflecting the hegemonic ambitions of the US.[25] The Philippine policies were viewed as 'a product of instructions from the United States government'.[26] According to Chinese scholar Fu Chu, 'the US imperialists not only militarily invade Taiwan, but also support its lackeys, like the Philippines and South Vietnam, in their attempt to invade our South China Sea islands, including the Nansha Islands'.[27]

After the breakdown of Sino–Soviet relations, the Chinese perceived threat from the Philippines eased, and the Democratic Republic of Vietnam came to be seen as the main security threat in the South China Seas: 'Vietnam's claim and operations there represent regional hegemonism', according to the *Beijing Review* (January 1, 1980, p. 24). The collapse of the Cold War made it possible for the PRC to further approach the Philippines and ASEAN and for Indochinese latecomers to enter ASEAN. Yet it also took away one of the important sources of ASEAN identity.

The East–West division was by no means the only or even the most important source of common identity, however. The bulwark of the common values and common identity of Southeast Asia centred on the concept of 'Asian values' which has been consolidated and actively promoted, especially by the Malaysian Prime Minister Mahathir.[28] The construction of 'Asian values' has derived its strength by contrasting Asian values with the values of the 'West' or the 'North'.[29] In specific disputes this has meant resorting to a new identity paradigm to play down the public tension caused by disputes.

For example, in the Malaysian–Indonesian dispute over the islands of Ligitan and Sipadan, the effort to resort to common values and identity was exemplified in a public statement by the Secretary General for Indonesia's Home Affairs Ministry, Major General Nugroho, who said that differences in opinions between Malaysia and Indonesia in territorial issues are understandable because of 'maps inherited from their colonial masters'.[30] Instead of blaming his opponent, Nugroho framed the dispute as resulting from the deeds of a common 'other', the colonialists.

The emergence of a new identity paradigm in Southeast Asia has also had some worrying developments. Since the end of the Cold War a division has emerged between supporters of Asian values (Singapore, Malaysia, the PRC, and Suharto's and Wahid's Indonesia) on the one hand and supporters of globalized Western concepts of human rights and democracy (Thailand, the Philippines and Habibie's Indonesia) on the other. This split is sometimes also expressed in the religious/civilizational division between Christians and Muslims.

The criticism levelled against Malaysia's prime minister for his detention of Deputy Prime Minister Anwar Ibrahim clearly highlighted the new division, where the Philippines, Indonesia and Thailand referred to Western principles of democracy and human rights in their condemnation of Mahathir. The Philippine criticism was, in fact, related to a militarized Malaysian–Philippine dispute, as many Philippine officials and scholars believed Malaysia to have constructed a two-storey building on the Investigator Shoal, an area that the Philippines was claiming, partly as a retaliation against President Estrada's harsh criticism of Mahathir.[31]

The Western distrust of the judicial system of a country promoting 'Asian democracy' was visible in how the Philippines handled the situation: President Fidel Ramos ordered the Philippine Air Force on a rescue mission to bring back to the Philippines all those Philippine citizens who felt their lives to be under threat in Singapore.[32] This incident took place exactly at the same time as another promoter of 'Asian values', the PRC, intensified its presence in Mischief Reef in the Spratly Islands claimed by the Philippines. Again the Philippine reaction demonstrated its 'Western', 'non-Asian' identity: instead of quietly playing down the issue, the Philippines sent a mission carrying 38 international journalists to the area.[33]

It seems clear that the pillar of peace built on the principle of a shared identity in the South China Sea is weakening and the rift between the West and Asia seems to be causing divisions even within ASEAN. The position of the Christian, globalist, democratic Philippines in this division is especially problematic.

COMMON MECHANISMS OF DISPUTE MANAGEMENT

Conflict management and the creation of ASEAN

The creation of ASEAN can arguably be seen as the result of efforts by some Southeast Asian states to create an association that could provide the framework for successful management of disputes amongst themselves. If this view is accepted, the creation of ASEAN can be seen as determined by the desire of its original member-states (Indonesia, Malaysia, the Philippines, Singapore, and Thailand), to handle existing and potential inter-state disputes through peaceful measures and thus minimize the risk of militarized conflicts. There was, in other words, a desire to secure a peaceful and cooperative environment in the sub-region of Southeast Asia – indeed, this was the decisive factor in the creation of ASEAN. Thus, ASEAN was from the outset an association for conflict management.

Empirical evidence lends support to this view of the *raison d'être* of ASEAN. During the first half of the 1960s, deep conflicts erupted between

Indonesia and Malaysia and between Malaysia and the Philippines, respectively. Furthermore, the two existing sub-regional organizations in Southeast Asia – the Association of Southeast Asia (ASA) created in 1961 with Malaysia, the Philippines and Thailand as members, and, subsequently, Maphilindo created in 1963 with Malaysia, the Philippines and Indonesia as members – failed to contain the two conflict situations.[34] The limitations and shortcomings of these two associations clearly indicated the need for a broader and more efficient association as a vehicle for regional cooperation and conflict management. To bring about a broader membership base in the new association, all the major non-socialist countries in Southeast Asia (except the Republic of Vietnam) joined ASEAN alongside Singapore in 1967.

Hence, managing the relations between the founding members of ASEAN was the main reason for establishing the Association. This is linked to the fear of internal communist and separatist movements in several of the ASEAN states in the 1960s and the need to minimize the risk of interference by neighbouring countries. A broader fear of international communism can also be identified, particularly directed at the PRC.

Given this background, dispute/conflict management has been of major importance within ASEAN. But what is implied by the ASEAN approach to dispute/conflict management? There are two basic aspects: first, the mechanisms as formulated in different ASEAN declarations and treaties, and second, the way in which the ASEAN members negotiate and how they reach a common understanding on various issues. Both these aspects will be examined below, first the mechanisms and then the ASEAN negotiation and decision-making processes.

Mechanisms for conflict management

Although ASEAN was created as part of a process aiming at peaceful management of conflicts among its members, the *ASEAN Declaration (Bangkok Declaration)*[35] adopted on 8 August 1967 did not specify exactly how this aim should be achieved. In fact more attention is devoted to the promotion of social and economic cooperation among the member-states of the Association than to conflict management. The references to conflict management in the Preamble of the Declaration are general in character as can be seen from the expressed desire to

> establish a firm foundation for common action to promote regional cooperation in South-East Asia in the spirit of equality and partnership and thereby contribute towards peace, progress and prosperity in the region...[36]

Also, in the part relating to the aims and purposes of the Association, the paragraph dealing specifically with the promotion of 'regional peace' is general rather then specific in its wording:

To promote regional peace and stability through abiding respect for justice and the rule of law in relationship among countries of the region and adherence to the principles of the United Nations Charter.[37]

Thus, the ASEAN Declaration spelled out the overall goals of ASEAN and set the stage for a process aiming at refining the way in which the Association should function and the mechanisms by which the aims should be achieved.

The evolution during the so-called 'formative years' (1967–76), which led to the signing of the *Declaration of ASEAN Concord* and the *Treaty of Amity and Cooperation (TAC) (Bali Treaty)*[38] on 24 February 1976, in connection with the First Summit Meeting of ASEAN held in Bali, can be seen as operationalizing the overall goals and objectives as expressed in the Bangkok Declaration.[39]

The Declaration of ASEAN Concord only relates to the member-states of ASEAN whereas the Bali Treaty is also open for accession to non-members. The Declaration of ASEAN Concord contains both general principles relating to the overall goals of the Association and principles relating to the specific goals of managing disputes and expanding cooperation among the member-states. One of the stated overall objectives is to strive for the establishment of a *Zone of Peace, Freedom and Neutrality (ZOPFAN)* in Southeast Asia. Emphasis is also placed on respect for the principles of 'self-determination, sovereign equality and non-interference in the internal affairs of nations'.[40]

The Bali Treaty provides specific guidelines in the field of conflict management, particularly in relation to the peaceful settlement of disputes.[41] According to Article 18 of the Bali Treaty, it 'shall be open for accession by other States in Southeast Asia' – i.e. in addition to the five founding members of ASEAN.[42] The Bali Treaty is divided into a Preamble and five Chapters. In terms of cooperation and settlement of disputes Chapters I, III and IV are most relevant.[43] In Chapter I, dealing with 'Purpose and Principles', Article 2 outlines the fundamental principles which should guide the relations between the signatories to the Treaty. The principles are:

a. Mutual respect for the independence, sovereignty, equality, territorial integrity and national identity of all nations;

b. The right of every State to lead its national existence free from external interference, subversion or coercion;

c. Non-interference in the internal affairs of one another;

d. Settlement of differences or disputes by peaceful means;

e. Renunciation of the threat or use of force;

f. Effective cooperation among themselves.[44]

The principles include three main factors for managing inter-state relations: non-interference in the internal affairs of other countries, peaceful settlement of disputes and overall cooperation.

In Chapter III, dealing with 'Cooperation', the areas in which mutual cooperation can be established and expanded are outlined and the linkages between cooperation, peaceful relations and non-interference are set out. The later is most evidently shown in Article 12 which states that the signatories:

> [I]n their efforts to achieve regional prosperity and security, shall endeavour to cooperate in all fields for the promotion of regional resilience, based on the principles of self-confidence, self-reliance, mutual respect, cooperation and solidarity which will constitute the foundation for a strong and viable community of nations in Southeast Asia.[45]

In Chapter IV, devoted to 'Pacific Settlement of Disputes', the first Article (13) outlines the way in which the signatories should behave in situations in which there is a risk that disputes may arise or where they have arisen. The Article stipulates that the signatories

> shall have the determination and good faith to prevent disputes from arising. In case disputes on matters directly affecting them shall refrain from the threat or use of force and shall at all times settle such disputes among themselves through friendly negotiations.[46]

Article 14 is devoted to the creation and envisaged role of a *High Council.* The Council shall be made up of a representative at the ministerial-level from each of the signatories and its role should be to take 'cognizance' of existing disputes or situation which could potentially threaten regional 'peace and harmony'. The High Council is envisaged as 'a continuing body', i.e. this indicates that it should have been established in 1976.[47]

Article 15 deals with the mediating role of the Council and such a role can be assumed by it in the event that no solution to a dispute is reached through 'direct' negotiation between the parties to the dispute. The role as mediator can be assumed by recommending to the parties to a dispute appropriate means of settlement; i.e. good offices, mediation, inquiry, or conciliation. The Council can also 'constitute itself into a committee' of mediation, inquiry or conciliation.[48]

Article 16 displays some limitations to the mediating functions of the Council by stating that the provisions of Articles 14 and 15 shall apply to a dispute only if the parties to the dispute agree to their 'application'. Literally this implies that only the High Council can decide whether to mediate in a dispute if the parties agree to the 'application' of the provisions in Articles 14 and 15, but that the parties to the dispute cannot bring the matter to the High Council. However, among some officials and researchers in the Southeast Asian region another interpretation is being put forward, namely that the High Council can only assume the role of mediator in a dispute if the parties involved agree to bring the dispute to the Council.[49] Article 16 also states that signatories who are not parties to such a dispute can offer assistance to settle it and the parties to the dispute should be 'well disposed towards such offers'.[50]

The Declaration of ASEAN Concord and the Bali Treaty provide ASEAN with the broad goals and aims of the Association and with the more specific mechanisms and code of conduct to achieve enhanced regional cooperation and to manage inter-state relations in general and the existing and potential disputes in particular. They also show that by the end of the 'formative years' the ASEAN members had achieved a high degree of understanding on how to manage inter-state relations within the grouping.

Since 1976 the only notable revisions of the Bali Treaty have been the two protocols amending it. The first protocol was adopted on 15 December 1987 in connection with the Third Summit Meeting of ASEAN in Manila.[51] The second protocol was adopted on 25 July 1998 in connection with the 31st ASEAN Ministerial Meeting (AMM) in Manila.[52]

In Article 1 of the first protocol, the amendment deals with the provisions relating to which states can accede to the Bali Treaty:

> States outside Southeast Asia may also accede to this Treaty by the consent of all States in Southeast Asia which are signatories to this Treaty and Brunei Darussalam.[53]

Article 2 contains an amendment to Article 14 in the Bali Treaty and relates to the formation of a High Council with representatives from all the signatories. The amendment is the following text added to the original one:

> However, this article shall apply to any of the States outside Southeast Asia which have acceded to the Treaty only in cases where that state is directly involved in the dispute to be settled through the regional processes.[54]

In the second protocol the amendment to the Bali Treaty relates to Article 18, Paragraph 3 of the Treaty and is amended thus:

> States outside Southeast Asia may also accede to the Treaty with the consent of all States in Southeast Asia, namely, Brunei Darussalam, the Kingdom of Cambodia, the Republic of Indonesia, the Lao People's Democratic Republic, Malaysia, the Union of Myanmar, the Republic of the Philippines, the Republic of Singapore, the Kingdom of Thailand and the Socialist Republic of Vietnam.[55]

These two protocols and the amendments in them imply that the Bali Treaty is open for accession also by non-Southeast Asian states, provided that the Southeast Asian signatories give their consent. The non-Southeast

Asian states can also be represented in the High Council if they are directly involved in disputes to be settled through the 'regional processes'. By adopting such amendments the ASEAN members have agreed to extend the conflict management process and mechanisms of the Bali Treaty to countries outside the Southeast Asian region and to disputes not limited to Southeast Asian states. However, it is noteworthy that countries from outside the Southeast Asian region are not allowed to be members of the High Council when it deals with disputes involving only Southeast Asian states. This is, presumably, to prevent outside interference in intra-regional disputes.

Conflict management in ASEAN's negotiation and decision-making processes

The ASEAN states have managed to build confidence, familiarity and understanding of each other's positions on different issues through a system of informal and formal meetings between the leaders, ministers and senior officials of the member-states. Achieving a high level of interaction, cooperation and understanding between the original member-states of ASEAN was a gradual process during the formative years leading up to the First Summit Meeting in 1976. ASEAN is also known from its decision-making process, which requires that all decisions be reached by consensus. Particular emphasis has been put on promoting and achieving regional resilience based on the internal resilience of each of the member-states through economic development which would result in greater political support for the governments and lead to enhanced political stability.

ASEAN's approach specifically to conflict management has primarily been geared towards preventing the outbreak of conflicts and stopping existing conflicts from disrupting inter-state relations. In the context of ASEAN's conflict management approach, a central element is the consultation process called *musyawarah*, which is informal in character and aims at conflict prevention. This approach has evolved from traditional arbitration practices in villages in Indonesia, Malaysia and the Philippines. The aim of *musyawarah* is to achieve unanimous decisions; i.e. consensus, known as *mufakat*. This has become a crucial part of the decision-making process within ASEAN. The consensus approach is an important mechanism in the conflict management process since it aims at preserving peaceful relations between the member-states of ASEAN by avoiding, defusing and containing issues which could escalate into open inter-state conflicts.[56]

What is the importance of conflict management in ASEAN?

The ASEAN approach to conflict management through the negotiation and decision-making processes as well as the mechanisms and provisions provided by the Declaration of ASEAN Concord and the Bali Treaty attest to the high priority placed by the member-states of ASEAN on managing and resolving inter-state disputes through peaceful means. However, achieving formal resolution of inter-state disputes within ASEAN should not be carried out in such a way as to disrupt the relations between the parties to the disputes. This implies that conflict resolution is both desirable and a goal for the ASEAN members, but not at the expense of maintaining stable inter-state relations within the Association.

The ASEAN approach to conflict management and border disputes in Southeast Asia[57]

In the following the ASEAN approach to conflict management will be assessed through an analysis of how border disputes in Southeast Asia have been and are being managed. The border disputes located in the South China Sea and the Gulf of Thailand were identified in Chapter 3. Here the border disputes that are not located in the South China Sea and the Gulf of Thailand are identified.

Since some of the border disputes have been settled while others remain unsettled, the overview of the disputes is divided into two categories; first, the border disputes which have been formally settled through agreements or through joint-development arrangements, and, second, the border disputes which have yet to be resolved.

SETTLED BORDER DISPUTES

- The first agreement settling a border dispute was reached on 27 October 1969 between Indonesia and Malaysia delimiting their continental shelf boundary in central and southern parts of the Strait of Malacca. On 17 March 1970 they signed an agreement delimiting their territorial sea boundary in the Strait of Malacca. Finally, on 21 December 1971 an agreement was reached relating to the continental shelf boundary in the northern part of the Strait of Malacca.[58]

- Also on 21 December 1971, an agreement was signed between Indonesia, Malaysia and Thailand relating to the establishment of a 'Common point' (tri-junction point) on the continental shelf. This enabled the three countries to link the point to their pre-existing maritime boundaries.[59] Four days earlier (17 December) Indonesia and Thailand had signed an agreement delimiting a part of their continental shelf boundary in the northern part of the Malacca Strait and Andaman Sea. On 17 December 1975 they agreed on a continuation of the boundary in the Andaman Sea.[60]

- Indonesia has also reached an agreement with Singapore on delimiting their territorial sea boundary in the Strait of Singapore on 25 May 1973.[61]

- Laos and Vietnam have delimited their border through a series of agreements reached between 1977 and 1990. On 18 July 1977 they signed a treaty delimiting the land boundary between the two countries. A complementary treaty was signed on 26 January 1986. A final agreement on the status of the border was signed on 1 March 1990 and was ratified on 8 November of the same year.[62]
- Malaysia and Thailand signed a treaty on 24 October 1979 relating to the delimitation of the territorial seas between the two countries in the Strait of Malacca.
- Myanmar (then Burma) reached an agreement with Thailand relating to the delimiting of the maritime boundary between the two countries in the Andaman Sea on 25 July 1980.[63]
- Laos and Myanmar have reached two agreements related to their land boundary, i.e. along the Mekong river. A 'Convention' was signed between Laos and Myanmar on 11 June 1994 relating to the 'fixation' of the international boundary between the two countries. The 'Convention' was ratified by the government in Myanmar on 21 December 1994 and by the National Assembly of Laos on 15 September 1994 and by the President of Laos on 13 March 1995. As early as 8 April 1994 the two countries and the PRC signed a 'Convention' relating to the delimitation of a tri-junction point where the borders between the three countries meet.[64]

UNSETTLED TERRITORIAL DISPUTES

- There is a dispute relating to the land boundary between Brunei and Malaysia over the Limbang Valley which is currently part of the Malaysian state of Sarawak.[65]
- Indonesia and Malaysia still have to reach an agreement on delimiting their continental shelf boundary in the western Celebes Sea. There is also the unresolved question of sovereignty over Pulau Sipadan and Pulau Ligitan off the eastern coast of Borneo. In addition they have overlapping claims to EEZ in the Strait of Malacca.[66] In recent years tension along the border between the Malaysian States of Sabah and Sarawak and the Indonesian part of the Island of Borneo (Kalimantan) has highlighted that the border is 'poorly' demarcated. [67]
- Indonesia and the Philippines have to agree on maritime boundaries in the Celebes Sea in the area between Miangas Island on the Indonesian side and Mindanao on the Filipino side in the northeastern part of the Celebes Sea.[68]
- Malaysia and the Philippines have to agree on maritime boundaries in the Sulu Sea and the Celebes Sea.[69] It should also be noted that

Malaysia and the Philippines have not yet formally settled the Sabah issue.

- Malaysia and Singapore have two territorial disputes to resolve. First, there is the question of ownership of Pedra Branca/Pulau Batu Puteh and the boundaries relating to jurisdictional zones in the area. Second, the two sides have to agree on the offshore boundary in the Strait of Johore and the Singapore Strait to the south of Singapore.[70] In the Singapore Strait the boundary would link up with the boundaries agreed upon by Indonesia and Malaysia and Indonesia and Singapore, respectively.
- Between Malaysia and Thailand there are disputed areas along the land border which remain to be settled.[71]
- Between Thailand and Laos there are disputed areas along the land border. The border is partly made up of the Mekong river.[72]
- Between Thailand and Cambodia there are disputes relating to the land border.[73]
- Between Thailand and Myanmar the 2,400 km land border is mostly undemarcated and the area of dispute that has caused most tension in recent years is along the Moei river. Furthermore, despite the 1980 agreement (see above) there are still two disputes to be resolved in maritime areas. One relates to overlapping claims to some small features and the other to the delimitation of the territorial seas of the two countries in a limited area of the Andaman Sea.[74]
- Between Vietnam and Cambodia there are disputes relating to the land border. [75] [76]
- Cambodia and Laos have to settle their differences relating to the demarcation of their land boundary.[77]

OBSERVATIONS

There is no clear-cut trend relating to the success or lack of success in settling the various border disputes among the ASEAN members. Some countries have settled more border disputes than others but none of the member-states has settled all its border disputes. Indonesia and Thailand, respectively, have been among the more successful in settling border disputes with other members. However, the clashes between Thailand and Myanmar resulting from their border disputes show that some disputes are in urgent need of settlement or at least conflict management to defuse the periods of acute tension. Another observation are the problems that Cambodia is encountering in handling its border disputes with its three neighbours – Laos, Thailand and Vietnam – in particular with Vietnam. Overall, the Southeast Asian region is witnessing a trend towards resolving border disputes.

An interesting development in recent years relates to some of the remaining territorial disputes among the original ASEAN members. Malaysia and Singapore and Malaysia and Indonesia, respectively, have decided to bring their disputes over islands to the International Court of Justice (ICJ) in the Hague. Between Malaysia and Singapore the two prime ministers agreed on the principle of deferring the matter to the ICJ on 6 September 1994. Three rounds of talks have been held to discuss the formal submission of the case of Pedra Branca/Pulau Batu Puteh to the ICJ. At the third round of talks in Kuala Lumpur on 14 April 1998, an agreement was reached on the text of the Special Agreement to refer the issue to the ICJ. The agreement has yet to be signed and ratified by the two governments.[78] Between Indonesia and Malaysia the Indonesian president and the Malaysian prime minister agreed on the principle of deferring the matter to the ICJ on 6 October 1996. The formal written agreement to forward the issue of Pulau Sipadan and Pulau Ligitan to the ICJ was signed by the foreign ministers of the two countries on 31 May 1997 and ratified by both countries during the same year.[79] This agreement came into force on 14 May 1998 upon the exchange of the ratification instruments.[80] A 'joint notification letter' was signed by the two foreign ministers in New York on 1 October 1998.[81] Finally, on 2 November 1998, Indonesia and Malaysia jointly apprised the International Court of Justice of their dispute.[82] It can also be noted that at the sixth ministerial meeting of the Malaysian-Indonesian Joint Commission in mid–August 1997, the two sides decided to postpone bilateral talks on the Sipadan–Ligitan issue and to maintain the 'status quo' pending a ruling from the ICJ.[83]

This is a novel pattern of behaviour in the management of border disputes among the ASEAN members. To bring such disputes to the ICJ can be seen as a positive move if the parties to the dispute cannot reach a compromise. However, it can also be seen as a shortcoming of the ASEAN framework for conflict management, or at least an indication that there is still room for enhanced cooperation between the ASEAN states in the field of conflict management.

If the provisions of the Bali Treaty are interpreted to mean that the parties to a dispute can take the matter to the High Council, then it is noteworthy that the two conflicts were not brought to the High Council before being brought to the ICJ. However, if the interpretation is made that only the High Council can decide whether to mediate in a dispute, then the procedure applied by the parties to the two disputes has been in accordance with the provisions of the Bali Treaty.

If the first line of interpretation is pursued it should be noted that the High Council has yet to be established and thus, it might not have been seen as an option by the parties to the two disputes.[84] This seems to have been the case in the dispute between Malaysia and Singapore. However, in the Indonesian–Malaysia dispute, Indonesia had earlier proposed that the issue should be settled through the framework of the Bali Treaty and the High Council, but Malaysia favoured the alternative of referring the matter to the ICJ.[85] The reluctance to bring the conflicts to the High Council can possibly be explained by the fact that Malaysia is involved in other unsettled border disputes with several other ASEAN members. Malaysia might be worried that the other members would allow such disputes to influence their attitude in a negative way, seen from the Malaysian perspective.[86]

Viewed from the perspective of making the ASEAN framework for conflict management more efficient, the ASEAN members ought to bring their disputes to the High Council and exhaust the regional mechanisms for conflict management before turning to the international arena and to organisations such as the ICJ. Alternatively, the High Council ought to decide on whether to mediate or not in disputes before the parties bring such disputes to the ICJ. This would by necessity imply that the High Council has to be established.

TOWARDS ENHANCED PEACEFUL MANAGEMENT OF BORDER DISPUTES IN SOUTHEAST ASIA

If the achievements in conflict management among the ASEAN-states are assessed from the perspective of the prevention of military conflicts, the track-record of ASEAN is impressive since no dispute has led to a militarized inter-state conflict between the original member-states since 1967. However, this does not mean that all the territorial disputes have been successfully settled, nor that disputes in general do not arise. Some territorial disputes have been resolved while others remain unresolved. The unresolved disputes have been contained and defused through various conflict management mechanisms.

The expansion of ASEAN membership in the 1990s has brought additional territorial disputes into the realm of the Association, thus complicating the task of managing them. The overview above has shown that among the disputes involving the new member-states, some have been settled while others remain unsettled. It has also illustrated that the level of tension relating to the unsettled border disputes varies considerably.

The preferred way to handle territorial disputes between the various Southeast Asian countries is through bilateral dialogue and negoti-ations. However, in recent years two border disputes – between Malaysia and Singapore and between Indonesia and Malaysia, respectively – have been brought to the ICJ. This displays a willingness among some ASEAN members to seek international arbitration when the bilateral efforts to resolve territorial disputes fail to achieve a successful outcome.

The bilateral efforts to manage and settle the border disputes can be facilitated by the mechanisms for conflict management created by ASEAN, by enhancing the effectiveness of these mechanisms. This relates to ASEAN's role as facilitator rather than as an active third-party mediator in the disputes. However, it does not preclude that the role of ASEAN itself is enhanced, as long as it is within the limits set by the ASEAN framework for conflict management and providing there is political consensus among the parties concerned that ASEAN should play such a role.

In this context the possible role played by the ASEAN framework for conflict management is important. The question to be asked is how to make it even more suited to meet the challenge of the border disputes and the tension which sometimes results. The first step in such a process could be the establishment of the High Council. This seems to be problematic in view of the fact that nearly 25 years after the signing of the Bali Treaty, the Court is still not in place. This indicates that the informal and formal political cooperation among the ASEAN members needs to be enhanced in order to remove the lingering feelings of suspicion about the intentions of fellow member-states. There is also the fact that a High Council created on the basis of the provisions of the Bali Treaty could wield considerable power, due to the decisions and judgements it could make relating to territorial disputes in which the Council decides to mediate, or which might be brought to it by the parties to such disputes, depending on the interpretation made of the relevant provisions of the Bali Treaty. This would also imply that bilateral disputes could become multilateralized. Making the High Council a decision-making body would increase the degree of institutionalization within ASEAN and this would not be conducive to the more informal approach favoured by the Association. The multilaterization impact of establishing the High Council would not be an attractive scenario for member-states who are also involved in disputes with other ASEAN members and/or states. This is because they might fear that the opposing party to a dispute might have a higher degree of diplomatic influence or leverage within the ASEAN grouping.

These are legitimate concerns and they should be given careful consideration if a High Council is eventually established by ASEAN. In order to shape the Council into a constructive mechanism for conflict management, it has to be seen more as a confidence-building forum than a decision-making body.

To effectuate a positive role for the High Council along the lines suggested above, it should be set up as a forum to which member-states could turn if negotiations between the parties to the disputes fail. A High Council, if established, with a strong focus on mediation, may be an attractive alternative to the ICJ. This line of argumentation is based on the interpretation of the Bali Treaty whereby parties to a dispute can bring such a dispute to the High Council.

In this context it is not argued that parties to a dispute should not bring border disputes to the ICJ no matter the circumstances. On the contrary, the ICJ can still be used as an instrument of 'last resort' if bilateral and regional conflict management approaches and efforts fail to lead to a settlement acceptable to all parties.

The above analysis has displayed the complexities involved in managing the border disputes in Southeast Asia and has helped to shed light on the difficulties involved. This is important since Southeast Asian countries are involved in disputes also in the South China Sea area. The ongoing efforts to manage those disputes are presented and analysed in Chapter 8.

CONFLICT POTENTIAL IN THE SOUTH CHINA SEA AREA: SIGNS TO WATCH

While there are clear positive developments toward political stability in the South China Sea area – such as the growth of objective economic interdependence, the deepening and broadening of the institutional-ization of the regional political dialogue and the architecture of security, combined with the increasing power of the legislature in the Southeast Asian territorial disputes, there are also issues that need to be followed with some anxiety.

The development of the perceived divide between Westernized/ rich/globalized/Christian areas on the one hand and the poor/Asian/ Muslim/communist parts of the region on the other is certainly one worrying tendency. If we remember that all serious conflicts and militarized disputes in the South China Sea area have been between countries in opposing identity-groups, this growing division should be taken seriously. It seems likely that, within the system of self-regulating, established and stable states there will be mechanisms to maintain a healthy dialogue and prevent the 'demonization' of the 'other side'.

However, in the context of a transnationalization of the Southeast Asian security structure, the soft security construction may prove too weak to prevent the growth of hostility. The weakening of the national security order in Indonesia and in the Philippines (and to a much lesser extent perhaps also in the PRC) has meant that there could be a revival of militias and regular defence force personnel/units operating transnationally on their own ideological, ethnic and religious projects, out of reach of the central government. The prospect of rogue elements of Indonesia's military hindering tourism or the exploitation of natural resources in an area that has been claimed, but whose dispute has been settled on the highest political level, would not be surprising given a historical perspective. It could be said that the use of people's militias and the informal connections of these militias with the regular coercive apparatus has always been the pattern of Indonesian military strategy (independence struggle 1945–49; struggle to regain West Irian 1954–61; confrontation with Malaysia 1963–65; violence in East Timor 1999). In this kind of a setting the international mechanisms of extended ASEAN conflict management may be too weak to respond.

There are also other contingencies where the identity divide, together with drastic changes in the traditional state-centred security structure, could trigger confrontation. All of them would prove testing for Southeast Asian political stability because of the 'national elite'-centred conflict management mechanisms. A further weakening of the political control of the Indonesian central administration on the Indonesian flanks could create new types of threats in the South China Sea area. For example,what would happen in the disputed waters north of the Indonesian Natuna Islands if parts of Indonesia (including the province of Riau, in which separatism has been a problem) started to separate?

The transformation of the normative construction should also be followed closely. The democratization of ASEAN countries and Taiwan in particular (but the economic liberalization of the PRC) is rendering the old personalistic, secretive, elitist foundations of stability and conflict management more difficult. The important question is whether the consolidation of the new foundations, the growing objective interdependence, strengthening institutionalization in conflict management, and the greater reliance on the legal discourse in the argumentation can be rapid enough to compensate for the weakening of the old elements of stability.

Finally, it goes without saying that the development of the role of the PRC as a regional power is of crucial importance. The current development is very optimistic as positive interdependence between the PRC and ASEAN grows and both parties exercise extreme self-restraint to nurture this mutually advantageous development. Yet there is no guarantee that the current positive evolution will continue. Thus the development of the global and regional role of the PRC needs to be followed closely, because that is essential for the development of the regional and international escalation potential of territorial disputes in the South China Sea.

NOTES

1 Ramses Amer wrote the section Common Mechanisms of Dispute Management. Timo Kivimäki wrote the Introduction, Common Interests, Common Identity and Conflict Potential in the South China Sea.

2   See, for example, Howard P. Jones, *Indonesia, a Possible Dream* (Mas Aju: Singapore, 1974).

3   This observation is based in Kivimäki's interview with General Hasnan Habib, in Jakarta, in January 1991.

4   See, for example, the first paragraph of the *Declaration of ASEAN Concord*, Indonesia, 24 February 1976, in www.Aseansec.org/summit/concord.htm

5   As cited in Djiwandono, J. Soedjati, 'Intra-ASEAN Territorial Disputes: The Sabah Claim', *Indonesian Quarterly* vol. 22, no. 2 (1994), p. 49.

6   It is worth noting, however, that indicators of ASEAN economic inter-dependence (intra-ASEAN trade, for example) show that in objective terms the establishment of ASEAN took place during a drastic decline of inter-dependence. Yet the subjective sense of interdependence was higher due to the developmentalist orientation of ASEAN leaders (see Kivimäki, 'The Long Peace of ASEAN', *Journal of Peace Research* vol. 1, 2001).

7   Jusuf Wanandi, 'The Future of ARF and CSCAP in the Regional Security Architecture', in Jusuf Wanandi (ed.), *Regional Security Arrangements*. Jakarta: CSIS (1996), p. 31; see also Trood, Russell, 'The Asia Pacific Region, Economics and New Concepts of Security', in Hadi Soesastro and Anthony Bergin (eds) 1996, *The Role of Economic Cooperation Structures in the Asia Pacific Region*. Jakarta and Canberra: CSIS and ADSC (pp. 119–20).

8   See, for example, Amer, Ramses, 'Expanding ASEAN's Conflict Management Framework in Southeast Asia', *Asian Journal of Political Science* vol. 6, no. 2, pp. 33–56 (hereafter Amer, 'Expanding ASEAN'); Busse, Nikolas, 'Constructivism and Southeast Asian Security', *Pacifica Review* vol. 12, no. 1, pp. 39–60; Snitwongse, Kusuma, 'Achievements through Cooperation', *Pacifica Review*, vol. 11, no. 2, pp. 183–194.

9   Chi-Kin Lo, *China's Policy Towards Territorial Disputes: The Case of South China Sea Islands* (London: Routledge, 1989), p. 167.

10   See, for example, 'News Briefing by Chinese Foreign Ministry', *Beijing Review*, 24–30 April 1995, pp. 21–22; 1–7 May 1995, p. 23 and 17–23 April 1995.

11   Guo Xing Ji, 'China vs. South China Sea Security', *Security Dialogue* vol. 29, no. 1 (March 1998), pp. 101, 111.

12   See, for example, Chris Roberts, *Chinese Strategy and the Spratly Islands Dispute* (Canberra: ANU, SDSC Working Paper no. 293, 1996); Larry M. Wortzel, 'China Pursues Great-Power Status', *Orbis*, vol. 38, no. 2, Spring 1994.

13   Kurus, Bilson, 'Understanding ASEAN: Benefits and Raison d'Être', *Asian Survey*, vol. 33, no. 8 (1993), p. 852; Weatherbee, Donald E., *ASEAN and Pacific Regionalism*. Bangkok: ISIS, 1989.

14   Kurus, Bilson, 'The BIMB-EAGA: Developments, Obstacles and Future Direction', *Borneo Review* vol. 8, no. 1 (1997), pp. 1–13.

15   '1st Meeting of the Malaysia-Philippines Joint Commission for Bilateral Cooperation. Speech by Foreign Minister of Malaysia', *Foreign Affairs Malaysia*, vol. 26, no. 4 (1993), pp.54–58.

16   John McBeth, 'Oil-Rich Diet: Beijing Is Asked to Explain Its Maritime Appetite', *Far Eastern Economic Review*, 27 April 1995, p. 28.

17 Chi-Kin Lo, *op. cit.*, pp. 76–78.

18 R. Haller-Trost, *The Territorial Dispute between Indonesia and Malaysia over Pulau Sipadan and Pulau Ligitan.* International Boundary Research Unit. Boundary and Territory Briefing 2:2 (Durham: University of Durham Press 1995), p. 4; See also *Strait Times,* 7 July 1982; *Asiaweek,* 23 July 1982.

19 Hadi Soesastro, *ASEAN in a Changed Regional and International Political Economy* (Jakarta: Center for Strategic and International Studies, 1995), pp. iii–ix.

20 *Business Times,* Singapore, 5–8 June 1991.

21 *Strait Times,* 30 December 1987.

22 *Business Times,* 27 January 1992.

23 In the 1960s Indonesia's confrontation with Malaysia cut Indonesia's economic ties with Singapore, through which most of Indonesia's exports entered world markets. Even though confrontational policies were objectively thinking very harmful for Indonesia, economic matters did not command priority in Indonesia's calculation, and thus the confrontation went on.

24 Kay Möller, 'East Asian Security: Lessons from Europe', *Contemporary Southeast Asia,* vol. 17, no. 4 (1996), p. 363.

25 Chi-Kin Lo, *op. cit.*, pp. 32–34.

26 *People's Daily,* 26 May 1950.

27 Fu Chu, cited in Chi-Kin Lo, *op. cit.*, p. 33.

28 See, for example, Mahathir bin Mohammad, *Regionalism, Globalism and Spheres of Influence* (Singapore: ISEAS, 1989).

29 Mahathir stresses that Asian values are not materialistic and they are not 'liberal' vis-à-vis crime, the use of drugs or disregard for family values. For this, see Lawson, Stephanie, 'Culture, Relativism and Democracy: Political Myths about "Asia" and the "West"', in Richard Richard Robison (ed.), *Pathways to Asia: The Politics of Engagement.* (St Leonard's: Allen & Unwin 1996); Tanji, Miyume and Stephanie Lawson, '"Democratic Peace" and "Asian Democracy": A Universalist-Particularist Tension', *Alternatives,* vol. 22 (1997), pp. 133–155.

30 Quoted in Haller-Trost, *op. cit.*, p. 5.

31 *Far Eastern Economic Review,* 8 July 1999, p. 14. The same division between Singapore and the Philippines was demonstrated in the rapid militarization of a dispute over the execution of a Philippine maid in Singapore in 1995.

32 See *Asian Recorder* (Delhi), 16–22 April, vol. XXXXI, no. 16 (1995), p. 24729.

33 *Asian Recorder,* 12–18 March, vol. XXXXI, no. 24 (1995), p. 24860.

34 Kamarulzaman Askandar, 'ASEAN and Conflict Management: The Formative Years of 1967–1976', *Pacifica Review,* vol. 6, no. 2 (1994), pp. 63, 66–67; Mely Caballero-Anthony, 'Mechanisms of Dispute Settlement: The ASEAN Experience', *Contemporary Southeast Asia,* vol. 20, no. 1 (April 1998), pp. 44–45; Ranjit Gill, *ASEAN Coming of Age* (Singapore: Sterling Corporate Services, 1987), pp. 8–9, 13; François Joyaux, *L'Association des Nations du Sud-*

Est Asiatique (ANSEA), Que sais-je? no. 3153 (Paris: Presses Universitaires de France, 1997), pp. 31–37.

35 The terms ASEAN Declaration and Bangkok Declaration will be used interchangeably in this section.

36 Quoted from text of the 'ASEAN Declaration', reproduced as 'Appendix 1' in Vinita Sukrasep, *ASEAN in International Relations* (Bangkok: Institute of Security and International Studies, Faculty of Political Science, Chulalong-korn University, 1989), p. 96. The text of the Declaration can also be found on the web site of ASEAN (http://www.asean.or.id/).

37 Sukrasep, *op. cit.*, p. 97.

38 The terms TAC and Bali Treaty will be used interchangeably throughout the study.

39 Askandar argues that the First Summit Meeting marked the end of the 'formative stage' of ASEAN regionalism and that the signing of the Declaration of ASEAN Concord and the Bali Treaty marked the beginning of the 'second phase' (Askandar, *op. cit.*, p. 68).

40 Derived from the text of the 'Declaration of ASEAN Concord' reproduced as Appendix B in M. Rajendran, *ASEAN's Foreign Relations. The Shift to Collective Action* (Kuala Lumpur: Arenabuku Sdn. Bhd., 1985), p. 270. The text of the Declaration can also be found on the web site of ASEAN (http://www.asean.or.id/).

41 See text of the 'Treaty of Amity and Cooperation in Southeast Asia' reproduced as Appendix C in ibid., pp. 275–278. The text of the Treaty can also be found on the web site of ASEAN (http://www.asean.or.id/).

42 Rajendran, *op. cit.*, p. 278.

43 Ibid., pp. 275–278.

44 Ibid., p. 275.

45 Ibid., p. 277.

46 Ibid.

47 Ibid.

48 Ibid.

49 This can be exemplified by the fact that this interpretation was prevalent in Amer's discussions with officials and researchers in Malaysia in August 1998.

50 Rajendran, *op. cit.*, p. 277.

51 The full text of the 'Protocol Amending the Treaty of Amity and Cooperation in Southeast Asia' has been reproduced in Sarasin Viraphol and Werner Pfenning (eds), *ASEAN–UN Cooperation in Preventive Diplomacy* (Bangkok: Ministry of Foreign Affairs, 1995), pp. 277–279. The text of the Protocol can also be found on the ASEAN website (http://www.asean.or.id).

52 See text of the 'Second Protocol Amending the Treaty of Amity and Cooperation in Southeast Asia' (hereafter 'Second Protocol'). (Obtained by Amer from the Ministry of Foreign Affairs of Malaysia, Kuala Lumpur, in August 1998.)

53 Viraphol and Pfenning, *op. cit.*, pp. 277–278.

54 Ibid.

55 *Second Protocol*, p. 1.

56 Askandar, *op. cit.*, pp. 63–65; and, Caballero-Anthony, *op. cit.*, pp. 51–55 and 57–62. Caballero-Anthony also discusses third-party mediation and she notes that it was not until 'quite' recently that third-party mediation was officially adopted by ASEAN as a form of dispute management (see ibid., p. 61). On intra-ASEAN negotiations, see also Pushpa Thambipillai and Johan Saravanamuttu, *ASEAN Negotiations: Two Insights* (Singapore: Institute of Southeast Asian Studies, 1985).

57 For more detailed analyses of the territorial disputes among the ASEAN members, see Ramses Amer, 'Expanding ASEAN'; Ramses Amer, 'Managing Border Disputes in Southeast Asia', *Kajian Malaysia, Journal of Malaysian Studies*, Special Issue on Conflict Management in Southeast Asia, vol. 23, nos. 1–2 (June–December 2000), pp. 30–60.

58 Vivian L. Forbes, *Indonesia's Maritime Boundaries*, A Malaysian Institute of Maritime Affairs Monograph (Kuala Lumpur: Malaysian Institute of Maritime Affairs [MIMA], 1995), pp. 18–19, 21–24, 40–41, 46 as well as Annexes E1 and E2; and 'Indonesia–Malaysia (Continental Shelf) (1969)' and 'Indonesia-Malaysia (Territorial Sea) (1970)', in Jonathan I. Charney and Lewis M. Alexander, *International Maritime Boundaries Volume I*, (Dordrecht, Boston and London: Martinus Nijhoff Publishers and the American Society of International Law, 1993) pp. 1019–1037 (hereafter Charney and Alexander, 'Maritime Boundaries vol. I').

59 Forbes, *op. cit.*, pp. 18–19, 35–36, 44, as well as Annex I; and 'Indonesia–Malay–sia–Thailand (1971)', in Jonathan I. Charney and Lewis M. Alexander, *International Maritime Boundaries Volume II* (Dordrecht, Boston and London: Martinus Nijhoff Publishers and the American Society of International Law, 1993), pp. 1443–1454 (hereafter Charney and Alexander, 'Maritime Boundaries vol. II').

60 'Indonesia–Thailand (Malacca Strait and Andaman Sea) (1971)' and 'Indonesia–Thailand (Andaman Sea) (1975)', in Charney and Alexander, *op. cit.* (note 59), pp. 1455–1463, 1465–1472; Forbes, *op. cit.*, pp. 18–19, 35–36, 39, as well as Annexes H1 and H2.

61 Ibid., pp. 18–19, 24–25, 41, also Annex G; and 'Indonesia–Singapore (1973)' in Charney and Alexander, *Maritime Boundaries vol. I*, pp. 1049–1056.

62 It can be noted that during the second Indochina conflict some areas of Laotian territory were put at the disposition of the Democratic Republic of Vietnam by the Lao People's Revolutionary Party; these areas have been restored to Laos in accordance with an agreement dated 10 February 1976. For details on the settlement and demarcation of the land border between Laos and Vietnam see Bernard Gay, *La nouvelle frontière lao-vietnamienne. Les accords de 1977–1990*. Histoire des frontières de la péninsule indochinoise – 2, Travaux du Centre d'histoire et civilisations de la peninsule indochinoise publiés sous la direction de P.B. Lafont (Paris: L'Harmattan, 1995). See also a report carried *by VNA News Agency* reproduced in *British Broadcasting Corporation, Summary of World Broadcasts, Part Three, Far East*, 2975 B/6–7 (19 July 1997) (hereafter *BBC/FE*).

63 Kriangsak Kittichaisaree, *The Law of the Sea and Maritime Boundary Delimitation in South-East Asia* (Singapore, Oxford and New York: Oxford University Press, 1987), pp. 47–48, 52, 74–75. The text of the agreement has been reproduced as Appendix 4 in ibid., pp. 184–185. See also 'Burma (Myanmar)–Thailand (1980)' in Charney and Alexander, *Maritime Boundaries vol. II*, pp. 1341–1352.

64 For details on the settlement and demarcation of boundary between Laos and Myanmar, see Bernard Gay and Ouan Phommachack (eds), *La nouvelle frontière Lao-Myanmar (Les Accords de 1993–1995)*. Histoire des frontières de la péninsule indochinoise – 3, Travaux du Centre d'histoire et civilisations de la peninsule indochinoise publiés sous la direction de P.B. Lafont (Paris: L'Harmattan, 1999). The 'Convention' between Laos and Myanmar of 11 June 1994 entered into force following the exchange of the instruments of ratification on 8 May 1995; see ibid., p. 18.

65 For more details, see Mark Clearly and Simon Francis, 'Brunei: The Search for a Sustainable Economy' in *Southeast Asian Affairs 1994* (Singapore: Institute of Southeast Asian Studies, 1994), pp. 67–68; Tim Huxley, 'Brunei: Defending a Mini-State', in Chin Kin Wah (ed.), *Defence Spending in Southeast Asia*, Issues in Southeast Asian Security (Singapore: Regional Strategic Studies Programme, Institute of Southeast Asian Studies, 1987), p. 240; Pushpa Thambipillai and Hamzah Sulaiman, 'Brunei Darussalam: After a Decade of Independence', in *Southeast Asian Affairs 1995* (Singapore: Institute of Southeast Asian Studies, 1995), p. 121.

66 J.R.V. Prescott, *The Maritime Boundaries of the World* (London and New York: Methuen, 1985), pp. 226–230 (hereafter Prescott, 'The Maritime Boundaries'); Mark J. Valencia, *Malaysia and the Law of the Sea. The Foreign Policy Issues, the Options and Their Implications* (Kuala Lumpur: Institute of Strategic and International Studies [ISIS Malaysia], 1991), pp. 46–48, 80–84, 135. For details pertaining to the dispute over the islands, see David M. Ong, 'International Court of Justice – Case between Indonesia and Malaysia Concerning Sovereignty over Pulau Litigan and Pulau Sipadan', *International Journal of Marine and Coastal Law*, vol. 14, no. 3 (August 1999), pp. 400–414.

67 Information derived from N. Ganesan, *Bilateral Tensions in Post-Cold War ASEAN*, Pacific Strategic Papers 9 (Singapore: Regional Strategic and Political Studies Programme, Institute of Southeast Asian Studies, 1999), p. 30.

68 Prescott, *The Maritime Boundaries*, p. 230; Forbes, *op. cit.*, pp. 37, 45 and 47.

69 Prescott, *The Maritime Boundaries*, pp. 218–221, 230; Valencia, *op. cit.*, pp. 54–66, 80–85, 136–137.

70 Ibid., pp. 31–35, 37, 136.

71 Amer's discussions with researchers in Kuala Lumpur in December 1996 and in August 1998. It can be noted that following talks between the Malaysian and Thai prime ministers in late February 1997 it was reported that they had agreed to resolve the 'demarcation problem' relating to the land see *BBC/FE/*2856 B/4–5 (1 March 1997).

72 Amer's discussions with officials in Bangkok in December 1998, April 1999 and November 2000.

73 Amer's discussions with officials in Bangkok in December 1998, April

1999 and November 2000. See also Victor Prescott, *The Gulf of Thailand* (Kuala Lumpur: Maritime Institute of Malaysia [MIMA], 1998).

74 Amer's discussions with officials in Bangkok in April 1999 and November 2000.

75 For details on disputes between Cambodia and Vietnam relating to the land and sea borders, see Ramses Amer, 'The Border Conflicts between Cambodia and Vietnam', *Boundary and Security Bulletin*, vol. 5, no. 2 (Summer 1997), pp. 80–91; Amer, 'Vietnam and Its Neighbours: The Border Dispute Dimension', *Contemporary Southeast Asia*, vol. 17, no. 3 (December 1995), pp. 299–301.

76 Just as in the case of the maritime territorial disputes between the two countries (see Chapter 3), they did sign agreements relating to the land border during the 1980s. These agreements were not recognized by all parties within Cambodia for most of the 1990s but in recent years Cambodia has indicated an acceptance of the agreements. However, new bilateral talks on the status of their borders between the countries have been initiated to reach a solution to remaining disputed issues. Therefore, in the context of this chapter the land border dispute between Vietnam and Cambodia is not classified as settled for the same reason as outlined in Chapter 3.

77 This was acknowledged by the then Cambodian first prime minister Ung Huot in early June 1998 (*BBC/FE*/3250 B/1 [11 June 1998]).

78 Amer's discussions with officials in Kuala Lumpur in August 1998. See also *BBC/FE*/2098 B/2 (12 September 1994); and *Joint Press Statement. The Third Malaysia–Singapore Meeting to Submit the Case of Pedra Branca/Pulau Batu Puteh to the International Court of Justice, Kuala Lumpur, 14 April 1988* (Kuala Lumpur: Press Release, Ministry of Foreign Affairs Malaysia, 14 April 1998). (Obtained by Amer from the Ministry of Foreign Affairs of Malaysia, Kuala Lumpur, in August 1998.)

79 Amer's discussions with officials in Jakarta in December 1996. Amer's discussions with researchers in Kuala Lumpur in December 1996 and with officials and researchers in Kuala Lumpur in August 1998. See also *BBC/FE*/ 2738 B/3 (9 October 1996).

80 Ong, *op. cit.*, p. 399.

81 *BBC/FE*/3347 B/4 (2 October 1998). Report carried by *Radio Republic of Indonesia*. The 'joint notification letter' is necessary in accordance with the procedures of the ICJ.

82 Ong, *op. cit.*, p. 399.

83 *BBC/FE*/2998 B72 (15 August 1997); 3001 B/4–5 (19 August 1997).

84 As indicated in Amer's discussions with officials in Kuala Lumpur in August 1998.

85 Amer's discussions with officials in Jakarta in December 1996. See also *BBC/FE*/2098 B/2 (12 September 1994); 2103 B/2 (17 September 1994). For the Malaysian position see for example ibid., 2098 B/2; 2103 B/2; 2134 B/2 (24 October 1994).

86 Malaysia has unsettled territorial disputes with all other original member-states of ASEAN as well as with Brunei and Vietnam, but not with Cambodia, Laos and Myanmar.

PART III

PEACE PROSPECTS

8

ONGOING EFFORTS IN CONFLICT MANAGEMENT

Ramses Amer

INTRODUCTION AND DIFFERENTIATION

In the context of this chapter the management of the conflict situations in the South China Sea is analysed from a broad perspective rather than by going into the particular details of bilateral negotiations and talks and multilateral initiatives that seek to defuse tension and avoid confrontation. Factual details will mainly be used to exemplify the complexities involved.

From the outset it is necessary to differentiate between the bilateral conflict situations and the multilateral conflicts over the Spratly archipelago and in the Gulf of Thailand, respectively. The main reason for making such a distinction is that a bilateral conflict situation can be addressed and dealt with through purely bilateral talks or bilateral agreements to seek international mediation, whereas a multilateral conflict situation does not lend itself to such approaches as several countries are involved; in such cases multilateral approaches are necessary.

The situation is further complicated by the fact that the Spratly conflict is, if not directly, at least indirectly linked to some of the bilateral conflict situations in areas around the Archipelago. This is because one or more claimants may link other conflict situations to the Spratly dispute or may use the Spratly archipelago to claim maritime zones in surrounding areas of the South China Sea. The complexity of the overall conflict situation is most clearly displayed between the PRC and Vietnam.

BILATERAL CONFLICT SITUATIONS

In discussing conflict management of the bilateral conflict situations, the preferred approach adopted by the involved countries is a combination of discussions, consultations and formal talks on the issues at stake. This does not differ much from the approaches of the involved countries to other territorial disputes. The conflict situations in the South China Sea are either addressed as issues in their own right, in bilateral contacts (i.e. through consultations, discussions and/or formal talks), or they are incorporated in overall discussions between the two countries involved in a given conflict situation. The frequency of discussions and/or talks in any given dispute depends on a variety of factors including the perceived urgency to deal with the issues at stake, depending on political, economic and broader security perspectives of the involved countries. A necessary precondition for the initiation of discussions and talks relating to a bilateral territorial dispute is that both parties agree that there is in fact a dispute and that the situation needs to be addressed. As noted in the overview of agreements reached thus far, the negotiations on bilateral disputes have resulted in four formal agreements on boundary delimitation; i.e. between Indonesia and Malaysia, between Malaysia and Thailand, between Thailand and Vietnam, and between the PRC and Vietnam, respectively, and in two agreements on joint development in disputed areas; i.e. between Malaysia and Thailand and between Malaysia and Vietnam, respectively. There are also ongoing talks relating to unsettled territorial disputes. For example, between Vietnam and Indonesia[2] and between Vietnam and Cambodia.[3] Furthermore, talks are under way between Vietnam, Malaysia and Thailand relating to the area in the Gulf of Thailand where the claims of the three countries overlap.[4]

The Sino–Vietnamese disputes

To illustrate the attempt to handle a complex bilateral conflict situation, an overview of the Sino–Vietnamese approach to talks and discussions will be outlined.[5] The PRC and Vietnam have initiated a system of talks and discussions relating to the border disputes which is both highly structured and extensive. From bottom to top it looks as follows:

- expert-level talks (on a regular basis);
- government-level talks, i.e. deputy/vice-minister (once yearly);
- foreign minister-level talks (on a regular basis);
- high-level talks, i.e. secretaries-general of the Chinese Communist Party and the Communist Party of Vietnam, presidents and prime ministers (at yearly high-level summits).

Talks at the expert level go back to October 1992; up to late 1995 the talks focused mainly on the land border demarcation and the delineation of the Gulf of Tonkin. The talks at the government level began in August 1993. On 19 October 1993 the two sides reached an agreement on the principles for handling the land border and Gulf of Tonkin disputes. It was further agreed to set up joint working groups at the expert level to deal with the two issues. The working group on the land border held its first meeting in February 1994 and the working group on the Gulf of Tonkin met for the first time in March 1994. Talks at the expert-level on the border disputes in the South China Sea proper, the so-called 'sea issues', were initiated in November 1995.

The major achievements from the bilateral negotiations on border disputes have been the signing of a Land Border Treaty on 30 December 1999[6] and the signing of an agreement on the delimitation of the territorial waters, the EEZs and the continental shelves in the Gulf of Tonkin on 25 December 2000.[7] Little progress, if any, has been achieved with regard to the territorial disputes in the South China Sea proper, i.e. the competing sovereignty claims to the Paracel and Spratly archipelagos as well as the overlapping claims to waters and continental shelf areas to the East of the Vietnamese coast.

Despite the talks, the border disputes between the PRC and Vietnam have been the most serious source of tension in bilateral relations since full normalisation of relations in November 1991. All the border disputes, i.e. along the land border, in the Gulf of Tonkin and in the South China Sea, caused serious tension in bilateral relations from May to November 1992. The differences relating to oil exploration in the South China Sea and to the signing of contracts with foreign companies for oil exploration were particularly deep from April to June 1994, in April and May 1996, and in March and April 1997. During 1998 there was no extended period of tension relating to the border disputes but shorter periods can be noted, such as in January along the land border and in the South China Sea during the months of April, May, July and September. During 1999 the focus was on reaching a settlement of the land border dispute. During 2000 the focus shifted to reaching a settlement of the Gulf of Tonkin dispute. No significant tension was caused by any of the border disputes during these two years.

This overview illustrates the difficulties involved in managing the conflict situation and although talks have been initiated on the disputes in the South China Sea proper, there are still many differences. For example, the PRC and Vietnam have yet to agree on which disputes to include on the agenda, with Vietnam pushing for the inclusion of the Paracels as an issue alongside that of the Spratlys, whereas the PRC will only discuss the latter issue. Furthermore, Vietnam regards the Chinese moves to sign contracts with foreign oil companies and to engage in oil exploration in areas in parts of the South China Sea where Vietnam does not recognise the PRC's extensive claims to EEZ and continental shelf areas as attempts to turn areas in which Vietnam's claim was previously uncontested, into contested ones. These areas were formerly termed 'historical waters' by the PRC but, through its legislation and statements the PRC has gradually turned them into the EEZ and continental shelf of the Paracel and Spratly archipelagos.

The differences between the PRC and Vietnam relating to the PRC's EEZ and continental shelf claims extending from the Paracels and Spratlys into surrounding areas of the South China Sea show that varying interpretations of the relevant provisions of the 1982 UNCLOS further complicates the conflict situation. It is noteworthy that differences relating to oil exploration have been the single most important factor causing tension in bilateral relations since normalisation of relations between the two countries in late 1991. This highlights the importance of the 'oil factor' in the context of the Sino–Vietnamese conflict situation.

THE 'OIL FACTOR' AND ITS IMPORTANCE IN THE CONFLICT SITUATIONS

The 'oil factor' also comes into play in other conflict situations in the South China Sea area. It is often seen as a major factor in the conflict situation around the Spratly archipelago – although no evidence of substantial oil deposits has yet been found within the archipelago. In sea-bed areas in parts of the South China Sea substantial oil deposits have been found and commercially viable exploitation is taking place beyond the coasts of Brunei and the Malaysian state of Sarawak, beyond the east coast of Peninsular Malaysia and beyond the Vietnamese coast. As exemplified by the PRC's claims to EEZ and continental shelf zones around the Spratly and Paracel archipelagos, control over islands, cays and reefs in the South China Sea proper, in the Gulf of Thailand and in the Gulf of Tonkin can be used in order to substantiate potential claims to maritime zones in which oil deposits may be found in the future. To gain control over areas in which oil exploration could prove to be commercially sustainable is of great importance for the countries bordering the South China Sea area, since such exploitation could potentially make some countries self sufficient in terms of oil production or reduce their need to import oil, depending on the size of the deposits and on the needs of each country. Furthermore, oil as an export commodity is attractive to the claimants.

THE SPRATLY CONFLICT SITUATIONS AND SEARCH FOR A SOLUTION

Relevance of a bilateral 'code of conduct'

If the focus of attention is directed at the conflict situations around the Spratly archipelago, it can be observed that many of the efforts by the countries directly involved are devoted to conflict management. This has been shown above between the PRC and Vietnam, and between the PRC and the Philippines and between the Philippines and Vietnam, which resulted in agreements on a 'code of conduct' between the Philippines and the PRC in August 1995[8] and between the Philippines and Vietnam in November 1995.[9]

In assessing the usefulness of the 'code of conduct', it is important to take into consideration developments in the South China Sea in recent years. As noted above, the PRC and Vietnam did not experience any serious tension relating to their disputes in the South China Sea during 1999 and 2000.

A closer look at other developments in recent years shows that there have been periods of tension, occasionally deep tension, between the Philippines and the PRC in the South China Sea. In 1999 China's occupation of Mischief Reef (the occupation dates back to early 1995) continued to be a source of controversy and the dispute over Scarborough Shoal has caused continued tension – in particular in November, when two ships from the navy of the Philippines were stuck there. Furthermore, several incidents involving naval units from the Philippines and Chinese fishing boats were reported.[10] The bilateral tension in the Scarborough Shoal area continued into early 2000 and during the first half of the year there was also tension relating to activities of Chinese fishing boats which even led to the death of a Chinese fisherman in late May.[11] There have been bilateral talks relating to the situation in the South China Sea between the Philippines and the PRC. In late March 1999 the First Expert Group Meeting on Confidence-Building Measures was held in Manila; the second meeting was held in late October.[12]

In connection with the official visit to the PRC by the then President of the Philippines, Joseph Estrada, in mid-May 2000, the foreign ministers of the two countries signed a joint statement on the framework for co-operation between the two governments. Section 9 of the joint statement is devoted to the disputes in the South China Sea and reads as follows:

> The two sides commit themselves to the maintenance of peace and stability in the South China Sea. They agree to promote a peaceful settlement of disputes through bilateral friendly consultations and negotiations in accordance with universally-recognised principles of international law, including the 1982 United Nations Convention on the Law of the Sea. They reaffirm their adherence to the 1995 joint statement between the two countries on the South China Sea and agree not to take actions that might complicate or escalate the situation. The two sides expressed their determination to follow through the work of the China–Philippines Working Group on Confidence Building Measures to enhance peace and stability in the

region. They reiterate that they will contribute positively towards the formulation and adoption of the regional Code of Conduct in the South China Sea.[13]

This agreement led to a period characterised by increased stability and less tension. In October the armed forces chief of the Philippines visited the PRC to discuss the situation in the Spratlys with his Chinese counterpart.[14] In January 2001 the secretary of defence of the Philippines visited the PRC for talks with his Chinese counterpart.[15] However, in early February renewed tension relating to Scarborough Shoal was reported. According to the Philippines, the problems were caused by the activities of four Chinese fishing vessels in the area. The PRC protested against the presence of the Filipino Navy in the area and against actions carried out against the Chinese fishing vessels.[16] There was also Filipino concern about the Chinese-built 'structures' in the area.[17] The tensions continued into March with mutual accusations and official complaints.[18] In late March initial talks between the two parties took place in Beijing, when a special envoy of the president of the Philippines visited the PRC.[19]

Furthermore, in 1999, for the first time in years, there was tension between Vietnam and the Philippines in the South China Sea. In October the Philippines protested against the shooting at one of its armed forces plane by Vietnamese soldiers based on Tennent Reef in the Spratly archipelago.[20] Vietnam responded by stating that the armed forces plane of the Philippines had 'seriously' violated Vietnam's sovereignty. Furthermore, the Vietnamese forces had 'restrained' themselves and 'merely warned' the Filipino planes which flew at a low altitude over Tien Nu (Tennent) Reef.[21] Two incidents in 2000 can also be noted. First, in March 2000 Vietnamese fishermen were arrested by the navy and coastguards of the Philippines on Fearless Shoal near the southern tip of Palawan.[22] Second, in May it was reported that the Philippines were closely monitoring the activities of Vietnamese vessels in the Spratlys.[23]

Thus, tension occurred despite the existing 'code of conduct' between the respective parties. Since the tension between the PRC and the Philippines in the South China Sea has been so evident over the past few years, it indicates that a 'code of conduct' in itself is no guarantee that actions and incidents will not cause tension over the disputed areas.[24]

Multilateral approaches

Multilateral approaches to the management of the Spratly conflict situation can be seen as a multifaceted dialogue process involving both state and non-state actors. The multilateral process at the level of the state includes the ASEAN Regional Forum (ARF) which brings together all the claimants, except for Taiwan, alongside other regional powers and the global powers for discussions on security-related issues including the situation in the South China Sea. A further measure is the ASEAN–PRC dialogue which relates to both political and economic relations and which also involves discussions on the overall situation in the South China Sea. The Association of Southeast Asian Nations (ASEAN) is also relevant in this context as it brings together all the Southeast Asian claimants to the whole or parts of the Spratly archipelago. ASEAN has issued statements on the South China Sea situation and in this context – the 1992 ASEAN Declaration on the South China Sea being the most important one. The Declaration's main feature is the emphasis placed on the necessity to resolve the disputes by peaceful means without resort to the use of force. Furthermore all parties concerned are urged to exercise restraint in order to create a positive climate for the eventual resolution of all disputes.[25]

The role that ASEAN can play is a rather complex one, since five of its member-states are involved in conflict situations within the South China Sea proper and four have sovereignty claims to all or parts of the Spratly archipelago. This creates a situation in which ASEAN cannot play the role of a third-party mediator between the PRC and other claimants, as these claimants are member-states of the Association. In conflict situations involving only ASEAN members, the conflict management mechanisms of the Association can come into play.[26]

Of particular interest in the context of this study is the way in which the situation in the South China Sea has been brought on to the agenda in the context of the ASEAN–PRC dialogue. One core issue is the search for a mutually agreeable 'code of conduct' for the South China Sea. The difficulty in reaching an understanding and an agreement on the content and scope of a 'code of conduct' for the South China Sea has focused on how to reconcile an ASEAN proposal and a Chinese proposal.[27] However, within ASEAN the process of agreeing on the content and scope of the proposal has been a difficult one and there are indications that some differences still persist, most notably relating to the 'scope of application' of a future 'code of conduct', i.e. which areas of the South China Sea should be encompassed by the 'code of conduct'.[28] ASEAN has to reconcile the views and interests of the five member-states bordering on the South China Sea proper and the interest of the four member-states with sovereignty claims in the Spratlys, in particular the three countries that control various features of the archipelago, i.e. Malaysia, the Philippines and Vietnam. Another relevant dimension of the intra-ASEAN process is how the member-states perceive the PRC and the potential threat that the PRC might pose to the region. This is exemplified by the fact that Myanmar and Thailand have good and close relations with the PRC – extending to the military field – and no territorial disputes with the PRC, whereas Vietnam alongside Brunei Darussalam, Indonesia, Malaysia and the Philippines have territorial disputes with the PRC in the South China Sea. Different perceptions complicate the process of formulating a clear-cut policy towards the PRC which can address not only the situation in the South China Sea but also broad issues such as the benefits of economic cooperation and the merits of a policy of constructive engagement as well as issues on which the ASEAN countries have different perceptions.

These multilateral discussions relating to the various conflict situations in the South China Sea provide a boost for confidence-building measures and avenues for the parties to get together and discuss the situation. They aim at defusing tension, promoting the use of peaceful means to handle the situation and respecting the status quo. The latter can be seen as a minimalist approach to conflict management since it does not address the current state of affairs and aims only at preventing the conflict situations from escalating into open militarised confrontation. However, in a potentially volatile situation such as the one in the South China Sea, even a minimalist approach contributes to the management of the currrent situation.

It can be noted that the Spratly issue as such is not discussed in the multilateral forums outlined above, at least not those involving the PRC. Instead, the references, statements and declarations relate to the situation in the South China Sea. The reason for this is the PRC's expressed preference to handle the Spratly dispute bilaterally with each of the other claimants. Thus, the PRC opposes multilateral talks on the Spratly issue as such. However, the PRC is amenable to multilateral discussions on the overall situation in the South China Sea and ways in which the stability in the area can be maintained.[29]

Among the multilateral contacts at the level of non-state actors are the many contacts between researchers and other experts at a number of conferences and workshops. In this context it is worth noting the 'workshops' arranged on a yearly basis in Indonesia, with Canadian support, which bring together experts from various fields in the countries involved in the Spratly conflict. These workshops allow for the opportunity to discuss issues that do not directly touch upon the sovereignty question. They also aim at increasing the level of understanding between the participants and to identify possible avenues for future cooperation on issues that are of a politically less sensitive nature. Another forum for discussion between scholars and policy-makers is the Council for Security Cooperation in the Asia Pacific (CSCAP). Within CSCAP, security-related issues are subject to discussion, including the situation in the South China Sea and the Spratly dispute. The CSCAP activities are often referred to as the 'second-track' process as compared to the state-level activities which are referred to as 'first-track'. Thus, CSCAP is part of the overall process of confidence-building in the Asia-Pacific.

In the current situation relating to the Spratly conflict, the multilateral dialogue processes between state and non-state actors cannot bring about a formal resolution to the conflict. Nevertheless, these processes do positively contribute to enhanced confidence-building and to a better understanding among the claimants to the Spratly archipelago about the position and attitude of the other claimants. This creates better conditions for efficient conflict management and eventually for a possible formal resolution to the conflict situation. The positive impact also extends to the managing of the bilateral conflict situations in the South China Sea area. The bilateral dialogues and ongoing negotiations are not only of great importance for managing and eventually resolving the bilateral disputes; they also contribute to the management of the multilateral dispute around the Spratly archipelago, in particular the bilateral contacts be-tween the claimants to all or parts of the archipelago.

In this context efficient conflict management and eventual formal resolutions of the bilateral conflict situations in the South China Sea area and of the Spratly conflict do not depend on the actions of outside parties but upon the policies and attitudes of the parties to the various conflict situations. In other words, it is the political willingness of the various claimants to peacefully manage the disputes and to achieve the formal resolution of the conflict situations that is the key factor. This is a necessary precondition in order to avoid tension and confrontation in the South China Sea and in the processes that will eventually lead to a resolution of the conflicts in the area. Thus, it is a question of implementing policies aiming to achieve efficient conflict management and eventual formal resolutions of the conflicts and of acting in such a way as to promote a pattern of interaction that will lead to such an outcome. The challenge of doing so rests with the parties to the various conflict situations.

Joint development or exploration as conflict management?

A pertinent question in this context is whether joint development or joint exploration arrangements relating to natural resources, and more prominently to oil, would be a possible way of defusing and managing the remaining conflict situations relating to territorial disputes in the South China Sea area. After all, this is the way in which the disputes between Malaysia and Thailand and between Malaysia and Vietnam, respectively, have been managed in the Gulf of Thailand. It could be a way of managing the trilateral dispute involving the three countries in the Gulf of Thailand. Would such an approach be possible in the South China Sea proper? The countries involved in the Spratly conflict seem to be amenable to the notion of joint development or joint exploration of natural resources. This would imply that they shelve their territorial disputes over the Spratlys, or at least put them aside, and instead focus on cooperation in exploring the natural resources inclusive of oil. Theoretically this seems like a positive scenario but the PRC's position has to be clarified before such a scheme could be seriously discussed. It is not a question of whether or not the PRC is interested in joint development but instead a question relating to which areas the PRC is referring to when proposing and arguing in favour of joint development. Does the PRC mean the Spratly archipelago as such or the vast areas of the South China Sea to which the PRC lays claim? The latter would be interpreted by the Southeast Asian countries bordering on the South China Sea proper as if the PRC were trying to get access to their continental shelf areas by proposing joint development and joint exploration there. In fact Vietnam has indicated that this is how it interprets the PRC's proposal for joint development.[30]

The key role of the parties to the disputes in conflict management

By way of conclusion, it can be stated that the key to efficient conflict management and eventually to formal conflict resolution is basically one of political will. To suggest that the problem is that technical solutions cannot be found and formulated by the countries to the conflicts is wrong, and leads one to question the stated position of many politicians and experts in those countries. For example, it is not a problem of knowing how to formulate the text of a 'Spratly Treaty' nor of identifying the possible schemes for dividing the disputed areas, but rather how to reach a political understanding and eventually a consensus on the need and feasibility of such arrangements.[31] The agreements reached thus far on either border delimitation, e.g. between Thailand and Vietnam in the Gulf of Thailand, or on joint development, e.g. between Malaysia and Thailand in the Gulf of Thailand, are testimony to the capabilities of politicians and experts from the countries involved to reach agreements on how to manage and/or formally resolve their territorial disputes.

NOTES

1   The approach used in this chapter is derived from Ramses Amer, *Conflict Situations and Conflict Management in the South China Sea*, UPSK Occasional Paper, no. 5/00 (Bangi, Selangor: Unit Pengajian Strategi dan Keselamatan [Strategic and Security Studies Unit], Universiti Kebangsaan Malaysia, 2000).

2   Author's discussions with officials in Hanoi in December 1998, May 1999 and November 2000. See also Ramses Amer, 'Vietnam and Its Neighbours:

the Border Dispute Dimension', *Contemporary Southeast Asia*, vol. 17, no. 3 (1995), pp. 304–305.

3   Author's discussions with officials in Hanoi in December 1998, May 1999 and November 2000. See also Ramses Amer, 'The Border Conflicts between Cambodia and Vietnam', *Boundary and Security Bulletin*, vol. 5, no. 2 (1997), pp. 80–91; Ramses Amer, 'Expanding ASEAN's Conflict Management Framework in Southeast Asia: the Border Dispute Dimension', *Asian Journal of Political Science*, vol. 6, no. 2 (1998), pp. 47–48 (hereafter Amer, 'Expanding ASEAN').

4   Author's discussions with officials in Hanoi in December 1998, May 1999 and November 2000 as well as with officials in Bangkok in December 1998, April 1999 and November 2000.

5   Unless otherwise stated, the information relating to Sino–Vietnamese territorial disputes is derived from Ramses Amer, 'The Territorial Disputes between China and Vietnam and Regional Stability', *Contemporary Southeast Asia*, vol. 19, no. 1 (1997), pp. 86–113; Ramses Amer, *The Challenge of Managing the Border Disputes between China and Vietnam*, EAI Working Paper, no. 16 (24 November 1998) (Singapore: East Asian Institute [EAI], National University of Singapore); Ramses Amer, *The Management of the Border Disputes between China and Vietnam and its Regional Implications*, EIAS Publications, Briefing Papers, BP 00/03 (Brussels: European Institute for Asian Studies [EAIS], October 2000); Ramses Amer, 'The Sino–Vietnamese Approach to Managing Border Disputes', *Maritime Briefing*, vol. 3, no. 5, Durham: International Boundaries Research Unit, University of Durham, (2002 forthcoming).

6   Nguyen Hong Thao, 'The China–Vietnam Border Delimitation Treaty of 30 December 1999', *Boundary and Security Bulletin*, vol. 8, no. 1 (Spring 2000), pp. 87–90.

7   Information about the agreement can be found in the text of the joint statement on comprehensive cooperation issued on 25 December 2000 in connection with a high-level Sino–Vietnamese summit in Beijing. The joint statement has been reproduced in 'Déclaration Vietnam–China sur la coopération au nouveau siècle', *Agence vietnamienne de l'information (AVI)* (25 Dec. 2000); 'Joint Viet Nam-China Statement for Comprehensive Cooperation (take two)', *Vietnam News Agency (VNA)* (26 December 2000. From the web site of Vietnam News Agency (http://www.vnagency.com.vn).

8   For details relating to the negotiations and agreement, see *British Broadcasting Corporation, Summary of World Broadcasts, Part Three, Far East* 2378 B/4–5 (10 August 1995), 2379 B/3 (11 August 1995) and 2380 B/2–3 (12 August 1995) (hereafter *BBC/FE*); *Foreign Broadcast Information Service: Daily Report. East Asia*–95–155 (11 August 1995), pp. 50, 95–157 (15 August 1995), pp. 76–77 and 95–158 (16 August 1995), pp. 46–47.

9   For details relating to the negotiations and agreement see *BBC/FE*/2456 B/4 (9 November 1995); and 2459 B/2 (13 November 1995).

10   Ibid., B/5–6 and G/1 (21 July 1999); 3666 G/7 (15 October 1999); 3688 G/3–4 (30 October 1999); 3690 B/7–8 (12 November 1999); 3694 B/3–4 (17 November 1999); and 3706 B/8 (1 December 1999). See also 'High Seas Chase Denied' and 'Demand to Cease Encroachment' in the section on the

'South China Sea', in *Boundary and Security Bulletin*, vol. 7, no. 4 (Winter 1999–2000), pp. 47–48.

11 *BBC/FE/*3748 B/6 (27 January 2000); 3760 B/5–6 (10 February 2000); 3778 B/4 (2 March 2000); 3783 B/4 (8 March 2000); 3788 B/5 (14 March 2000); 3789 B/3–4 (15 March 2000); 3791 B/4–5 (17 March 2000); 3795 B/3–4 (22 March 2000); 3842 B/5 (17 May 2000); 3853 B/3–4 (30 May 2000); 3854 B/5–6 and G/4 (21 May 2000); 3855 B/4–5 (1 June 2000); 3856 B/4 (2 June 2000); and 3858 G/3 (5 June 2000). See also 'PRC Vessels Sighted Near Shoal', in the section on the 'South China Sea', in *Boundary and Security Bulletin*, vol. 8, no. 1 (Spring 2000), p. 50.

12 *BBC/FE/*3492 B/4–5 (25 March 1999); and 3682 B/8 (3 November 1999).

13 Ibid., 3843 G/3 (18 May 2000).

14 Ibid., 3977 B/5–6 (21 October 2000).

15 Ibid., 4044 G/2 (15 January 2001).

16 Ibid., 4061 B/7 (3 February 2001); and 4065 G/2 (8 February 2001).

17 Ibid., 4078 B/5 (23 February 2001); and 4080 B/4 (26 February 2001).

18 Ibid., 4097 B/4 (17 March 2001); 4098 G/1 (19 March 2001); 4100 B/6 and G/3 (21 March 2001); 4102 B/5 (23 March 2001); and 4107 B/6–7 (29 March 2001).

19 Ibid., 4107 G/1.

20 Ibid., 3678 B/5–6 (29 October 1999); and 3679 B/8.

21 Ibid., 3680 B/5 (1 November 1999).

22 Ibid., 3788 B/5.

23 Ibid., 3842 B/5.

24 In the context of displaying tension between claimants in the South China Sea, it can be noted that in 1999 there was also tension between the Philippines and Malaysia. In June the Philippines protested against Malaysia taking control of two features in the Spratlys (ibid., 3565 B/5 (19 June 1999)). In October combat planes from the Philippines and Malaysia 'nearly engaged' while flying over the Malaysian-controlled Investigator Shoal in the Spratlys. The Philippines did not issue a formal protest over the incident (ibid., 3681 B/4 [2 November 1999]). According to Malaysia there was not a 'standoff' and no 'engagement' between the military planes of the two countries. In fact the Malaysian planes were 'unarmed' (ibid., 3682 B/6–7 [3 November 1999]).

25 The text of the 1992 ASEAN Declaration on the South China Sea can be found on the web site of ASEAN (http://www.asean.or.id/).

26 For studies focusing on ASEAN and its conflict management mechanisms, see among others: Amer, *Expanding ASEAN*, pp. 33–56; Kamarulzaman Askandar, 'ASEAN and Conflict Management: The Formative Years of 1967–1976', *Pacifica Review*, vol. 6, no. 2 (1994), pp. 57–69; and Mely Caballero-Anthony, 'Mechanisms of Dispute Settlement: The ASEAN Experience', *Contemporary Southeast Asia*, vol. 20, no. 1 (1998), pp. 38–66. See also Chapter 7 of the present volume.

27 Discussions between ASEAN and the PRC relating to a possible 'code of conduct' for the South China Sea took place in connection with the ARF meeting in Singapore in late July 1999; in connection with discussions following the Third ASEAN Informal Summit in Manila in late November 1999, at the 'First Meeting of the ASEAN–China Working Group on the Regional Code of Conduct on the South China Sea' held in Hua Hin, Thailand on 15 March 2000, in connection with the Sixth ASEAN–China Senior Officials Consultations held in Kuching, Malaysia on 25–26 April 2000; at the Second meeting of the joint working group on the regional code of conduct held in Kuala Lumpur, Malaysia, on 26 May 2000; and at the Third meeting of the joint working group held in Hanoi on 11 October 2000. The meetings up to May 2000 are listed in accordance with information carried by the web site of ASEAN (http://www.asean.or.id/). Information about the October meeting in Hanoi is derived from 'ASEAN–China working group on the Code of Conduct meets', *News Bulletin*, no. 325 (13 October 2000). From the web site of *Nhan Dan* (http://www.nhandan. org.vn/).

28 Differences in opinion between Malaysia and Vietnam relating to the 'scope of application' of a possible 'code of conduct' were brought up in discussions between the author and scholars and officials in Bangkok and Manila in November 2000.

29 For a detailed analysis of the PRC's policies and behaviour in the multilateral and bilateral dialogues relating to the situation in the South China Sea, see Lee Lai To, *China and the South China Sea Dialogues* (Westport, CO and London: Praeger, 1999). Other studies on the PRC and the South China Sea include Greg Austin, *China's Ocean Frontier. International Law, Military Force and National Development* (St Leonards: Allen & Unwin and Canberra: Department of International Relations and the Northeast Asia Program, Research School of Pacific and Asian Studies, Australian National University, 1998); Frédéric Lasserre, *Le Dragon et la Mer. Stratégies géopolitiques chinoises en mer de Chine du Sud* (Montréal: L'Harmattan Inc., 1996); Lo Chi-kin, *China's Policy towards Territorial Disputes. The Case of the South China Sea Islands* (London and New York: Routledge, 1989); Mark J. Valencia, *China and the South China Sea Disputes*, Adelphi Paper, no. 298 (Oxford: Oxford University Press and the International Institute for Strategic Studies [IISS] 1995).

30 Of interest in this context are the statements made by Vietnam's deputy-foreign minister Vu Koan in an interview published by the Japanese newspaper *Sankei Shimbun* on 22 August 1994. He elaborated on Vietnam's standpoint with regard to the PRC's proposal to engage in joint development in areas of the South China Sea and said that the problem was in which area this would take place and that the PRC's 'intention' in proposing joint development was to justify a Chinese presence within Vietnamese waters under the 'name' of joint development. (Excerpts of the interview in *Sankei Shimbun* have been translated and reproduced in *BBC/ FE*/2085 B/1 [27 August 1994].)

31 Mark Valencia has drafted the text of a possible 'Spratly Treaty': see 'Annex 1' Mark J. Valencia, *Malaysia and the Law of the Sea. The Foreign Policy Issues, the Options and Their Implications* (Kuala Lumpur: Institute of Strategic

and International Studies [ISIS Malaysia], 1991), pp. 139–146; Mark J. Valencia, 'Spratly Solution Still at Sea', *Pacifica Review*, vol. 6, no. 2 (1993, pp. 164–168). For an extensive analysis of various models for sharing the resources in the South China Sea, see Mark J. Valencia, Jon M. Van Dyke and Noel A. Ludwig, *Sharing the Resources of the South China Sea* (The Hague, Boston and London: Martinus Nijhoff Publisher, 1997). (For a broader presentation and discussion relating to scholarly work on possible technical solutions to the South China Sea disputes, see Chapter 9 below.)

9

WHAT COULD BE DONE?

Timo Kivimäki, Liselotte Odgaard

and Stein Tønnesson[1]

The efforts of the disputants of the South China Sea territories have so far done much more to *contain* the conflicts than to resolve the disputes behind them or transform the structures of conflict behind the disputes. In fact the criticism often levelled against the Southeast Asian security arrangements is that the causes of conflicts are not discussed or resolved, rather they are merely swept under the carpet.[2] However, this should not delude those who analyse the potentials for peace to conclude that the only measures that are available are those that already have been tried.

When moving towards an analysis of the ways in which those outside of the region could support the South China Sea peace processes, the discussion starts with a short classification of the instruments available for conflict prevention and conflict management in the area. The term 'conflict management' is taken here in a very broad sense, as defined in the previous chapter. It includes all possible means to prevent conflicts, prevent their escalation, end them, address their root causes, limit their destructive capability, etc.

One should keep in mind that the definition adopted here is not universal. In some writings, the term 'conflict management' is related to the idea of living with conflict and trying to limit its destructiveness, without really seeking to end it permanently. Sometimes the term also has a militaristic interpretation, where conflict management means more or less containment of the violent expressions of conflict by means of defence, deterrence and a code of conduct in conflict behaviour. In some writings this conceptual practice is very much felt as the only way to deal with conflicts, and thereby the militaristic conflict management school reduces conflict studies to military studies or security studies. This is not the meaning in which the concept is used in this study.

The wide range of activities within the category of conflict management can be divided into three categories: the containment of violence, dispute resolution and conflict transformation. The reason why this categorization is useful is that most of the conflict management activity so far has restricted itself to one or two of the three categories. A general categorization developed in comparative conflict studies can open up horizons for activities and strategies that have not been considered previously.

The first of the three approaches to conflict management relates to the *direct containment of violence*. In this approach, military means play an important role as the intention is not really to go deeply into the causes of conflicts but just to live with conflict by inhibiting the effects of its violent expression through defence, deterrence, and agreements about the rules of conflict behaviour. Violence containment is directed at the means of conflict and it aims at the prevention of the escalation of the conflict. This approach does not in itself try to resolve the dispute behind the conflict behaviour let alone the conflict structures that give rise to the disputes. Instead, the intention is merely to control violence and try to contribute to the defence of people.

The approach of the containment of violence has been recognized in the present Western political debate and it is represented in the partnership for peace and peacekeeping philosophy. When thinking of the potentials for the containment of violence in the South China Sea, one should start with the different measures to ensure a military stalemate where none of the powers has an incentive to initiate violence. The military expressions are related to the basic elements of deterrence and the defence equation. The logic of defence and deterrence is still the bottom line in the area; a structure of hard bones on which softer security elements can be built. The efforts to build up codes of conduct are an encouraging, softer, cooperative strategy of conflict management in this category.

The second approach, *dispute resolution*, aims at the settlement of the dispute by offering alternative solutions, persuading the disputants or one of them into compromises, or providing good offices in a dialogue by claimants of the South China Sea area. This approach has for a long time represented the only mindframe of international diplomacy. Yet this is probably the category of conflict management that has the most untapped potential in the South China Sea, because of the tradition of downplaying issues that divide Asians (conflicts) and concentrating instead on matters that unite.

In order to settle conflicts, one does not necessarily have to accept the conflict setting as a given and aim at the containment of violence or dispute resolution within that dispute setting. Instead, one could investigate the possibility of changing the dispute setting in some way. For example, often the demonized identity-structures (perceptions of other claimants as enemies) need to be changed before dispute resolution can even begin: in order to see any point in negotiating on the issues of disagreement, parties need to realize that they are not facing demons but ordinary human beings. By transforming demonized identity structures into more cooperative ones, the setting of the dispute changes from 'military negotiation' into one of cooperation. Thus conflict management should not be entirely focused on concrete issues of dispute or violence. The idea that prevention of conflicts and the promotion of security are merely matters of objective military resources, rather than identities, should be abandoned: London and Liverpool might not have defensive power resources against each other, yet, their common security identity (lack of identity structures that should be transferred) has always meant that these resources have not been considered necessary.

The philosophy in the *conflict transformation approach* is that in disputes there are invariably causes or reasons more fundamental than the ones that are expressed at the level of the disputes. Often, disagreements caused by economic, political, identity or discursive structures give rise to concrete disputes, which then escalate into armed conflicts. Here, economic structures deal with questions of the distribution of income and accumulation of wealth in economic interaction between agents of a different sort. Political structures are similarly related to the distribution of power resources. Identity structures refer to how people perceive groups and relations between groups; they are important because they construct the potential sides in conflicts. Very much related to identity structures are discursive structures, which define the bases and limits for civilized verbal argumentation in societies. The way in which different groups perceive norms and interpretations of the reality, which is relevant to a dispute/conflict, is crucially important from the point of view of conflicts. In a peaceful discursive structure there are some generally accepted bases for argumentation in politics; moreover, there are no groups that lack common grounds for debate and argumentation or there are interlinking groups – groups that would find some elements of the argumentative basis of both groups legitimate.

Since all categories of conflict management – the containment of violence, dispute resolution and conflict transformation – can be used in the South China Sea, there is no reason to choose between these three approaches. Instead the potentials of each will be discussed by starting with conflict containment.

POTENTIALS FOR CONTAINING VIOLENCE

The debate on security in the Asia-Pacific in the post-Cold War era tends to contest the premise that much change in the fundamental dynamics of this region has taken place. A recurring argument holds that although the international politics of the Asia-Pacific are in flux, at heart they remain an object lesson in the realist understanding that power politics dominate the international realm. For example, Rozman notes that the US has good reason to worry that the PRC and Russia will use inequalities in resources and power as an excuse for irresponsibly hampering steps toward a safer future.[3] Gao argues that the PRC's honeymoon with the US came to an end in 1999, ruling out a friendly partnership between the two regional great powers,[4] while Miles argues that the PRC's perception that the US is failing to take into account its security concerns might strengthen anti-US sentiment to the detriment of a future strategic partnership.[5] Yahuda states that as yet there is no basis for the establishment of stable relationships based on shared rules, conceptions of legitimacy and common assumptions in the Asia-Pacific.[6] Ross argues that the Asia-Pacific is marked by the US–PRC bipolar conflict that is stable. As such, it is conducive to the development of a relatively peaceful and cooperative great power order.[7]

This chapter recognizes that the dynamics of military power balancing remain fundamental, but argues that it provides the region of Southeast Asia with a measure of stability that encourages cooperation between the local powers. The implosion of the Soviet Union has provoked a realignment of the remaining powers and their security outlook which promotes the emergence of a structure of deterrence principally based on a mutual display of force between the US and the PRC. It is argued that a structure of deterrence provides the region with a measure of stability, allowing for a rapprochement between the PRC and Southeast Asia to take place.[8]

The South China Sea is an arena for the testing of the compatibility between the security policies of the PRC and Southeast Asia. The ongoing low-intensity dispute over rights to territory and maritime space in this area marks the establishment of the PRC as a Southeast Asian power. A strategy for managing the conflict potential inherent in this realignment of powers is deterrence. Consequently, the purpose of this chapter is to address how violent conflict behaviour in the South China Sea can be contained by means of deterrence. The US is the only regional power with the military means to counter the PRC's power projection capabilities. Therefore, the US holds the key to the consolidation of a stable structure of deterrence.

To address these issues, first the Southeast Asian principle of the non-use of force will be looked at. It is argued that this principle has remained a core strategy for keeping violence at bay since the inception of ASEAN. Second, the confrontation between PRC and Southeast Asian security policies in the South China Sea will be analysed. It will be argued that the insecurity surrounding the PRC's maritime strategy constitutes a potential threat towards the Southeast Asian principle of the non-use of force. Third, the determining influence of the US on the management of the balance of power between the PRC and Southeast Asia will be addressed. It will be argued that the US military presence is a precondition for the development of a structure of deterrence allowing for the preservation of the principle of the non-use of force as the basis of order in Southeast Asia. Finally, developments that might shatter this outcome will be addressed. It will be argued that the mix of force and diplomacy which the US uses to address security issues in the wider region of East Asia determines whether a structure of deterrence is consolidated in Southeast Asia.

The ASEAN principle of the non-use of force

Violent conflict amongst the Southeast Asian ASEAN member states has been circumscribed through the establishment of the principle of the non-use of force between states. Originally, this policy was adopted by the Philippines, Thailand, Malaysia, Indonesia and Singapore, who decided to establish ASEAN in 1967 against a background of repeated outbreaks of hostility, especially between Indonesia and Malaysia, as well as communist threats towards regime stability.

The *raison d'être* of ASEAN was first and foremost preventative: to obviate internal as well as external threats to state security from producing violent conflict in their neighbourhood. Reconciliation between Indonesia and Malaysia in 1966 produced the idea that if conflict amongst the member states of ASEAN could be avoided, then resources could be concentrated on economic and social development. Moreover, the non-use of force externally would allow the states to direct resources towards suppressing the internal communist opposition perceived as the principal threat towards state security in the majority of the member states.[9]

The principle of the non-use of force was not merely motivated in ASEAN-internal security problems, but also by the great power rivalry in the vicinity of the member states. The primary contestants were the US, the Soviet Union and the PRC. Their competition for influence induced the ASEAN member states to conduct diverse policies towards the external powers.[10] Despite these policy differences, the ASEAN member

states were unified in a determination to insulate their regional environment from the violent encounters staged by the great powers in
Indochina. The Indochina threat provided the states with a common
security focus centred on the need to avoid any kind of provocation that
might spark off great power intervention. The protracted conflicts in
Indochina highlighted the importance of refraining from the use of
force amongst the remainder of the Southeast Asian states to ensure
some measure of a united front towards unstable surroundings.

After the end of the Indochina wars, Vietnam, Laos, Cambodia and
Myanmar opted for ASEAN membership. By admitting them to the
association, ASEAN would at the same time spread its policy of the non-
use of force to previously war-ridden states. To include Indochina as a
subscriber to the policy of the non-use of force would be an important
first step in demonstrating the acceptability of this policy outside of the
original reach of ASEAN. One advantage of the ASEAN expansion was
that committing Indochina to a policy of the non-use of force would
greatly diminish the likelihood of a violent conflict breaking out among
any of the Southeast Asian contestants in the South China Sea. Moreover, additional pressure would be applied to the PRC to reach an ac-
commodation in the South China Sea disputes without using instruments of violence.

PRC and Southeast Asian Security Policies in the South China Sea

The ten Southeast Asian countries have committed themselves to the
principle of the non-use of force. However, uncertainty prevails as to
whether the PRC is a genuine subscriber to this doctrine. The uncertainty
stems from the PRC's record of military activities in the South China Sea
combined with her change in military strategy from a northbound continental perspective to a southbound maritime perspective. Traditionally,
the PRC's military strategy has focused on the army, preparing for
engagement in major land wars, and the threat of nuclear retaliation. But
with the Soviet Union's withdrawal from great power rivalry in the mid-
1980s, the likelihood of an attack from the north waned. Instead, the threat
of maritime clashes rose to the top of the PRC's military command's
agenda as the economic development of the coastal regions took off.[11]

In the late 1980s, the military high command agreed on a new
maritime strategy termed the active offshore defence strategy. One of its
explicit goals is to protect offshore islands and maritime interests such
as exploration projects and sea-lanes of communication.[12] Thus, from
concentrating on coastal defence, the PRC now focuses on obtaining
offshore capabilities, making no secret of its long-term aspirations to
enter the ranks of the regional maritime powers Japan and the US.[13]
The PRC navy's extension of the maritime space of exercises and

136

training to 200 nautical miles from the Chinese mainland indicates that the PRC is well on the way to possessing offshore capabilities.[14] PRC control of the South China Sea is not on the cards. However, the change in military strategy indicates that in future, the PRC will be able to engage in limited war in the South China Sea.

Among the ASEAN member states, the southern naval orientation of the PRC's military is perceived as a potential threat towards regional peace and stability. The alleged PRC threat is more pronounced in some Southeast Asian states than in others. The Philippines is the most enthusiastic supporter of a confrontational stance against the PRC. By contrast, Malaysia is a very reluctant subscriber to the PRC-threat scenario. This internal fracture in ASEAN on how to deal with the PRC may disrupt the prospects of forging a unitary approach towards this regional great power.

Although the ASEAN member states hold divergent views and policies on the PRC, they also have a proven record of mustering unity of purpose when faced with common issues considered central to regional security. The spectrum of PRC policies within ASEAN from provocative to conciliatory strategies are united by fundamental agreement that territorial and maritime disputes in the South China Sea are potentially destabilizing. For example, Malaysia concludes a summary of developments in the Spratly dispute by stating that 'the potential for military encounters cannot be ignored thus becoming a source of instability in the Asia Pacific region'.[15]

The armed forces may want to exaggerate the likelihood of the outbreak of military confrontation in the Spratlys. However, the fact that this dispute is ranged before other external security concerns indicates that maritime disputes in the South China Sea are at the centre of strategic planning.

When PRC activities have been considered threatening to stability in the South China Sea, the ASEAN member states have summoned sufficient unity to produce a common response. The 1992 ASEAN Declaration on the South China Sea, following the PRC's adoption of a law allegedly defining the Spratly area as part of PRC territory, recommends that all South China Sea issues be resolved without resort to force.[16] This position was repeated in 1995, with the ASEAN Statement on the Recent Development in the South China Sea following the PRC's occupation of Mischief Reef urging all concerned to resolve differences by peaceful means.[17] Similarly, Malaysia ended up supporting draft work on a code of conduct for the South China Sea, despite initial reservations about provoking the PRC on this issue.[18] The Malaysian decision does not merely indicate temporary compliance; it also denotes adherence to the common ASEAN policy positions on the South China Sea, which includes the establishment of common rules of behaviour.[19]

The suspicion that the PRC may be willing to use military force to defend its territorial and maritime interests in the South China Sea is based not merely on perception, but also on the PRC's involvement in confrontations in the area. Two incidents have caused particular concern. First, the naval clash between the PRC and Vietnam in 1988, which accompanied the PRC's entrance to the scramble for effective occupation in the Spratlys and reportedly cost the lives of at least 70 Vietnamese soldiers, [20] brought the PRC's military presence into the backyard of Southeast Asia. The battle took place when Vietnam was in a weak position, having lost the support of the Soviet Union. Although Vietnam at the time was an isolated state with no formal ties to ASEAN and with a history of violent clashes with the PRC, the PRC's willingness to use force in maritime Southeast Asia potentially threatened the ASEAN policy of the non-use of force.

The second incident to add substance to Southeast Asian security concerns has been the PRC's involvement in the prolonged Mischief Reef affair. Situated 135 nautical miles from Palawan, Mischief Reef is one of the Spratly features closest to the Philippine coastline.[21] Since the PRC's occupation of the feature in 1995, it has been a bone of contention between the PRC and the Philippines, involving repeated diplomatic wrangling and occasional provocative acts between the two countries' armed forces. The PRC did not use force against the Philippines to occupy Mischief Reef since the feature had only been claimed, but not occupied by the Philippines. But as was the case with the 1988 incident, the PRC occupied Mischief Reef when the Philippines were in a position of weakness, subsequent to the closure of the US military bases.[22] Moreover, by the late 1990s, PRC claims that fishermen's shelters were the only facilities on Mischief Reef resembled unconvincing attempts to deny that construction of satellite communication facilities and accommodations for radar and gun emplacements had been carried out.[23] The uncertainty surrounding the PRC occupation serves as a warning that no state in the South China Sea can assume insulation from the PRC's power projection capabilities.

PRC activities in the South China Sea during the last decade suggest a willingness to utilize the temporary weaknesses of Southeast Asian states to further PRC national interests. It does this by military means in a security environment no longer constrained by Soviet power projection. It cannot be ruled out that the PRC's disinclination towards territorial expansion during the Cold War was caused by relative weakness at the time instead of disinterest in restoring alleged PRC territorial and maritime space. The fact that representatives of the PRC navy refer to Zengmu Ansha or James Shoal at the far end of the South China Sea as the southern limit of PRC sea-space does nothing to allay this suspicion.[24] The insecurity surrounding PRC intentions in the South China Sea opens up the possibility that the PRC might attempt to further expand her presence insofar as the Southeast Asian states are incapable of countering PRC military power in the area. Because the South China Sea constitutes a first line of defence for the majority of Southeast Asian states, they cannot afford to ignore what may be a PRC attempt to become a Southeast Asian power disregarding the policy of the non-use of force.

The US and the balance of power in the South China Sea

The principal response of the states of Southeast Asia to the security threat posed by the PRC has been to deter the PRC from using force in their neighbourhood. In contrast to the PRC, the majority of the Southeast Asian states are unable to project military power beyond their own territory.[25] Despite modernization efforts directed at developing their naval and airforce capabilities, the military weakness of the Southeast Asian states is revealed by the fact that most of them are not capable of patrolling the maritime zones recognized to be under their jurisdiction. Hence, the prospects of their countering PRC offshore capabilities is remote. This comparative disadvantage is enhanced by the absence of a common defence identity amongst the ASEAN member states.[26] Numerous territorial, maritime and ethnic disputes within ASEAN effectively prevent the member states from heading in this direction. Moreover, the provocation towards the PRC that plans for an intra-ASEAN defence alliance would entail rules out substantial defence integration in Southeast Asia.

Consequently, Southeast Asia has to rely on the US to balance PRC military power. In the post-Cold War era, there is no immediate challenger to the dominant position of the US. As a result, the US prefers to let regional powers settle disputes that are not of consequence to global peace and stability or to the national interests of the US. Until 1995, the Spratly dispute was perceived as a dispute of no immediate consequence for the US position. Therefore, the US administration maintained a policy of non-interference on this issue insofar as the sea-lanes remained unaffected. The principle of non-interference was echoed by then Secretary of State James Baker:

> [T]he US would like to see a peaceful resolution of the various claims to the Spratlys, the claims in some cases being quite conflicting. We have taken no legal position with respect to those and it would be our hope that somehow they could be resolved peacefully.[27]

The hesitant attitude of the US in the early 1990s caused some concern amongst the Southeast Asian countries that they might not be able to rely on the US as military balancer in future. For example, Siti

Azizah Abod from the Malaysian defence ministry stated that 'the Asian governments are concerned that Washington has neither the political will nor the resources to underwrite the security of Southeast Asia or involve itself in regional conflicts that are nationalistic rather than ideological in nature'.[28]

However, the 1995 Mischief Reef incident prompted the US to consider the PRC's policy on the South China Sea as an indication of possible hegemonic ambitions of the PRC in the region, requiring a clarification of US limits of tolerance in the area. After the airing of Southeast Asian concerns about the extent of US commitment to the region's security, the US administration sharpened its position, stating that it would view 'with serious concern any restriction on maritime activity in the South China Sea that was not consistent with international law'.[29]

No change in the substance of US policy on the South China Sea was announced. However, the attempts to dissociate the US from events in the area had been replaced by warnings that the US would not tolerate any interference with shipping in the South China Sea. The secretary of state of the second Clinton administration, Madeleine Albright, maintained a cautious attitude toward events in the South China Sea, stating that the US is 'concerned with the growing tension over territorial claims in the South China Sea. We will be urging them to exercise restraint and to find ways to build confidence and move towards resolution.'[30]

In the late 1990s, the US was also less coy about singling out the PRC as a violator of stability. The US House of Representatives explicitly called for bringing pressure to bear on the PRC to scale down its military activities in the South China Sea in the 1995 China Policy Act.[31] Similarly, in 1999 state department spokesman James Rubin urged the PRC to 'avoid actions that increase tensions in the region'.[32]

In line with the policy of non-interference unless the sea-lanes are endangered, the US rejected Philippine requests for military assistance in connection with the Mischief Reef incident, refusing to invoke the 1951 Mutual Defense Treaty as a basis for US involvement. However, confusion persists as to whether the US would aid Philippine forces if attacked in the eastern part of the South China Sea. Although the US has stated that it considers the Spratly area as international waters, the joint US–Philippine military exercises, resumed in 2000, involved the defence of troops attacked in the South China Sea. Former US Defense Secretary Cohen's statement that the US will aid Philippine troops if attacked in disputed areas has only added to the vagueness surrounding US involvement in the South China Sea.[33] The statement as well as Cohen's suggestion that the Philippines convene a conference on the South China Sea sponsored by the US has added to the perplexity concerning the extent of US involvement in this area. This is not necessarily a sign of indecision.

Instead, it may signify an unwillingness to clarify US intentions in the South China Sea until the PRC makes a similar clarification of her policy in the area.

The US is aware that the rising power of the PRC may result in a future challenge to US dominance, and that the South China Sea remains one of the hot spots where the first signs of a future challenge may emerge. In view of the inchoate military capabilities of the Southeast Asian states, the US remains the principal balancer of the PRC. Consequently, the US has maintained its strategy of forward deployment in Eastern Asia. Widespread domestic dissatisfaction in the Philippines with the preservation of Clark Air Force Base and Subic Bay led to their closure in 1992. The loss of the largest overseas US military installation and the largest ship-repair and refuelling facility of the US in the Pacific required a change in the bilateral defence arrangements between the US and Southeast Asian states.

During the Cold War era, Malaysia and Indonesia resented the potentially destabilizing effects of the US military presence in Southeast Asia. However, in the 1990s they recognized that US balancing is a precondition of regional stability. Hence, for the first time, all ASEAN member states called for the US to maintain a secure military balance in the region at the 1992 ASEAN foreign ministers' meeting in Manila. Support for the current level of US military presence appears to be substantial in the higher echelons of Southeast Asian societies. Even in Malaysia, only 31.3% of Southeast Asian executives consider the US military presence in Asia too large.[34] The US, for her part, welcomed the general acceptance amongst Southeast Asian countries that 100,000 US troops remain deployed in Asia.[35] The then US Secretary of State James Baker stated that 'withdrawal from Clark and Subic Bay ... has not altered our interest in, nor commitment to, Asian security'.[36]

In contrast to the permanent stationing of large contingents of US troops in Japan and South Korea, the type of access undertaken by the US in Southeast Asia in the 1990s constitutes a network of bilateral arrangements facilitating inter-operability. As compared to the permanent bases of the Cold War, the network of arrangements allow for a flexible deployment of US military power corresponding to the insecurity as to where and when violent conflict might erupt. The increasingly frequent visits of senior military officials from the US to Southeast Asian countries in the second half of the 1990s underscore the importance that the US attaches to the establishment of this military cooperation network.

The expansion of security cooperation and military access between the US and Southeast Asian states centres on port calls, repair facilities, logistics support, training and joint military exercises.[37] The main countries in the network of military cooperation are Singapore and the

US alliance partners Thailand and the Philippines. Singapore has been at the forefront in recommending support for a continued US presence in Asia.

The 1990 Access Memorandum of Understanding provides the foundation for the location in Singapore of a naval logistics unit, US access to a pier capable of accommodating an aircraft carrier, as well as periodic US naval and air training. Thailand continues to allow US ships and aircraft transit, refuelling and visiting rights. Moreover, Cobra Gold constitutes the largest joint training agreement involving US troops in Southeast Asia. Since 1995, the US has been able to transfer fighter aircraft to the Philippines, and US marine commandos have trained Philippine troops in the vicinity of the Spratlys.

In May 1999, the Philippine Senate approved an accord allowing US troops to resume major naval visits and large-scale joint exercises suspended in 1996. The first exercises took place in January and February 2000.[38] The exercises were accompanied by the arrival of US surplus military equipment for the Philippines.[39] Examples of military cooperation with the US on a smaller scale include transit and visiting rights as well as periodic exercises with Brunei. In addition to naval visits, Indonesia and Malaysia have made available maintenance and repair facilities for US ships and aircraft. US exercises have also taken place in Malaysia in the 1990s. The US has made incremental moves to establish nascent military relations with Vietnam, Laos and Cambodia, although relations with the latter have been left hanging due to internal political instability. Hence, Myanmar is the only state in Southeast Asia entirely excluded from the network, instead relying on the PRC for military assistance.

The Southeast Asian states consider the US military presence to shield them from direct confrontation with the PRC. Consequently, the ASEAN member states want to leave room for continued military exercises in a future code of conduct for the South China Sea.[40] This attitude is in line with the continued US commitment to regional balancing. In the main, US power projection capabilities in Southeast Asia have been maintained, as indicated by the establishment and renewal of military cooperation agreements in the area.

Preliminary steps have been taken to establish a nascent strategic partnership between the US and the PRC. Official visits of the US and PRC heads of state in 1997 and 1998, naval visits, defence university exchanges and senior-level defence dialogues have formed part of these efforts.[41] In the South China Sea, the US and the PRC have participated in a joint scientific project on marine science and technology since 1995.[42]

A series of disagreements between the US and the PRC has imperiled the prospects of a strategic partnership. Among the most serious incidents have been PRC opposition to the NATO air strikes in Yugoslavia, the

NATO bombing of the PRC embassy in Belgrade, the revelations that espionage has allowed the PRC access to detailed information on advanced US defence technology, the US–Chinese aircraft collision over the South China Sea in 2001 and the US withdrawal from the Antiballistic Missile (ABM) Treaty.[43] These events have strained the engagement policy close to breaking point. Although efforts have been made on both sides to pour oil on troubled waters, the notion of a strategic partnership remains a statement of intent rather than an established practice.

Nothing in the more fundamental patterns of military balancing supports the expectation that a strategic partnership is emerging between the US and the PRC. This development has been reflected in statements by leading US officials and analysts implying that great power rivalry is becoming the dominant characteristic of US–PRC relations. For example, Princeton political scientist Aaron L. Friedberg has stated that 'the US is beginning to face up to the fact that we are likely over the next few years to be engaged in an ongoing military competition with China. Indeed, in certain respects, we already are'.[44]

The future US involvement in regional security arrangements should not be exaggerated. The argument that the US is opting for regional hegemony appears to entail such exaggeration. The importance that the US attaches to the participation of local powers in conflict resolution, combined with US reluctance to play an active role in disputes not directly affecting its interests, does not support the proposition that the US has hegemonic ambitions in the Asia-Pacific.

Instead, a structure of deterrence appears to be in the making. Deterrence is directed at the intentions of the opponents: if the deterrent forces are estimated to prevent the opponent from achieving gains through aggression, the opponent will refrain from attack. Hence, the ability of the entities to project power is constrained by a mutual display of force between the US and Southeast Asia on the one hand and the PRC on the other hand. The efforts of the PRC to become a Southeast Asian power have driven home the point that the ASEAN member states can no longer ignore the potential for violent conflict in their neighbourhood. To maintain a regional order based on the principle of the non-use of force, most of the states have maintained or revitalized security arrangements with the US, seeing the latter as the only power able to provide a credible match to the military capabilities of the PRC.

Prospects for a consolidation of the structure of deterrence

The regional order developing in Southeast Asia in the post-Cold War era is based on deterrence. The principal precondition that this structure is consolidated as a stable regional pattern is that the US continues to add substance to it by balancing the military power of the PRC.

The consolidation of a stable structure of deterrence conducive to regional peace and stability may be disrupted by four developments. First, a departure from the US position of non-involvement in local disputes could produce a military response from the PRC. The increase in consultation, coordination and cooperation taking place between the PRC and Southeast Asia within the structure of deterrence at the informal and formal level may come to be considered part of a separation process from US regional involvement. If collaboration between the PRC and Southeast Asia develops beyond the present preliminary stage, the US may not continue to take a back seat position. Instead, the US may opt for a strengthening of the military ties with states such as the Philippines and Thailand to preserve deterrence as the fundamental characteristic of PRC–Southeast Asian relations.

The presidency of the Republican George W. Bush is not likely to change US foreign policy in the direction of increased regional involvement. Members of the Republican-dominated US Congress have called for a tougher stance towards PRC military activities in the South China Sea.[45] However, Bush is likely to stop short of adopting a very tough policy on the PRC that might require greater US regional involvement because such a development would run counter to the less internationalist profile of the present US administration.[46] As noted by security analyst Jusuf Wanandi, the realities of power in the US will make the Bush presidency drop some of its harsh rhetoric and moderate policies that could upset stability in the Asia-Pacific.[47] The combination of strategic competition coupled with moderate regional involvement entails a consolidation of, instead of a departure from, the structure of deterrence evolving in the region.

Second, violent conflict in the Taiwan Strait could spill over into the South China Sea. Bush has announced that the US will be directly involved if war not provoked by Taiwan breaks out in the Taiwan Strait, the most sensitive issue in US–PRC relations.[48] If violent conflict between the PRC and the US erupted in the area, the US might put pressure on the Philippines for enhanced access to repair, refuelling and transit facilities. This situation might reactivate the dispute over the Spratlys where the PRC has allegedly built military installations in the vicinity of the Philippines. Moreover, Taiwan has military installations on the largest island of Itu Aba, another reason why the Spratly area may be included in violent conflict involving Taiwan.

This scenario must be considered unlikely. First, the Spratly Islands are situated too far from the Taiwan Strait to be immediately useful for countries involved in military activities between Taiwan and the PRC. Second, without the permanent Philippine bases, the US will have a hard time persuading the Philippines to become involved in a crisis due to the major threats towards its national security that such assistance would entail. Finally, the PRC does not have much interest in an unprovoked attack on Taiwan in view of the high risk of a US military response coupled with the strength of the Taiwanese military forces. As long as the political establishment of Taiwan continues a moderate policy focusing on reconciliation and continued negotiation on the issue of a rapprochement between the two Chinas, the Chinese mainland can afford to wait for a better opportunity for reunification to arise. Although a deterioration in Taiwan–PRC relations was initially feared as a result of the victory of Chen Shui-bian in Taiwan's presidential elections, he has proved to be a pragmatic politician who takes care to avoid provoking the PRC into military actions.

Third, implementation of the plans for a theatre missile defence (TMD) covering Japan, South Korea and Taiwan would threaten to skew the balance of power to the disadvantage of the PRC, risking a military response from the latter. Bush has made no secret of his support for a continuation of the missile defence plans, adding to the PRC's concern over its increased isolation in the region.[49] Realization of the plans for a theatre missile defence is likely to jeopardize stability because the moderate strategic deterrent capabilities of the PRC would be seriously degraded. Communist China has a history of violent encounters when pressure mounts against its security, even if this might provoke a military response from a superior power. The shelling of the Taiwanese-occupied offshore islands of Quemoy in 1958, the PRC's brief war with India in 1962, the border skirmishes with the Soviet Union in 1969, and the PRC invasion of Vietnam in 1979 are cases in point.[50] Although these incidents have been defensive or preventive military actions of limited duration, they serve as a warning that the PRC is willing to use military force if her security interests are not taken into consideration.

At present, the South China Sea is the weak link in the chain of military cooperation agreements surrounding the PRC due to US hesitancy towards issuing military guarantees in this area. As a consequence, it is also a likely setting for a PRC military demonstration against encirclement. Hence, the South China Sea may provide the arena, but not the cause, for the use of force that may threaten regional stability, in particular if the US chooses to respond to a PRC provocation.

Although this scenario stands a chance of coming to fruition, the prospects of its realization should not be exaggerated. It should be noted that the technical, financial and political feasibility of theatre missile defence remains in doubt.[51] Although research and testing continues, the realization of the more ambitious plans is far off on the horizon. Consequently, Bush may have to retreat from his campaign promises for a robust system adding sea, air and space-based interceptors and including Japan and Taiwan under a regional umbrella. Adding to the likelihood of a Bush retreat is the argument by Cirincoine of the Carnegie Endowment that the primary driver behind the politicization of missile defence has been domestic politics rather than technology or the threat of a missile attack.[52] The technological limits of the project and the realities of power in the Asia-Pacific are likely to induce moderation on the part of the US.

Fourth, increased Japanese responsibility for security in Asia may similarly destabilize the region and risk provoking the PRC to take military action. Particularly worrisome is the 1997 expansion of the US–Japan defence guidelines, allowing the principal Asian ally of the US to give logistical support in crises occurring in the Far East and surrounding areas. In 2001, substance was added to these plans with the Japanese decision to let its self-defence forces assist the US war on terrorism in a non-combat role. The PRC is undoubtedly the weaker part in Asia compared to the US and Japan, both in terms of military power and technological capabilities. In view of its relative weakness, the PRC reaps her own benefits from continued US control with Japanese defence. The increasing calls during the 1990s for constitutional revisions allowing Japan to exert political influence on a par with its economic power, produced fears of a revival in prior Japanese aspirations for regional supremacy.[53]

The prospects of a remilitarized Japan are sufficiently threatening to PRC security interests that a moderate US military presence is considered a necessary evil.[54] This benefit is reduced if the renewed US–Japan defence agreement proves to be the first step in a process aiming at instituting Japan as a political great power in Asia on a par with the PRC. Such a development is not conducive to stability. The PRC and the US are realpolitik opponents *par excellence.* Although this relationship entails tight constraints on the possibilities for cooperation, it is not a barrier to stability. By contrast, the hegemonic aspirations of early twentieth-century Japan make it a much more provocative regional balancer than the US. This view is not only detectable in PRC strategic thinking, but is also widespread in Southeast Asian countries such as Malaysia and Indonesia. Therefore, Japanese political influence conducive to great power status may not only provoke the emergence of a PRC–Russian alliance, but may also splinter the unity of ASEAN. The US would not be able to maintain control of such a profound restructuring of the strategic environment in Asia.

This scenario represents the most likely and as such also the most immediate caveat to the consolidation of a structure of deterrence, because the process of allowing Japan a greater role in regional security management is already under way. The mounting pressure on the PRC in the Northeast may call for a reaction in the Southeast, prompting the PRC to secure increased control in this area. Consequently, the South-east Asian states are walking a tightrope between reliance on US military balancing and reassurance from the PRC that cooperation rather than containment is the principal aim of Southeast Asian security policies. Aware of this precarious situation, ASEAN has kept quiet on the 1996 Taiwan Strait incident between the US and the PRC and retained a neutral position towards the revision of the US–Japan defence agreement.[55]

However, the ASEAN member states do not have much influence on the triangular relationship between the US, Japan and the PRC. Therefore, the principal barrier towards the realization of this scenario is the US interest in maintaining ultimate control with the military power of Japan. A Japan with political power on a par with its economic power would also be a much less reliable alliance partner of the US. The US does not need another security problem adding to the complexity of the inter-related issues of the rising power of the PRC and the Chinese and Korean reunification prospects. As a consequence, Japan is likely to remain a second-rank power compared to the US. Due to the precarious position of Japan in Asia, it is likely to continue to view this subordinate position as a price worth paying for continued US protection.

FROM DETERRENCE TO CODES OF CONDUCT

A structure of deterrence involving the US as the principal balancer of the PRC provides Southeast Asia with the level of military security and reassurance necessary to allow for the development of stronger co-operative ties with a PRC that is potentially threatening. The gradual advance of the PRC into the South China Sea combined with the slow but steady progress in upgrading the armed forces to offshore level has been a cause for increasing concern in Southeast Asia. The US has kept an eye on the Spratly dispute as an indicator of possible expansionist foreign policy intentions of the PRC. The ASEAN member states perceive the PRC's presence in the Spratlys as a potentially violent intrusion into their neighbourhood.

The states of Southeast Asia are not sufficiently strong to counter the PRC's power projection. Consequently, the states are drawing closer to the US. For these relatively weak states, the US is indispensable in order to balance the military power of the PRC. In parallel with her opponents, the PRC perceives the display of force on her southern flank as a potential threat based on a strategy of containment. The mutual insecurity surrounding the intentions of opponent powers allows for the emergence of a structure of deterrence. This development does not necessarily indicate that regional stability is deteriorating. Instead, it may ensure

147

that the policy of the non-use of force between states is accepted as a fundamental principle of state interaction in the South China Sea. Moreover, a structure of deterrence provides states not used to collaborating with the fundamental military reassurance that gives them the confidence to search for avenues of cooperation.

A stable structure of deterrence constitutes a precondition for agreement among the local powers on a set of rules defining what constitutes acceptable behaviour in the South China Sea. Common standards of behaviour represent a method of countering future outbreaks of violence. These standards lie somewhere in between everyday state practice and international law *par excellence*, in the sense that they are expressions of repeated, constant, generally accepted practices of long duration. On the basis of such continuous practices, states might agree on a set of soft rules, providing cooperative instruments as opposed to the sanctions accompanying the hard rules of international law.[56]

The 1992 ASEAN recommendation of a code of conduct for the South China Sea constitutes a call for the establishment of a formal standard aimed at conflict containment.[57] The recommendation implied that confirmation of the basic principles of state conduct applicable to the South China Sea was called for because the contending parties showed an increasing propensity to adopt national legislation incompatible with globally recognized principles of international law. A code of conduct is not a substitute for a strong political framework between the PRC and Southeast Asia. However, insofar as a structure of deterrence is consolidated, a foundation for the establishment of a common set of rules that serves to contain conflict in the South China Sea is in place. Bearing in mind this precondition, the following section explores the prospects of agreement between the PRC and ASEAN on a code of conduct for the South China Sea.

Code of conduct – what could be done to create a defensive and crisis stable setting?

An agreement between the PRC and ASEAN on a code of conduct for the South China Sea depends on the ability of the parties to frame the principles in a way that supports the consolidation of deterrence as well as cooperation. To create a stable setting for conflict management, the PRC and ASEAN need to establish rules in areas where rapprochement, consultation and cooperation have already taken place in practice. Furthermore, negotiations need to de-emphasize issues that are not multilateral as well as issues that are beyond the reach of PRC–ASEAN decisions. Issues belonging to the first category are competitive occupations, economic interests, environmental problems, safety of navigation and communication and scientific research. Issues belonging to the second category are military deployments and exercises and bilateral disputes.

Suggestions for discussions on bilateral territorial disputes as part of the talks on a code of conduct are detrimental to the prospects of future agreement. To reach an agreement, it is vital that negotiations concentrate on reconciling the views of the PRC and ASEAN. Attempts at including bilateral territorial disputes, such as the Vietnamese suggestion to include the Paracels, would prevent agreement from being reached because it would increase internal disagreement among the ASEAN countries on the amount of demands to be placed on the PRC. Furthermore, any hope that the PRC is willing to negotiate bilateral issues such as the Paracels in a multilateral forum is futile. The successful bilateral negotiations between the PRC and Vietnam on their Gulf of Tonkin dispute indicate that bilateral disputes should be dealt with in bilateral fora.

Competitive occupations serve to sustain the status of the Spratly dispute as a regional hot spot. This reading of the situation is detrimental to the prospects for stability because it suggests that the littoral states focus on the need to maintain contingency plans for the worst case scenario of war. Moreover, it contradicts the progress made throughout the 1990s in building confidence between the contending parties. Consequently, the PRC and Southeast Asia should focus on how to prevent further occupations from taking place.

By contrast, military deployments and exercises are not entirely within the realm of PRC–Southeast Asian regulation. Some military exercises in the South China Sea involve external powers. For example, the annual exercises between the US and the Philippines encompass the South China Sea. Located at the southwestern entrance to the South China Sea, Changi naval base at Singapore may also give rise to disagreement during negotiations since it is frequented by the US Seventh Fleet. In light of the continuous US presence in the region, the PRC is not likely to accept a ban on the construction of military installations in the South China Sea. A code of conduct can do nothing to stop the consolidation of a structure of deterrence in the South China Sea. However, it can help to ensure that deterrence is stable by preventing the volatility following from competitive occupations. In practice, the number of competitive occupations has decreased in the late 1990s. Partly this is due to the fact that most features large enough to hold buildings and installations have already been taken. Moreover, since the naval battle between the PRC and Vietnam in 1988, the claimant states have taken steps to avoid any violent conflict resulting from occupations.

So far, negotiations have resulted in mutual agreement that some measure of restraint should be applied in the use of threats and armed force against civilians. China seems to have ignored Southeast Asian calls for a common commitment to refrain from the occupation of new features. However, this may be due to the fact that the request is accompanied by a suggestion to restrict construction work on disputed features. Since ASEAN wants to leave room for the continuation of military exercises involving the US, they need to accept that China will adopt countermeasures such as installing satellites on features occupied in the South China Sea.

Economic interest is an area where a modest measure of rapprochement has occurred between the claimant states. Economic interests are primarily directed towards the exploration and exploitation of fish, mineral and hydrocarbon resources. However, the informal talks on a model of joint development for resource exploration and exploitation are not likely to make much progress until a code of conduct has been accepted defining rules of acceptable behaviour that will prevent the states from pursuing national interests without regard for the interests of the surroundings. The fact that negotiations on a code of conduct have been taken to the formal level, whereas joint development talks have been maintained at the informal level, confirms that the states recognize the need for behavioural regulation before cooperation on joint development in the South China Sea can be contemplated.

Environmental problems, scientific research and safety of navigation and communication are areas where limited cooperation has been established. The initiation of training programmes in the South China Sea on issues such as biodiversity, education of mariners, standardization of data and methods, as well as the amalgamation of country-specific data in marine scientific research, are small but significant steps towards cooperation in non-controversial areas. Negotiations have confirmed that cooperation in the above mentioned areas should form part of a prospective code of conduct.

Formal discussions on a code of conduct between the PRC and the ASEAN countries indicate that the littoral states of the South China Sea have already reached a level of mutual trust sufficient for discussing concrete steps towards defining what constitutes acceptable state conduct. The principal pitfall lies in areas related to military activities. This is not surprising, given the fact that China and Southeast Asia are on opposite sides in the emerging deterrence structure. At present, the parties seem to be issuing competitive demands in the areas of deployment, construction work and exercises. They are not likely to reach agreement in these areas. Instead, these elements constitute impediments to progress in negotiations. A more feasible strategy would be tacit mutual acceptance that deterrence is already in place and therefore allowances must be made for the states to consolidate their military postures. Instead, efforts could be concentrated on reaching an agreement so that no further competitive occupations can take place. This would aid in transforming the South China Sea from a hot spot into a setting for armed, but peaceful rapprochement between the local powers.

POTENTIALS FOR DISPUTE RESOLUTION

While it is true that only the countries directly concerned can resolve the conflict in the South China Sea, it may still be useful – even for outsiders – to discuss possible solutions. If it could be established that an equitable solution were possible, it might be a little bit easier for the governments in the region to acquire the necessary political will. In the last few years, ASEAN has engaged China in negotiations with the aim of agreeing on a regional code of conduct. If successful, this may not only be an important confidence-building measure, but also help prevent conflicts and pave the way for regional cooperation in certain areas, such as environmental protection.

Although there has been no movement in the direction of resolving the sovereignty disputes over the Paracel and Spratly Islands, or to delineate maritime zones in the central part of the South China Sea, it may be useful to consider ways by which the regional countries can, when sufficient political will has been established, resolve these disputes. Without an agreement on the delineation of maritime zones, it seems difficult to imagine that the countries around the South China Sea can find efficient ways to manage their fish stocks, provide environmental protection, attract major oil companies to explore for oil and gas, suppress piracy, and acquire the necessary technology to intervene in case of a major oil spill. And if countries elsewhere in the world have been able to resolve their territorial disputes, why should the countries around the South China Sea not have the same ability? It will be up to the regional countries themselves to resolve the disputes. Suggestions from outsiders on how to do so will be valuable only to the extent that they are embraced or seen as useful by governments or other interested parties in the region. Still it should be emphasized that countries outside the region, indeed in the rest of the world, also have an interest in maintaining secure sea-lanes, and in the preservation of peace in East Asia, where some of the world's most powerful states are situated.

Dispute resolution formulas

Some commentators have considered the disputes in the South China Sea too complex to make resolution a realistic prospect, at least in our lifetime. Other scholars have been inspired precisely by the complexity of the jurisdictional disputes to come up with creative solutions. In the 1980s and 1990s, Mark J. Valencia at the East–West Center in Hawaii presented a series of alternative proposals on how the South China Sea could be delimited into zones of national jurisdiction.[58] The proposals were based on the presumption that the conflict would be resolved diplomatically, through arbitration or a court ruling, rather than militarily. Ways of resolving the conflict were also discussed at the annual Managing Potential Conflicts workshops in Indonesia.

The proposals that have been discussed are basically of three types: The first suggests that, in the absence of a resolution of the sovereignty disputes, the claimant countries should establish Joint Development Zones (JDZs) or Joint Management Zones (JMZs). These proposals could seek inspiration from the Timor Gap Treaty, and from the JDZs established in the Gulf of Thailand between Thailand and Malaysia and between Vietnam and Malaysia. Indeed it has been claimed that the Gulf of Thailand is 'at the forefront' globally of joint development arrangements.[59] The idea of establishing a multilateral JDZ in the South China Sea was long associated with Indonesian Ambassador Hasjim Djalal's so-called 'doughnut theory', which argued that there would be an area of High Seas left in the middle of the South China Sea (more than 200 nautical miles from all shores) and that this area could form the basis for a JDZ regime. The idea was discussed at the workshops, and a particular area was identified as having the greatest potential, but because of indecision on the part of some of the claimant states, no steps were taken to actually carry out the project.[60]

Cooperative schemes less ambitious than outright JDZs or JMZs have also been discussed. The purpose would then be to carry out oceano-graphic research and research on biological diversity, protect the natural environment, and manage fish stocks. There is much urgency to this both in view of the serious environmental situation, and in view of the fact that the regional states have an obligation to undertake protective measures under the Convention on Biological Diversity. It therefore seems most desirable to encourage the regional states to establish cooperation in these fields. The Chinese code of conduct proposal may provide an opening for this. The technical working group on biological diversity, and other technical working groups under the Indonesian workshops, have come up with some concrete proposals, and cooperative projects could emerge under inspiration from the United Nations Environmental Programme's (UNEP) new Strategic Action Plan.

The second, more traditional kind of proposal for dispute resolution has aimed at resolving the sovereignty dispute to the Paracel and Spratly Islands on the basis of international law. The merit of each state's claim must be considered, and each feature or island group must be allocated to the country that has the strongest claim in law. Several scholars and commentators have assumed that the sovereignty disputes concerning the islands must be resolved before one can get on with delimiting maritime zones. Most legal scholars, however, have been reluctant to discuss the merits of the various sovereignty claims. They defer their judgment until being engaged by the parties or by a court. Some scholars, however, have dared to discuss the merits of the various claims, coming to somewhat different conclusions. In a volume published together with the leading South China Sea specialist Mark J. Valencia, the legal scholar Jon M. Van Dyke has pointed to the fact that it may actually be dangerous to start by resolving the sovereignty disputes:

> In fact, the allocation of the features [to some of the claimants] might accentuate rather than resolve strategic concerns, as well as exacerbate such disputes if the recognized owners one day insist on claiming EEZs and continental shelves extending from the islands.[61]

If one or a few states gain sovereignty to the islands, this may exacerbate the conflict and possibly lead to a highly inequitable distribution of maritime zones among the countries concerned. For these reasons, and also because it is unlikely that the countries will agree to let the sovereignty disputes go to mediation, the second approach seems neither reasonable nor practicable.

Precisely for the above reason, Valencia, Ludwig and Van Dyke have included among their several models on how to divide the South China Sea, one where the islands as such have no influence on the delimitation. Instead the zones are delineated on the basis of distance from the coasts of the surrounding countries, with a system of moderate compensation for geographically disadvantaged states. This has inspired a third kind of proposal which suggests that the conflict could be resolved diplomatically by the regional countries themselves, on the basis of the LOS Convention of 1982, but without resolving the tortuous question of sovereignty to the Spratlys.

The key element in this proposal is that all claimant states realize that under the LOS Convention (paragraph 121.3) the Spratly Islands, since they do not allow for human habitation or an economic life of their own, cannot generate more than 12 nautical mile territorial waters. The dispute over sovereignty to the islands and their 12 nautical mile territorial waters can therefore be shelved for quite some time, while the states define their EEZ and continental shelf claims on the basis of distance from their coasts, and negotiate median lines. Then, when most of the South China Sea and the continental shelf have been divided into national zones, the question of what to do with the High Seas remaining in the middle must be addressed. And the Spratly Islands with their 12 nautical mile territorial waters could be made into a regional, jointly managed marine park, where all economic activity is prohibited. This proposal has been outlined in three articles, which present a six-stage strategy for conflict resolution.[62] The following is a brief outline of the proposal:

First stage. China and Vietnam negotiate bilaterally on the Gulf of Tonkin (Beibu Gulf). They abandon earlier plans to consider the Gulf as 'historical waters' with status as internal waters, and instead divide the Gulf between them by applying a median line. This is what the two countries did in December 2000.[63] They also agreed on a fishing cooperation treaty, with the dual purpose of providing access for Chinese fishermen to resources on the Vietnamese side, and ensuring the preservation of essential fish stocks. It remains to be seen if the agreement has been successfully implemented, and if the two sides are able to cooperate in resource management.[64]

Second stage. The governments in Beijing and Taipei establish a joint team to defend China's interests in the South China Sea and work out a coordinated negotiation strategy vis-à-vis the Philippines, Malaysia, Brunei and Vietnam. This may seem utopian, but Chinese and Taiwanese scholars and policy-makers know one another from the Indonesian workshops, and also from intra-Chinese workshops on the South China Sea, which have been organized in Hainan. Furthermore, cooperation in the South China Sea may be a way to enhance a closer relationship between mainland China and Taiwan now that Taipei has lifted its restrictions on investments and trade with the mainland.[65]

Third stage. China and Taiwan make a 'small bargain' with the Philippines over Scarborough Shoal (a feature west of Luzon that is not a part of either the Paracels or the Spratlys). They agree that there is one rock on the shoal (*Hyungan* or Yellow Rock) that satisfies the condition for being an island in the legal sense, and that therefore has a right to 12 nautical miles of territorial waters, but they also agree that it does not have a right to a continental shelf or EEZ. Then they shelve the sovereignty dispute to the shoal as such and its territorial waters. In order to protect its natural environment (invaluable coral reefs) they decide to prohibit any kind of economic activity in the disputed zone, and jointly establish the means to enforce the prohibition.

Fourth stage. The 'small bargain' is used as a model for a 'big bargain' concerning the Spratlys and the Paracels. All claimant countries concede that none of the Spratly Islands satisfy the conditions for having a right to more than 12 nautical mile territorial waters. Then they shelve the sovereignty dispute to the islands and reefs as such, as well as their territorial waters. In return, Vietnam and the other claimants recognize Chinese sovereignty over the Paracels, and also concede that some of the Paracel Islands satisfy the conditions for having a right to a continental shelf and a 200 nautical mile EEZ. This concession, which will be difficult to swallow for Vietnam, will be necessary in order to obtain Chinese agreement to limiting the maritime zones of all the Spratlys to only 12 nautical miles. Vietnam's reward for making the concession will be to gain recognition of its national jurisdiction over a huge continental shelf and EEZ in the Vanguard Bank area west of the Spratlys, which does have geological structures that *may* contain significant quantities of oil and gas. Vietnam may also demand that China agree to demilitarize the Paracels.

Fifth stage. All claimant states draw new proper baselines along their coasts and islands, and precisely define their continental shelf and maritime zone claims, using proper base points on their coasts and coastal islands as a point of departure. Then everyone will see precisely where the claims overlap. Through a system of bilateral and multilateral conferences, the countries may then undertake the laborious work of negotiating median lines. The Paracels can be legitimately used as a basis for the Chinese claim, but no claimant can use Scarborough Shoal, the submerged Macclesfield Bank or the Spratlys as basis for the continental shelf or EEZ claims. In the end most of the South China Sea will have been delimited into maritime zones, except an area in the middle, which is beyond 200 nautical miles from all coasts. This will be High Seas, and the resources here will need to be managed by an international authority. (It is possible that the whole sea-bed under the South China Sea can come under national jurisdiction, since a continental shelf under certain conditions can go beyond 200 nautical miles to a maximum of 350 nautical miles. No point in the South China Sea is more than 350 nautical miles from all coasts.) After the fifth stage has been completed, only the sovereignty dispute to Scarborough Shoal and the Spratlys, and their territorial waters, will remain unresolved.

Sixth stage. All claimant countries transfer their alleged sovereignty to the Spratlys to a regional or international authority, which is set up to administer a system of marine nature parks. Within the parks all economic activity is prohibited, except environment-friendly tourism. The Spratlys are thus given back to their original inhabitants, the birds, fish and turtles.

The aim of this six-stage proposal has not been to establish a recipe for the claimant states to follow slavishly. The issues could no doubt be resolved in a different order. The proposal has two main purposes. The first is to show that the dispute in the South China Sea can be resolved equitably on the basis of the LOS Convention. The second is to demonstrate that this may be done without first resolving the tortuous issue of sovereignty to the Spratly Islands. The two guiding principles for the proposal are: (1) to start with the least difficult and least contentious disputes before proceeding to the more complex ones, and (2) to establish a basis or precedent on the first and easier stages for resolving the more difficult issues.

The main weakness with the proposal is that it can only be realized through arduous and drawn-out negotiations. This may then serve as an excuse for refraining from establishing cooperation in the environmental domain. The best course to follow may therefore be a combination of the first and third approaches mentioned above. The environmental situation is now so serious that the establishment of joint management regimes and environmental protection cannot wait until the maritime disputes have been resolved.

Is the conflict likely to be resolved?

The jurisdictional disputes in the South China Sea are complex, but they can be resolved in a relatively reasonable and equitable way if there is the necessary political will. The necessary preconditions are that the claimants respect one another and concede that they all have a legitimate right to defend their national interests. None of the states can realize the whole of their claims; they must be willing to compromise. The main stumbling block has not been ASEAN, but China, although in 2000–01 Malaysia caused serious disunity in ASEAN. Throughout the 1990s, China was more reluctant than any other claimant state to enter into genuine discussions about the most contentious issues. This also goes for discussion about joint cooperation schemes, although China has repeatedly declared itself in favour of such schemes.

Why has China been so hesitant? It may be that some circles in Beijing see an advantage in keeping up a maritime dispute in the South China Sea because it provides ways for China to send 'signals' to other states in the region when they are deemed to be acting in opposition to Chinese interests. It may also be that some Chinese decision-makers suffer from the illusion that China at some later stage in history will be more powerful than it is today, and therefore able to get a better deal from the other claimant countries. This is highly unlikely, for several reasons:

First, it is by no means certain that China will become more powerful, if we measure power relative to others. China has increased its prosperity and influence significantly since the 1970s, but this trend will not necessarily continue. It is also possible that other powers, such as India and Japan, will move into the region and complicate matters further.
Second, although China should continue to have higher economic growth than other countries in the region, this will not be enough to match the US technological supremacy within the military field. As long as China is seen as a possible threat, the other countries in the region will continue to seek US protection. The longer China delays the question of resolving the disputes in the South China Sea, the stronger is the risk of US involvement.

Third, even if China should significantly increase its economic and military power, it is most unlikely that the smaller claimant states will go for a deal where China gains hegemony in the South China Sea. The stronger China becomes, the more the other countries will see the U-shaped line and Chinese possession of the Spratlys as a threat to their own security. Growing Chinese strength will not necessarily lead to greater leverage in territorial disputes, but may instead provoke the other states in the region to join forces.

Some decision-makers in Beijing are likely to understand that China has a better chance to reach an acceptable settlement now than in the past, possibly also better than in the future. Still it does not seem that China is about to change its passive stance. One reason may be China's awkward system of decision-making, which makes it difficult to change direction unless a consensus is reached among an informal group of powerful elders. All branches of government seem to operate on the basis of a few publicized statements by the president, the prime minister, the president of the People's Congress, and a few other party veterans.

Li Peng, who was then prime minister and now serves as President of the People's Congress, laid down the principles for China's present South China Sea policy in 1990 when he proposed to shelve the disputes, and jointly develop resources. No similarly authoritative statement has been made since. Jiang Zemin, Zhu Rongji and a few others could revise China's policy by making a new statement. All agencies concerned would then have to refer to that statement, interpret it and follow it up one way or another. As long as there are no clear guidelines, the various agencies tend to have their own interpretations and agendas. The Navy modernizes and builds bases. Fishermen fish in disputed waters, and expect to be protected by the Navy. Oil companies try to attract foreign participation in exploring for oil, while the State Oceanic Administration and the National Environmental Protection Administration make scientific surveys and launch initiatives to protect the environment. Some of the coastal provinces, like Hainan, also have their own agendas.

To the extent that the activities of China's various bureaucracies and interest groups have international implications, the Foreign Ministry is meant to co-ordinate them. However, the role of the Foreign Ministry seems rather to consist in delaying or preventing initiatives than in pointing out a direction for coordinated efforts. Only in one sense has the Chinese Foreign Ministry been a force for change: it has done its best to improve diplomatic relations with the Southeast Asian states. This may have prepared the terrain for conflict resolution.

In order to carry out new policies, the Chinese top leaders will need to give the Foreign Ministry sufficient authority to carry out new policies. The system of advice around Jiang Zemin appears to be almost as convoluted as it was under Mao and Deng. No one seems to know for sure whose authority they can safely rely on when the leaders at the top fail to issue clear directives. To change policy in such a system is either an extremely slow process (when the top leaders remain silent), or happens very abruptly (when the top leaders reach consensus on a new initiative). In both cases it is difficult to develop a coherent strategy and coordinate its implementation. The difficulties may be even greater in the present situation, when China is preparing for a change in the top leadership.

Because of all these difficulties, it seems unlikely that China will radically change its approach. Thus the status quo will be maintained. This will have disastrous consequences for the environment, resource management and regional security. Perhaps the sea must be completely fished out, a major oil blow-out happen, a mega-tanker run aground on a coral reef, or two navies fight a battle before the regional governments establish the necessary political will to resolve their disputes.

CONFLICT TRANSFORMATION POTENTIAL

As mentioned in the analysis of the conflict potential in the South China Sea, the ASEAN process of regionalization has provided a framework for the transformation of structures of interaction towards a more peaceful direction. The formulas of ASEAN interaction have been utilized even in ASEAN–PRC cooperation. In the economic sphere, the increasing commitment to development and open economic activity has generally transformed many of the economic structures of conflict in the South China Sea area.

When looking at the potentials for further economic conflict transformation, it must be noticed that the ASEAN tendency towards further economic engagement with the PRC must be seen as beneficial to security in the South China Sea. In order to create a broader basis for the liberal motivations of the people to resist war between ASEAN and the PRC, it would be beneficial if the ethnic functionalization[66] of the ASEAN economies were reduced. If wider circles of the ASEAN population, not only or not even mainly the local ethnic Chinese, were to directly experience the benefits of broader economic integration, the structures of liberal peace could be consolidated more firmly.[67]

More directly related to the economic activities in the South China Sea area, the economic transformation of conflict structures would require a strengthening of the commitment to environmental values in the economic activity of the area. The same effect is in the valuation of the safety of the sea lanes of communication in the South China Sea. Since the settings of the protection of the environment and safety of passage in the South China Sea are clearly cooperative, the valuation of the environment and security is directly proportional to the subjective sentiment of common interests in the area. At the same time, if attention in economic activity is on natural resources or relative position in the competition to attract international investment, the setting of economic interaction is more bellicose. Thus regional economic development based on raw material (especially energy) and capital-intensive production that accords low value to the environment, is likely to create rather than transform economic structures of conflict. However, environmentally sound, regionally integrated production that involves large segments of the regional population is likely to transform economic structures of conflict in the area. Thus supporting the latter type of development is conflict transformation while supporting the former is not.

The volume of regional economic interaction also affects the identity- and perception-structures of the South China Sea. In the transformation of identity-structures of conflict – in the dismantling of perceptions of neighbouring country citizens as devils with horns – the most effective type of economic interaction is one that brings people of different nationalities together. Programmes to increase transnational tourism have been experimented with in the growth area arrangements within ASEAN (especially in Sijori and BIMB-EAGA). An expansion of this kind of economic activity beyond the borders of ASEAN, for example projects to promote Sino-Vietnamese tourism, should be beneficial from the point of view of indentity conflict transformation.

Also political institutionalization serves the purpose of the transformation of identity- and perception-structures of conflict. Here also the ASEAN formula of continuous dialogue between scholars, bureaucrats and politicians has a potential even beyond ASEAN, as it creates more realistic perceptions among the elite groups of the disputants. Supporting the institutionalization process that was analysed in Ramses Amer's chapter on existing processes in conflict management can help the transformation of conflict structures in the South China Sea area.

The special challenge in the supporting of political structures of peace is caused by the rapid change in the political setting of Southeast Asia. While the patterns of elite cooperation have often been secretive, elitist, personalistic and somewhat extralegal,[68] the Southeast Asian societies are democratizing. As a result it seems clear that there are pressures to change certain ASEAN practices. An important question from the point of view of inter-state security in the South China Sea region is whether the new, more legalistic and institutionalized (and thus less personalistic) ways of political dialogue can be strengthened before the old structures of inter-state peace collapse due to their inherent contradictions with the Southeast Asian societies. Bridges between the old and new types of dialogue can be built by supporting those types of political dialogue that are compatible with both the old style and the new.

For example, the legal norms of the UN Convention on the Law of the Seas are seen rather innovatively by Indonesia's former chief negotiator as instruments for cooperation rather than instruments of one claimant against the claims of another.[69] In this way the legal discourse in the argumentation is strengthened without renouncing the non-confrontational principles of consensual decision-making. Later, as the role of legal discourse has strengthened in the argumentation of the claimants, there can be ways to actually solve disputes by using judicial reasoning (as has been the case in the Indonesian–Malaysian dispute on Sipadan and Ligatan, for example).[70]

Thus from the point of view of inter-state security in the South China Sea area, efforts to strengthen the power of law in a non-confrontational way may help build bridges between the old and new political structures of peace. However, policies that aim at more democratic political structures by subverting the old structures of political stability, can be harmful for inter-state security. Playing up the disputes, instead of common interests by using the free media, may be damaging for the political structures of inter-state peace in ASEAN. Similarly, efforts to support democratization in Asia by encouraging regional nations to put pressure on each other in issues that are in the old political structure considered as domestic, may have negative consequences. These need to be waived against the utility of that strategy in the promotion of less violent, democratic, domestic political structures in Asia.

NOTES

1 Timo Kivimäki wrote the sections on Potential Approaches to Conflict Management and on Conflict Transformation Potential; Liselotte Odgaard wrote the section on Potentials for Containing Violence; Stein Tønnesson wrote the section on Dispute Resolution.

2 For this criticism, see for example Soedjati Djiwandono 1994, 'ASEAN Solidarity, More Surface than Substance', *Jakarta Post*, 27 July 1994.

3 Gilbert Rozman, 'A New Sino–Russian–American Triangle?', *Orbis*, vol. 44, no. 4 (Fall 2000), p. 547.

4 Mobo C.F. Gao, 'Sino–US Love and Hate Relations', *Journal of Contemporary Asia*, vol. 30, no. 4 (2000).

5 James Miles, 'Chinese Nationalism, US Policy and Asian Security', *Survival*, vol. 42, no. 4 (Winter 2000).

6 Michael B. Yahuda, *The International Politics of the Asia-Pacific, 1945–1995* (London: Routledge, 1996), p. 9.

7 Robert S. Ross, 'The Geography of the Peace: East Asia in the Twenty-first Century', *International Security*, vol. 23, no. 4 (Spring 1999).

8 See also Liselotte Odgaard, 'Deterrence and Cooperation in the South China Sea'. *Contemporary Southeast Asia*, 23: 2, August 2001, pp. 292–306;

Liselotte Odgaard, *Maritime Security between China and Southeast Asia: Conflict and Cooperation in the Making of Regional Order* (Aldershot: Ashgate 2002).

9   *The ASEAN Declaration* (Bangkok Declaration), Thailand, 8 August 1967 (http://www.asean.or.id/history/leader67.htm); F. Frost, 'Introduction: ASEAN since 1967 – Origins, Evolution and Recent Developments', in Alison Broinowski (ed.), *ASEAN into the 1990s* (London: Macmillan, 1990), pp. 4–7; Michael Leifer, *ASEAN and the Security of South-East Asia* (London: Routledge, 1989), p. 2.

10 Michael B. Yahuda, *The International Politics of the Asia-Pacific, 1945–1995* (London: Routledge, 1996), pp. 43–104.

11 John Wilson Lewis and Xue Litai, *China's Strategic Seapower: The Politics of Force Modernization in the Nuclear Age* (Stanford: Stanford University Press, 1994), pp. 220–221.

12 Mel Gurtov and Byong-Moo Hwang, *China's Security: The New Roles of the Military* (Boulder: Lynne Rienner, 1998), p. 114.

13 Liu Yi-chien in *Hong Kong Ta Kung Pao*, FBIS-CHI-1999-1011 Translated Text, 1 September 1999.

14 *Hong Kong Sing Tao Jih Pao*, FBIS-CHI-2000-0911 Translated Text, 11 September 2000.

15 Ministry of Defence, *Malaysian Defence: Towards Defence Self-Reliance* (Kuala Lumpur: Ministry of Defence, 1997), p. 16.

16 *ASEAN Declaration on the South China Sea*, Manila, The Philippines, 22 July 1992 (http://www.asean.or.id/history/leader67. htm).

17 *Statement by the ASEAN Foreign Ministers of Recent Developments in the South China Sea*, 18 March 1995 (http://www.asean.or.id/politics/scs95.htm).

18 The Associated Press, 'Malaysia Seeks to Contain Dispute over Spratly Islands', quoted in *Northeast Asia Peace and Security Network Daily Report*, 23 July 1999, (http://www.nautilus.org./napsnet/dr/calendar.html).

19 *Declaration on the South China Sea*, Manila, The Philippines, 22 July 1992 (http://www.asean.or.id/history/leader67. htm).

20 *Jakarta Post*, 4 July 1991.

21 *Jakarta Post*, 6 April 1995.

22 Ross Marlay, 'China, the Philippines, and the Spratly Islands', *Asian Affairs: An American Review*, vol. 23, no. 4 (Winter 1997), p. 205.

23 Mark J. Valencia, Jon M. Van Dyke and Noel A. Ludwig, *Sharing the Resources of the South China Sea* (The Hague: Martinus Nijhoff Publishers, 1997), pp. 79–82, 258.

24 Liu Yi-chien in *Hong Kong Ta Kung Pao*, FBIS-CHI-1999-1011. Translated Text, 1 September 1999.

25 Bates Gill, 'Enhancing National Military Capabilities in Asia-Pacific: Legitimate Needs versus Unwarranted Development', Mohamed Jawhar Hassan and Sheikh Ahmad Raffie (eds), *Bringing Peace to the Pacific: Papers Presented at the Tenth Asia-Pacific Roundtable* (Kuala Lumpur: ISIS Malaysia, 1996), p. 225.

26 *The Nation* (Bangkok), 11 February 1999.

27 *Far Eastern Economic Review*, 26 November 1992.

28 *Manila Business World*, FBIS-EAS-95-080, 24 April 1995.

29 C. Shelly, 'Spratlys and the South China Sea', *Position of the U.S. Department of State*, 10 May 1995.

30 *The Nation* (Bangkok) (Internet Version), FBIS-EAS-1999-0725, 26 July 1999.

31 *Summary of World Broadcast*, FE/2372 G/1, 3 August 1995.

32 *Hong Kong AFP*, FBIS-EAS-99-006, 6 January 1999.

33 *Hong Kong Zhonguo Tongxun She*, FBIS-CHI-99-025. Translated text, 25 January 1999; *Manila Business World* (Internet Version), FBIS-EAS-98-218, 6 August 1998.

34 *Far Eastern Economic Review*, 'Asian Executives Poll', 6 April 2000.

35 *The Nation* (Bangkok), FBIS-EAS-95-047, 9 March 1995.

36 *Far Eastern Economic Review*, 6 August 1992.

37 US Department of Defense, *The United States Security Strategy for the East Asia-Pacific Region 1998* (http://www.defenselink.mil/pubs/easr98).

38 *Far Eastern Economic Review*, 26 November 1992, 3 April 1997; *Le Monde Diplomatique*, March 1996; *Summary of World Broadcast*, FE/2370 S2/3, 1 August 1995; Winston Lord, 'Southeast Asia Regional Security Issues: Opportunities for Peace, Stability, and Prosperity', *Statement before the House International Relations Committee, Asia and Pacific Subcommittee*, by the Assistant Secretary of State for East Asian and Pacific Affairs, 30 May 1996 (http://www.state.gov/www/regions/eap/960530.html); The Associated Press, 27 May 1999 and Seattle Post-Intelligencer, 11 October 1999, quoted in *Northeast Asia Peace and Security Network Daily Report*, 27 May 1999, 12 October 1999 (http://www.nautilus.org/napsnet/latest.html).

39 *Hong Kong AFP*, FBIS-CHI-2000-0205, 5 February 2000.

40 *Tokyo Sankei Shimbun*, FBIS-EAS-2000-0816, 16 August 2000.

41 'Statement of Dr. Kurt Campbell Deputy Assistant Secretary of Defense for International Security Affairs Asian and Pacific Affairs before the House International Relations Committee 14 April 1999', *Northeast Asia Peace and Security Network Daily Report* (http://www.nautilus.org/napsnet/dr/calendar.html), 16 April 1999.

42 Office of Naval Research Asia International Field Office, Asia, *Ocean Science and Engineering Newsletter*, no. 19 (http://www.onr.navy.mil/onrasia/oceans/ali19.html), August 2000.

43 Reuters, 'China's Zhu Spells out Fears over NATO Bombings', 7 April 1999, quoted in *Northeast Asia Peace and Security Network Daily Report* (http://www.nautilus.org/napsnet/latest.html), 7 April 1999; *China News Digest*, Global News, no. GL99-060, Special Report: 'NATO Missiles Hit Chinese Embassy in Belgrade', 8 May 1999, (http://www.cnd.org); The Cox Report reprinted in *Financial Times*, 26 May 1999; 'Bush Offers China Talks on Arms as U.S. Pulls out of ABM Treatty', *The New York Times*, 14 December 2001

44 *The Washington Post*, 26 May 2000, quoted in *Northeast Asia Peace and Security Network Daily Report* [http://www.nautilus.org/napsnet/latest.html], 26 May 2000.

45 Congress of the United States, House of Representatives, *Report: Codel Rohrabacher Fact Finding Mission to Kuwait, Taiwan and the Philippines*, 15 December 1998, (http://www.afpc.org/issues/codelrohr.htm).

46 'Special Report – World Media on George W. Bush's Foreign Policy', 19 December 2000, (http://www.usinfo.state.gov/products/medreac.htm).

47 *International Herald Tribune*, 15 December 2000, quoted in *Northeast Asia Peace and Security Network Daily Report* (http://www.nautilus.org/napsnet/latest.html).

48 'Special Report – World Media on George W. Bush's Foreign Policy', 19 December 2000, (http://www.usinfo.state.gov/products/medreac.htm).

49 *Far Eastern Economic Review*, 14 December 2000.

50 Liselotte Odgaard, 'Deterrence and Cooperation in the South China Sea'. *Contemporary Southeast Asia*, 23: 2, August 2001, pp. 292–306; Liselotte Odgaard, *Maritime Security between China and Southeast Asia: Conflict and Cooperation in the Making of Regional Order* (Aldershot: Ashgate 2002).

51 Ryukichi Imai, 'Ballistic Missile Defense, Nuclear Non-Proliferation, and a Nuclear Free World', Special Report, 21 December 2000, can be obtained from (NAPSNet@nautilus.org).

52 *Far Eastern Economic Review*, 3 August 2000.

53 Masao Kunihiro, 'The Decline and Fall of Pacifism', *The Bulletin of the Atomic Scientists*, vol. 53, no. 1 (January/February 1997).

54 Wu Xinbo, 'U.S. Security Policy in Asia: Implications for China–U.S. Relations', *CNAPS Working Paper* (Washington, DC: The Brookings Institution, 2000), (http://www.brook.edu/fp/cnaps/papers/2000_wu.htm).

55 *Bangkok Post*, FBIS-EAS-97-202, 21 July 1997.

56 Eibe Riedel, 'Standards and Sources. Farewell to the Exclusivity of the Sources Triad in International Law?', *European Journal of International Law*, vol. 2, no. 2 (1991).

57 *ASEAN Declaration on the South China Sea*, Manila, The Philippines, 22 July 1992 (http://www.asean.or.id/history/leader67. htm).

58 See the appendices in Mark Valencia, Jon Van Dyke and Noel Ludwig, *Sharing the Resources of the South China Sea*. The Hague: Martinus Nijhoff, 1997 (paperback edition: University of Hawaii Press, 1999).

59 Nguyen Hong Thao, 'Joint Development in the Gulf of Thailand,' *Boundary and Security Bulletin*, vol. 7, no. 3 (1999), pp. 79–89.

60 Hasjim Djalal acknowledges that the joint development concept is useful only when the disputed area can be clearly identified: 'In some disputed areas, the application of the joint development concept, as envisaged by Articles 74 and 83 of UNCLOS, might be useful as long as the zone of dispute is or can be identified.' Hasjim Djalal, 'Indonesia and the South China Sea Initiative', *Ocean Development and International Law*, vol. 32, no. 2 (April–June 2001), p. 103.

61 Mark Valencia, Jon Van Dyke and Noel Ludwig, *Sharing the Resources of the South China Sea*, p. 133.

62 Stein Tønnesson, 'Can China Resolve the Conflict in the South China Sea?' Singapore: *East Asian Institute Working Paper,* no. 39, 2000; 'China and the South China Sea: a Peace Proposal,' *Security Dialogue,* vol. 31, no. 3 (September 2000), pp. 307–326; 'Here's How to Settle Rocky Disputes in the South China Sea', *International Herald Tribune,* 6 September 2000 and *The Straits Times,* 7 September 2000.

63 If they are to live up to their obligations as defined in the LOS Convention, each of the two countries must also draw proper baselines along their coasts, following the low-water mark of the coastline wherever it is not 'deeply indented and cut into' or there is 'a fringe of islands ... in its immediate vicinity' (UNCLOS Article 7 [1]). Where these geographical conditions exist, such as along the Vietnamese coast north of Ha Long Bay, straight baselines would be warranted. The purpose of the baselines is to mark off internal waters from territorial waters and to serve as the basis for measuring the extent of the Vietnamese and Chinese territorial waters (12 nm), contiguous zone (12 additional nm) and EEZ (the rest) on both sides of the median line. Unfortunately, the two states have so far shown no intention of following the LOS Convention rules concerning the delimitation of maritime zones within their individual spheres. It remains to be seen, when the treaty text is published, if the two countries have cared to distinguish between the various kinds of zones established in the LOS Convention, which they have both ratified.

64 Zou Keyuan, 'Sino-Vietnamese Fishery Agreement in the Gulf of Tonkin'. *East Asia Institute Working Paper,* no. 77. Singapore, 23 May 2001.

65 For a political analysis of how Taiwan's South China Sea policy has been influenced by its shifting relations with mainland China, see Kristen Nordhaug, 'Explaining Taiwan's Policies in the South China Sea, 1988–1999', *Pacifica Review,* vol. 14, no. 4 (2001), pp. 487–508.

66 Ethnic functionalization here means that people of Chinese origin are disproportionally represented in ASEAN–PRC trade.

67 Very often the Southeast Asian Chinese business networks have been rather closed and even if the Chinese economic influence in most countries has been very beneficial, a more direct cross-ethnic integration would be more optimal in the creation of security communities, than integration through Chinese networks.

68 The whole mechanism of dialogue was developed in a context of rather conspiratory efforts of a group within the Indonesian military to find contacts in Malaysia, which according to the official Indonesian perception was still an enemy with which no contacts were allowed. See Dewi Fortuna Anwar, *Indonesia and ASEAN* (Singapore: Institute of Southeast of Southeast Asian Studies, 1994).

69 Interview with Hasjim Djalal, November 2000.

70 According to Soedjati Djiwandono, who has been an important intellectual behind the Indonesian negotiation panels in the South China Sea issues, the time is getting ripe for parties to accept rulings of the International Court in the Hague (interview in Jakarta, November 2000).

10

CONCLUSIONS

Timo Kivimäki

The aim of this volume has been to provide the reader with an introduction to the 'South China Sea game'. The first part offered an outline of the 'game setting' with players and their positions. The second part presented the strategic environment of the game with powers, interests and stakes of the players as well as the rules of the game. Economic, military, political and environmental aspects of the stakes were focused upon in greater detail. Finally, alternative strategy options available for the diplomacy of conflict prevention were analysed by dividing conflict management into three strategic categories: containment of violence, resolution of disputes and transformation of conflict structures.

In conclusion, it can be mentioned that the setting of the South China Sea disputes is quite complex. The history of the area, which is often referred to in arguments for various territorial claims, shows little evidence of any meaningful use made of the disputed areas by any of the claimants. In fact, it seems that these areas have only been economically meaningful when the small reefs and islands have disrupted sea lines of communication. The islands in the claimed areas have historically remained uninhabited. Furthermore, it seems that the claims presented in current political disputes often date back to a time before the concept of sovereignty had been introduced to the area. If one seeks to learn a lesson by examining historical patterns of conflict in the area, one notices that most of the wars here have been related to changes in the global geopolitical setting. Conflicts were caused first by colonialism, then by decolonization, later by the Cold War and the rivalry between superpowers such as the Soviet Union and the United States.

Territorial claims in the South China Sea can be divided into claims on water areas and claims on islands. The main disputants are Brunei, Cambodia, the People's Republic of China, Indonesia, Malaysia, the

Philippines, Taiwan, Thailand and Vietnam. The most serious recent disputes have been between Vietnam and the PRC, between the PRC and the Philippines, and between Malaysia and the Philippines.

The most disturbing aspect of the South China Sea disputes is the potential for environmental catastrophes and intensive conflicts. The former are mainly related to fishing practices, land-based pollution, destruction of coral reefs and – due to the disputes – a lack of transnational cooperation with regard to the protection of the environment. The latter are mainly due to weaknesses in military crisis stability in the area: the military doctrines and military capabilities of nations in the area fail to ensure any long-lasting guarantee of stability. The fact that great powers are involved and that the institutional setting and arms control are almost non-existent makes the disputes potentially dangerous – the more so because arms acquisition and evolving military doctrines may place the parties involved on a collision course.

The consolidation of a stable structure of deterrence conducive to regional peace and stability could be disrupted by four developments. First, any departure by the US from its position of non-involvement in local disputes could produce a military response from the PRC. Second, violent conflict in the Taiwan Strait could spill over into the South China Sea. Third, implementation of plans for a theatre missile defence (TMD) covering Japan, South Korea and Taiwan would threaten to skew the balance of power to the disadvantage of the PRC, thus creating the risk of a military response from the PRC. Fourth, increased Japanese responsibility for security in Asia might similarly destabilize the region, thus provoking the PRC to take military action.

The safety of the sea routes is also an important question, especially for Europe and Japan, as long as the development of alternative lines of communication (the Northern Sea route and the railway connections) between Northeast Asia and Northern Europe remain an unactivated potential.

In minimizing the potential threat to security interests in the area, this study has aimed to outline a menu of choice, rather than attempting to propose a coherent strategy or a contingency plan. Discussions with some of the parties to the South China Sea disputes (diplomats and scholars) have revealed that there are certain roles and positions that the international community can utilize in its efforts to prevent conflicts and environmental threats in the area. In fact, when Indonesia initiated the so-called Jakarta process of high-level informal dialogue on South China Sea questions, Canada was not considered as the only possible external power that could be asked for good services. In fact, Nordic countries would have been asked if Canada had not been interested.[1]

One of the main pillars of stability which holds potential for common reactions to the environmental threats is the rapidly developing institutionalization of ASEAN and PRC–ASEAN cooperation and dialogue. This development potentially strengthens some aspects of common regional identity, a feeling of common interest and a reliance on common mechanisms of conflict management. This development can thus be seen as essential social/political capital in containing violence, resolving disputes and transforming the conflict structures in the area.

While regional institutionalization is by definition a regional initiative, there are several ways to support and supplement it. In the field of violence containment, the ASEAN–PRC dialogue has made progress by creating codes of conduct, which are a major supplement to crisis stability in the area. In addition to political will, which has to be developed by the regional powers themselves, successful development of codes of conduct requires an answer to the question of which codes are most likely to promote crisis stability. While this kind of analysis might be very developed in Southeast Asia, local scholars certainly hold no monopoly on knowledge of the subject. Thus the international community could contribute to this investigation.

With regard to containment of violence, there is not much that external forces, with the possible exception of Japan and especially the United States, can do about the military equation in the area. However, it is in the interests of most nations to follow developments, be prepared for all contingencies, and perhaps support initiatives to limit the possible damage caused by a conflict in the South China Sea.[2]

In the field of dispute resolution, the main initiative lies once again with the regional powers, and the main problems are naturally related to the lack of political will among the claimant nations. The international community can support research, brainstorming and dialogue on dispute resolution. Research on possible solutions may inspire the political will, especially if innovative win-win solutions can be found. So far there have basically been three types of proposals.

The first suggests that, in the absence of a resolution of the sovereignty dispute, the claimant countries should establish Joint Development Zones (JDZs), or Joint Management Zones (JMZs). This kind of proposal could seek inspiration in the Timor Gap Treaty, and in the JDZ established in the Gulf of Thailand between Thailand and Malaysia. The idea of establishing a multilateral JDZ in the South China Sea has long been associated with Indonesian Ambassador Hasjim Djalal's so-called 'doughnut theory', which argued that there ought to be an area of high seas set aside in the middle of the South China Sea (more than 200 nautical miles from all shores), and that this area could form the basis for a JDZ regime. The idea was discussed at the workshops, and a particular area was pointed out, but because of hesitation among some of the claimant states, no steps were taken to actually carry out the project.

The second, more traditional kind of proposal has aimed at resolving the sovereignty dispute over the Paracel and Spratly Islands on the basis of international law. Legal scholars have been reluctant to discuss the merit of the various sovereignty claims, but scholars in other disciplines with a thorough knowledge of international law, such as Mark J. Valencia and Greg Austin, have discussed their merits and come to somewhat different conclusions.

The third idea, the so-called Tønnesson proposal, suggests that the conflict can be resolved diplomatically, on the basis of the LOS Convention of 1982, without resolving the tortuous question of sovereignty over the Spratlys. The key element in this proposal is that all claimant states should agree that the Spratly Islands, since these islands cannot support human habitation or sustain an independent economy, cannot be allotted more than 12 nautical miles of territorial waters. The dispute over sovereignty of the islands and their 12 nautical miles of territorial waters can then be shelved. At the same time the states could define their EEZ and continental shelf claims on the basis of distance from their coasts, while the median lines can be negotiated. After most of the South China Sea has been delineated in this way, the question of what to do with the high seas remaining in the middle must be addressed. The Spratly Islands with their 12 nautical miles of territorial waters can then be made into a regional, jointly managed marine park, where all economic activity is prohibited.

In the field of economic conflict transformation, the international community has many instruments for supporting economic integration in the area (development cooperation, trade policies). Due to the commonness of environmental concerns, environmentally sound, regionally integrated production involving large segments of the regional populations is likely to transform economic structures of conflict in the area. Thus, support lent to this type of development promotes transformation of conflict structures. In dismantling perceptions of citizens of neighbouring countries as devils with horns, the most effective type of economic interaction is the kind that brings people of different nationalities together. Programmes to increase transnational tourism have been implemented in growth area arrangements within ASEAN (especially in Sijori and BIMB-EAGA). An expansion of this kind of economic activity beyond the borders of ASEAN, for example projects to promote Sino–Vietnamese tourism, should be beneficial from the point of view of transformation of identity conflict structures.

Political institutionalization also serves the purpose of transforming structures of conflict built around identity and perception. In this case, too, the ASEAN formula of continuous dialogue between scholars, bureaucrats and politicians, has a potential stretching beyond ASEAN, since it creates more realistic perceptions among the disputants' elite groups. Supporting the institutionalization of environmentally sound international/transnational ocean management could serve the transformation of economical, political, and identity conflict structures at the same time. Finally, it can be concluded that transformation of discursive conflict structures could be expedited by projects that highlight and strengthen the legal bases of argumentation in maritime cooperation in the disputed areas.

The situation in the South China Sea is unpredictable, and there seems to be no guarantee that the relative peace of the past few years will continue. Instead of making predictions, this study has tried to highlight elements that work for and against peace. By following through on these elements it is possible to prepare for the development of the situation. Furthermore, this study has indicated some possible avenues to influence the situation from within as well as from outside the area. The conflicts in the South China Sea area are not imposed upon the disputants and the international community by some laws of nature. Instead, they are human creations and thus their management is also something for the disputants and for the international community to deal with.

NOTES

1   Discussions with Hasjim Djalal, Jakarta, November 2000.

2   There are several long-term strategies to reduce international dependence on sea lines of communication in the South China Sea area.

BIBLIOGRAPHY

SOURCES ON SOUTH CHINA SEA DISPUTES

In addition to being a bibliography for the present volume, this list includes suggestions for further reading which are taken mainly from the bibliography presented on the home page of Stein Tønnesson's research programme, 'Energy and Security in the South China Sea'. www.sum.uio.no/southchinasea. The said bibliography is being updated at http://www.prio.no/activities/southchinasea/bibliography.asp

(Anonymous). 'Maritime Risks and Threats in the Western Pacific'. Special Report. *Jane's Intelligence Review* (1 August 1995).

—— 'China Stirs up Tension on Mischief Reef'. *Jane's Defence Weekly*, vol. 30, no. 20 (18 November 1998)

—— 'In Brief. Philippines Sink Chinese Fishing Boat'. *Jane's Defence Weekly*, vol. 32, no. 4 (28 July 1999).

—— 'Country Briefing – Malaysia'. *Jane's Defence Weekly*, vol. 33, no. 13 (29 March 2000).

Abbot, Jason. 'Imagined Boundaries: Sovereignty over the Sea and International Law, the Case of the Spratly Islands Dispute'. Paper presented to the 38th ISA Convention 'The Westphalian System in Global and Historical Perspective'. Minneapolis, Minnesota, March 1998.

Abbot, Jason and Neil Renwick. 'Pirates? Maritime Piracy and Societal Security in Southeast Asia'. *Pacifica Review*, vol. 11, no. 1 (1996), pp. 7–24.

Acharya, Amitav. 'A Regional Security Community in Southeast Asia'. In Desmond Ball (ed.), *Transformation of Security of the Asia–Pacific Region*, Cass, Frank Publishers, 1996, pp. 175–200.

—— *Constructing a Security Community in Southeast Asia. ASEAN and the Problem of Regional Order.* London: Routledge, 2001.

Adger, Neil. 'Social Vulnerability to Climate Change and Extremes in Coastal Vietnam'. *World Development*, vol. 27, no. 2 (1999), pp. 249–269.

Aggarwal, Vinod and Charles E. Morrison (eds). *Asia-Pacific Crossroads. Regime Creation and the Future of APEC.* New York: St Martin's Press, 1998.

Alatas, Ali. 'South China Sea-views from ASEAN'. *Indonesian Quarterly*, vol. 18, no. 2 (1990), pp. 114–170.

—— 'Managing the Potentials of the South China Sea'. *Indonesian Quarterly*, vol. 18, no. 2 (1990), pp. 114.

—— 'Managing Potential Conflict in the South China Sea'. Address by H.E. Mr Alatas, Minister of Foreign Affairs, Republic of Indonesia at the Opening of the Fifth Workshop, Bukittinggi, 26 October 1994.

Albright, David and Corey Gay. 'Taiwan: Nuclear Nightmare Averted'. *Bulletin of the Atomic Scientists*, vol. 64, no. 1 (January 1998), pp. 54–60.

Alexander, Lewis M. 'Baseline Delimitation and Maritime Boundaries'. *Virginia Journal of International Law*, vol. 23, no. 4 (1983), pp. 504–536.

—— 'Uncertainties in the Aftermath of UNCLOS III: The Case for Navigational Freedoms'. *Ocean Development & International Law*, vol. 18, no. 3 (1987), pp. 333–342.

Alexander, Lewis M. and Jonathan I. Charney (eds). *International Maritime Boundaries*. Boston: Martinus Nijhoff (selection of relevant articles).

Almonte, Jose T. 'A Strategic Framework for Policymakers in Asia'. Paper presented at the Defence Asia Forum '97, Singapore, 15 January 1997.

—— 'Speaking with One Voice on the South China Sea Issue'. Paper presented at the ASEAN Experts on the Law of the Sea Conference, Metro Manila, 27–28 November 1997.

—— 'The Maritime Heartland of Southeast Asia'. *The Philippine Journal*, 2, 3 and 4 February 1998.

—— 'ASEAN Must Speak with One Voice on the South China Sea Issue'. Talk given at the South China Sea Confidence Building Measures Workshop, sponsored by the Pacific Forum CSIS and the ISDS, Mandarin in Oriental Hotel, Jakarta, Indonesia, 10–11 March 2000.

Amer, Ramses. 'Borders in Dispute'. *Trends*, no. 61 (September 1995), ISEAS, Singapore, p. 12.

—— 'Vietnam's Feuds: What Effect on Asean Bonds?' *Strait Times*, 3 October 1995, p. 24.

—— 'Vietnam and its Neighbours. The Border Dispute Dimension'. *Contemporary Southeast Asia*, vol. 17, no. 3 (December 1995), pp. 298–318.

—— 'Spratly konflikten'. *Världspolitikens Dagsfrågor*, no. 7 (1996).

—— 'The Territorial Disputes between China and Vietnam and Regional Stability'. *Contemporary Southeast Asia*, vol. 19, no. 1 (June 1997), pp. 86–113.

—— 'The Border Conflicts between Cambodia and Vietnam'. *Boundary and Security Bulletin*, vol. 5, no. 2 (1997).

—— 'The Sino-Vietnamese Border Disputes and Regional Security'. *The Business Times, Weekend Edition*, June 28–29 (1997), p. IV.

—— 'Expanding ASEAN's Conflict Management Framework in Southeast Asia: The Border Dispute Dimension'. *Asian Journal of Political Science*, vol. 6, no. 2 (1998).

—— 'Towards a Declaration on 'Navigational Rights' in the Sea-lanes of the Asia-Pacific'. *Contemporary Southeast Asia*, vol. 20, no. 1 (April 1998), pp. 88–102.

—— *The Challenge of Managing the Border Disputes between China and Vietnam*, EAI Working Paper, no. 16 (24 November 1998) Singapore: East Asian Institute (EAI), National University of Singapore.

—— 'The "Oil Factor" and the Conflicts in the South China Sea'. In *Olja – en förbannelse?* [Oil – A Curse?], Skrifter utgivna av Sällskapet för asienstudier 9, edited by Farid Abbaszadegan and Franz Wennberg. Uppsala, 1999.

—— 'Conflict Management and Constructive Engagement in ASEAN's Expansion'. *Third World Quarterly,* vol. 20, no. 5 (1999), pp. 101–148.

—— 'Sino-Vietnamese Relations: Past, Present and Future'. In Charlyle A. Thayer and Ramses Amer (eds), *Vietnamese Foreign Policy in Transition.* Singapore: Institute of Southeast Asian Studies, 1999.

—— *The Management of the Border Disputes between China and Vietnam and its Regional Implications,* EIAS Publications, Briefing Papers, BP 00/03. Brussels: European Institute for Asian Studies (EIAS), October 2000.

—— 'Managing Border Disputes in Southeast Asia'. *Kajian Malaysia, Journal of Malaysian Studies,* Special Issue on Conflict and Conflict Management in Southeast Asia, vol. 23, nos. 1–2 (June–December 2000), pp. 3–60.

—— *Conflict Situations and Conflict Management in the South China Sea,* UPSK Occasional Paper, no. 5/00. Bangi, Selangor: Unit Pengajian Strategi and Keselamatan (Strategic and Security Studies Unit), Universiti Kebangsaan Malaysia, 2000.

—— 'The Association of South-East Asian Nations and the South China Sea Disputes: Intra-Mural Implications and Foreign Relations Challenges'. A paper at the Panel on the South China Sea in honour of Professor Michael Leifer, Third European Association of Southeast Asian Studies Conference, London School of Economics and Political Science, 6–8 September 2001.

—— 'The Sino-Vietnamese Approach to Managing Border Disputes'. *Maritime Briefing,* vol. 3, no. 5, Durham: International Boundaries Research Unit, University of Durham, (forthcoming 2002).

Aprilani Soegiarto. 'Sustainable Fisheries, Environment and the Prospects of Regional Cooperation in Southeast Asia'. Paper presented to the Monterey Institute of International Studies Workshop on 'Trade and Environment in Asia-Pacific: Prospects for Regional Cooperation'. East–West Centre, Honolulu-Hawaii, 23–25 September 1994.

Asada, Mashiko. 'Revived Soviet Interest in Asia: a New Approach'. In Frank C. Langdon and Douglas A Ross (eds), *Superpower Maritime Strategy in the Pacific.* London: Routledge, 1990, pp. 35–71.

ASEAN. *ASEAN Strategic Plan of Action on the Environment.* Jakarta: ASEAN Secretariat 1994.

—— The First ASEAN State of the Environment Report. Jakarta: ASEAN Secretariat 1998.

—— Regional Forum. 'Draft Proposals on Maritime Issues under Agenda Item 6 – Submitted by China'. *Intersessional Support Group on Confidence Building Measures,* Sydney, 4–6 March 1998.

Auburn, Francis M., Vivian Forbes and John Scott. 'Comparative Oil and Gas Joint Development Regimes'. In Carl Grundy-Warr (ed.), *World Boundaries,* vol. 3 *Eurasia,* London: Routledge, 1994, pp. 196–212.

Austin, Greg. *China's Ocean Frontier: International Law, Military Force and National Development.* St Leonards: Allen & Unwin, 1998.

—— 'Impact of the South China Sea Issues on International Perceptions of China'. A paper at the Panel on the South China Sea in honour of Professor Michael Leifer, Third European Association of Southeast Asian Studies Conference, London School of Economics and Political Science, 6–8 September 2001.

Austin, Greg and Michael Thomas. 'Has Geo-economics Redefined Sovereignty in the East China Sea?' *The Asia-Pacific Magazine*, no. 13 (December 1998), pp. 31–33.

Bakke, Cecilie Figenschou. 'The Potential for Integration around the Gulf of Tonkin'. Unpublished paper presented at the conference 'Human and Regional Security around the South China Sea'. 2–4 June, Oslo.

Ball, Desmond. 'The Transformation of Security in the Asia/Pacific Region'. *The Journal of Strategic Studies, Special Issue*, vol. 18, no. 3 (September 1995), pp. 1–15.

Banlaoi, Rommel C. 'The ASEAN Regional Forum and the Management of Conflicts in the South China Sea'. A paper at the Panel on the South China Sea in honour of Professor Michael Leifer, Third European Association of Southeast Asian Studies Conference, London School of Economics and Political Science, 6–8 September 2001.

Bardacke, Ted. 'Malaysia–Thai gas deal may serve as model for SE Asia'. *Financial Times*, 23 April 1998.

Barnett, Robert W. *Beyond War. Japan's Concept of Comprehensive National Security*. Washington: Brassey's, 1984.

Bateman, Sam. 'ASEAN's Tiger Navies Catching Up or Building Up?' *Jane's Navy International*, vol. 102, no. 3 (1 April 1997).

—— East Asia's marine Resources and Regional Security, http://uniserve.edu.au/law/publ/icl...tudies_89/ms_marine_resources.html, [22. March 1999]

Bateman, Sam and Stephen Bates (eds). *Calming the Waters. Initiatives for Asia Pacific Maritime Cooperation*. Canberra Papers on Strategy and Defence no. 114, 1996.

—— *The Seas Unite: Maritime Cooperation in the Asia Pacific Region*. Canberra Papers on Strategy and Defence no. 118, 1996.

—— *Regional Maritime Management and Security*. Canberra Papers on Strategy and Defence no. 124, 1998.

—— *Shipping and Regional Security*. Canberra Papers on Strategy and Defence no. 129, 1998.

Beckman, Robert C., Carl Grundy-Warr and Vivian L. Forbes. 'Acts of Piracy in the Malacca and Singapore Straits'. International Boundaries Research Unit's *Maritime Briefing*, vol. 1, no. 4 (1994).

Bedi, Rahul. 'India, Vietnam in Co-operation Pact'. *Jane's Defence Weekly*, vol. 33, no. 14 (5 April 2000).

Beijing Review. 'The Truth About the Sino-Vietnamese Boundary Question'. no. 21, (May 25 1979), pp. 14–26.

Bennett, Michael. 'The People's Republic of China and the Use of International Law in the Spratly Island Dispute'. *Stanford Journal of International Law*, vol. 28, no. 2 (1992), pp. 425–450.

Bernhardt, Peter A. 'Straightjacketing Straight Baselines'. Paper presented on a workshop of The Law of the Sea Institute, The William S. Richardson School of Law, University of Hawaii, Honolulu, Hawaii, 13–15 January, 1986, pp. 85–101.

Betts, Richard K. *Nuclear Blackmail and Nuclear Balance.* Washington DC: The Brookings Institution, 1987.

Blake, Gerald H. *The Peaceful Management of Transboundary Resources.* London: Graham & Trotman, 1995.

Blanche, J.B. 'Chinese Bureaucrats Draw the Line in the South China Sea'. *Petroleum Economist,* no. 62 (July 1995), pp. 16–18.

Blanche, Bruce and Jean Blanche. 'South East Asia: Oil and Regional Stability in the South China Sea'. *Jane's Intelligence Review,* vol. 11 (1995).

—— 'An Overview of the Hydrocarbon Potential of the Spratly Islands Archipelago and its Implications for Regional Development'. *Petroleum Geology of South East Asia, Geological Society Special Publication,* no. 126 (1997), pp. 293–310.

Blussé, Leonard. 'Chinese Century: The Eighteenth Century in the China Sea Region'. *Archipel,* no. 58 (1999), pp. 107–129.

—— 'No Boats to China. The Dutch East India Company and the Changing Pattern of the China Sea Trade, 1635–1690'. *Modern Asian Studies,* vol. 30, no. 1 (1996), pp. 51–76.

Bodansky, Yossef. 'The Rise of the Trans-Asian Axis: Is It the Basis of New Confrontation?' *Defense and Foreign Affairs Strategic Policy,* vol. 22, no. 8 (1994).

Boillot, Jean-Joseph and Nicolas Michelon. 'The New Economic Geography of Greater China'. *China Perspectives,* no. 30 (July–August 2000), pp. 18–30.

Boillot, Jean-Joseph and Michelon, Nicolas. 'The South China Triangle and Taiwan'. *China Perspectives,* no. 30 (July–August 2000), pp. 32–41.

Booth, Anne. 'Southeast Asia: Towards a Sustained Recovery?' *Southeast Asia Affairs 2000.* Singapore: Institute of Southeast Asian Affairs, 2000.

Boutros-Ghali, Boutros. *Agenda for Peace.* 2nd edition with the supplement and related UN Documents. United Nations, New York, 1995.

Bowring, Phillip. 'China Is Slowly Winning a Long Game for the Sea'. *International Herald Tribune,* 28 January 1999.

Brevetti, Francine. 'Piracy Plagues the South China Sea'. *Seatrade Review,* (May 1994), pp. 21–23.

Bristow, Damon. 'Between the Devil and the Deep Blue Sea: Maritime Disputes between Association of South East Asian Nations (ASEAN) Member States'. *RUSI Journal,* vol. 141, no. 4 (August 1996).

British Broadcasting Corporation, Summary of World Broadcasts, Part Three, Far East 7074 A3/7–8 (10 July 1982).

Brömmelhörster, Jörn and John Frankenstein (eds). *Mixed Motives, Uncertain Outcomes. Defense Conversion in China.* Boulder, CO: Lynne Rienner, 1997.

Brookfield, Harold and Yvonne Byron (eds). *South-East Asia's Environmental Future: the Search for Sustainability.* The United Nations University, Kuala Lumpur: Oxford University Press, 1993.

Brown, E.D. 'Dispute Settlement and the Law of the Sea: The UN Convention Regime'. *Marine Policy,* vol. 21, no. 1 (1997), pp. 17–43.

Brown, Roxanna and Sten Sjöstrand. *Turiang: A Fourteenth Century Shipwreck in Southeast Asian Waters.* Los Angeles: Pacific Asia Museum, 2000.

Busse, Nikolas. 'Constructivism and Southeast Asian Security'. *Pacifica Review,* vol. 12 no. 1, (1999), pp. 39–60.

Buszynski, Leszek. 'ASEAN Security Dilemmas'. *Survival,* vol. 34, no. 4 (Winter 1992–93).

Buzan, Barry. 'A Framework for Regional Security Analysis'. In B. Buzan, Rother Rizwi *et al. South Asian Insecurity and the Great Powers.* London: Macmillan, 1986, pp. 3–33.

Buzan, Barry and Gerald Segal. 'Rethinking East Asian Security'. *Survival,* vol. 36, no. 2 (Summer 1994), pp. 3–21.

Caballero-Anthony, Mely. 'Mechanisms of Dispute Settlement: The ASEAN Experience'. *Contemporary Southeast Asia,* vol. 20, no. 1 (April 1998).

Calder, Kent E. 'Asia's Empty Tank'. *Foreign Affairs,* vol. 75, no. 2 (1996), pp. 55–69.

—— *Pacific Defence: Arms, Energy, and America's Future in Asia.* New York: William Morrow, 1996.

Campos, Jose Edgardo and Hilton L. Root. *The Key to the Asian Miracle. Making Shared Growth Credible.* Washington, DC: Brookings, 1996.

Carey, Merrick. 'Promise and Peril on the Pacific Rim'. *The 2000 Almanac of Seapower Seapower,* January 2000, pp. 59–65, at http://www.navyleague.org/seapower/promise_and_peril.htm.

Carpenter, Cole. 'Legal Aspects of Sino-American Oil Exploration in the South China Sea'. *Journal of International Law and Economics,* vol. 14, no. 3 (1980), pp. 443–484.

Carpenter, William and David Wiencek. 'Surveying the Asia-Pacific Security Setting'. *Asian Security Handbook.* (1996), pp. 3–18.

Carranza Jr., Ruben C. 'The Kalayaan Islands Group: Legal Issues and Problems for the Philippines'. *World Bulletin,* vol. 10, no. 5–6 (September–December 1994), pp. 48–73.

Catley, Bob and Makmur Keliat. *Spratlys: The Dispute in the South China Sea.* Singapore: Ashgate, 1997.

Center for International Political Economy. 'The Main Study – China and Long-range Asia Energy Security: An Analysis of the Political, Economic and Technological Factors Shaping Asian Energy Markets'. http://riceinfo.rice.edu/projects/.../publications/claes/main/main.html.

Chalmers, Malcolm. *Confidence Building in South-East Asia.* Boulder, CO: Westview, 1996, pp. 61–119.

—— 'Openness and Security Policy in the Southeast Asia'. *Survival,* vol. 38, no. 3 (1996), pp. 82–98.

Chang, Felix K. 'Beyond the Unipolar Moment; Beijing's Reach in the South China Sea'. *Orbis,* vol. 40, no. 3 (Summer 1996), pp. 353–374.

Chang Pao-min. 'A New Scramble for the South China Sea Islands'. *Contemporary Southeast Asia*, vol. 12, no. 1 (June 1990), pp. 20–39.

—— 'Sino-Vietnamese Relations: Prospects for the 21st Century'. In Carlyle A. Thayer and Ramses Amer (eds), *Vietnamese Foreign Policy in Transition*. Singapore: Institute of Southeast Asian Studies, 1999.

Chang Teh Kuang. 'China's Claim of Sovereignty over Spratly and Paracel Islands. A Historical and Legal Perspective'. *Case Western Reserve Journal of International Law*, vol. 23, (1991), pp. 399–455.

Chang Ya-chun. 'Beijing's Maritime Rivalry with the United States and Japan: The Search for Institutionalized Mechanisms of Competition'. *Issues & Studies*, vol. 34, no. 6 (June 1998), pp. 56–79.

Chao, John T. 'South China Sea: Boundary Problems Relating to the Nansha and Hsisha Islands'. *Chinese Yearbook of International Law and Affairs*, vol. 9 (1990), pp. 66–156.

Charney, Jonathan I. 'Central East Asian Maritime Boundaries and the Law of the Sea'. *American Journal of International Law*, vol. 89, no. 4 (October 1995), pp. 724–749.

Charney, Jonathan I. and Lewis M. Alexander. *International Maritime Boundaries Volume I*. Dordrecht, Boston and London: Martinus Nijhoff Publishers and the American Society of International Law, 1993.

Chemillier-Gendreau, Monique. *La souveraineté sur les archipels Paracels et Spratleys*. Paris: l'Harmattan, 1996.

—— 'Les États de l'ex-Indochine et les conflits territoriaux'. In Pierre Brocheux (ed.), *Du conflit d'Indochine aux conflits indochinois*. Paris: Éditions Complexe, 2000, pp. 103–120.

Chen Degong. *Xian Dai Guo Ji Hai Yang Fa* [The Modern International Law of the Sea]. Beijing: Zhongguo Shehui Kexue Chubanshe, 1988.

Chen Hurng-yu. 'The Prospects for Joint Development in the South China Sea'. *Issues & Studies*, vol. 27, no. 12 (1991), pp. 112–125.

—— 'A Comparison between Taipei and Peking in their Policies and Concepts regarding the South China Sea'. *Issues & Studies*, vol. 29, no. 9 (1993), pp. 22–55.

—— *Nanhai zhudao zhi faxian, kaifa yu guoji chongtu* [The discovery and development of the South China Sea islands and international conflicts]. Taipei: Guoli bianyiguan, 1997.

—— 'Comment on Documents Claiming Vietnamese Sovereignty over the Spratly and Paracel Islands'. *Issues & Studies*, vol. 35, no. 4 (July/August 1999), pp. 149–185.

—— 'The PRC's South China Sea Policy and Strategies of Occupation in the Paracel and Spratly Islands'. *Issues & Studies*, vol. 36, no. 4 (2000), pp. 95–131..

Chen Qimao. 'New Approaches in China's Foreign Policy. The Post-Cold War Era'. *Asian Survey*, vol. 33, no. 3 (1993), pp. 237–251.

China, People's Republic of. 'Joint Statement – Consultations on the South China Sea and other Areas of Cooperation'. 9–10 August 1995.

—— 'The Development of China's Marine Programs'. Information Office of the State Council, May 1998, Beijing.

—— 'Law of the People's Republic of China on the Exclusive Economic Zone and the Continental Shelf (Adopted at the Third Session of the Standing Committee of the Ninth National People's Congress of the People's Republic of China on 26 June 1998)'. *MIMA Bulletin.*

Chiu Hungdah. 'South China Sea Islands: Implications for Delimiting the Seabed and Future Shipping Routes'. *The China Quarterly* (1977), pp. 743–765.

Chong-Pin Lin. 'Chinese Military Modernization: Perceptions, Progress, and Prospects'. *Security Studies,* vol. 3, no. 4 (Summer 1994), pp. 718–753.

Chou Loke Ming and Hong Woo Khoo. 'Marine Science Training, Networking and Information in the South China Sea Region.' Paper presented to the First Working Group Meeting on Marine Scientific Research in the South China Sea, Manila, Philippines, 30 May–3 June 1993.

Chua Thia-Eng. 'Managing Marine Pollution in the East Asian Seas: A Regional Initiative'. *Integrated Coastal Zone Management,* Spring 2000 edition, pp. 189–197.

Chung Chien. 'Confidence-Building Measures in the South China Sea'. In Tien Hung-mao and Cheng Tun-jen (eds), *The Security Environment in the Asia-Pacific.* Studies of the Institute for National Policy Research, Armonk: East Gate Book, 2000.

Chung Chien-Peng. 'The PRC's Changing Moral and Realist Perceptions Toward Territorial Disputes'. *Issues & Studies,* vol. 36, no. 5 (2000), pp. 176–196.

Churchill, R.R. and A.V. Lowe. *The Law of the Sea.* Manchester: Manchester University Press, 1983 (3rd edn 1999).

Clad, James and J. Jefferson Edwards. 'South China Sea: New US Move Expected'. *Decision Brief, CERA* (July 1999).

Clagett, Brice M. 'Competing Claims of Vietnam and China in the Vanguard Bank and Blue Dragon Areas of the South China Sea'. Part I, *Oil Gas Law and Taxation Review* (UK), no. 10 (1995), pp. 375–388; Part II, no. 11 (1995), pp. 419–335.

Cloughley, Brian. 'Strategic and Security Issues. No Need for War in South China Sea'. *International Defence Review,* vol. 28, no. 6 (1 June 1995).

Coordinating Committee for Coastal and Offshore Geo-Science Programs in East and Southeast Asia (CCOP). *1996 CCOP Annual Report (A Review of Activities in 1996).* CCOP Technical Secretariat, Bangkok, Thailand.

Coquia, Jorge. 'Maritime Boundary Problems in the South China Sea'. *University of British Columbia Law Review,* vol. 24, no. 1 (1990), pp. 117–125.

Cordesman, Anthony H. *The Asian and Chinese Military Balance. A Comparative Summary of Military Expenditures; Manpower; Land, Air, Naval, and Nuclear Forces; and Arms Sales,* Washington, DC: Center for Strategic and International Studies, January 2000.

Cordner, Lee G. 'The Spratly Islands Dispute and the Law of the Sea'. *Ocean Development & International Law Journal,* vol. 25, no. 1 (1994), pp. 61–74.

Cossa, Ralph A. 'Security Implications of Conflict in the South China Sea: Exploring Potential Triggers of Conflict'. *CSIS PacNet Newsletter* at http://www.csis.org/pacfor/pac1698.html

Coulter, Daniel Y. 'South China Sea Fisheries: Countdown to Calamity'. *Contemporary Southeast Asia,* vol. 17, no. 4 (March 1998), pp. 371–388.

Cronin, Richard P. 'Japan'. In Richard Dean Burns (ed.), *Encyclopedia of Arms Control and Disarmament.* New York: Charles Scribner's Sons, 1993, vol. I, pp. 129–147.

Cruz de Castro, Renato. 'The Controversy in the Spratlys: Exploring the Limits to ASEAN's Engagement Policy'. *Issues & Studies,* vol. 34, no. 9 (September 1998), pp. 95–123.

Curtis, Gerald L. (ed.), *The United States, Japan, and Asia. Challenges for U.S. Policy.* New York: W.W. Norton, 1994.

Da Cunha, Derek. 'Whittling Away Asia's Security Bedrock'. *The Asian Wall Street Journal* (27 July 1993), p. 6.

—— 'What China's "Local" War Doctrine Means for East Asian Security'. *The Straits Times* (5 August 1993), p. 26.

—— 'The US Presence in the Asia-Pacific: Nodding Off'. *The Straits Times* (9 March 1995).

—— 'US Must Realign Naval Forces in Pacific to Keep Power Balance'. *The Straits Times* (30 May 1997), p. 62.

Dahlby, Tracy. 'Crossroads of Asia: South China Sea'. *National Geographic,* vol. 194, no. 6 (December 1998).

Danish Foreign Ministry. *Prevention and Resolution of Violent Conflicts in Developing Countries,* a public draft paper. Copenhagen, 1999.

Dao Van Thuy. 'Lap truong cua Trung Quoc trong tranh chap chu auyen tren hai auan dao Hoang Sa – Truong Sa va luat quoc te' [International law and China's position in the sovereignty conflict over the Paracel and Spratly archipelagos]. Thoi dai; revue vietnamienne d'études et de débats; Paris, no. 3, 1999, pp. 25–45.

Davis, Elizabeth Van Wie. *China and the Law of the Sea Convention. Follow the Sea.* Lewiston/Queenston/Lampeter: Edwin Mellen Press, 1995.

Dawson, Michael, Bernard Eccleston and Deborah McNamara. *The Asia-Pacific Profile.* London: The Open University, 1998.

De Dianoux, Hugues Jean. 'Les loges françaises dans l'Inde et au Bangladesh et les îles Spratly'. *Mondes et cultures* (published in Paris by the Académie française de l'Outre-Mer), vol. XLIV, no. 3, 1984.

Deans, Phil. 'Contending Nationalisms and the Diaoyutai/Senkaku Dispute'. *Security Dialogue,* vol. 31, no. 1 (March 2000), pp. 119–131.

Declaration of ASEAN Concord, Indonesia, 24 February 1976, in www. Aseansec.org/summit/concord.htm.

Denécé, Éric. 'Un enjeu essentiel de la sécurité en Asie du Sud-Est: la question des détroits'. *Revue Marine,* no. 152 (July 1991), pp. 31–35.

—— 'Straits and Seaways: Essential Stakes of South-East Asian Security'. *Asia Pacific Defence Journal* (Singapore), vol. 3, no. 1 (January/February 1993), pp. 40–44.

—— 'La liberté de navigation à travers les détroits d'Asie du Sud-Est'. *La lutte pour l'empire des mers,* Institut de Stratégie Comparée (ISC), 1995, pp. 263–289.

—— *Géostratégie de la mer de Chine méridionale et des bassins maritimes adjacents.* Paris: L'Harmattan, 1999.

—— 'Mer de Chine méridionale. Les ressources océaniques sont-elles seules au coeur des litiges?' *La Revue Maritime,* no. 453 (3ème trimestre 1999), pp. 21–31.

—— 'La situation juridique des archipels de mer de Chine méridionale'. *Annuaire du droit de la mer 1998,* vol. II. Paris: Pédone, 1999, pp. 273–284.

—— 'Les risques de conflits en mer de Chine méridionale'. *Défense nationale,* 56ème année (Feb. 2000), pp. 134–147.

Deng, Yong. 'Managing China's Hegemonic Ascension: Engagement from Southeast Asia'. *The Journal of Strategic Studies,* vol. 21, no. 1 (March 1998), pp. 21–43.

Denon, David B.H. 'China's Security Strategy. The View from Beijing, ASEAN and Washington'. *Asian Survey,* vol. 36, no. 4 (1996), pp. 422–439.

Deutsch, Karl W. *et al. Political Community and the North Atlantic Area. International Organization in the Light of Historical Experience.* Princeton, NJ: Princeton University Press, 1957.

Dewitt, David and Brian Bow. 'Proliferation Management in South-East Asia'. *Survival,* vol. 38, no. 3 (Autumn 1996), pp. 67–81.

Djalal, Dino Patti. *The Geopolitics of Indonesia's Maritime Territorial Policy.* Jakarta: Centre for Strategic and International Studies, 1996.

Djalal, Hasjim. 'Potential Conflicts in the South China Sea: In Search of Cooperation'. *Indonesian Quarterly,* vol. 18, no. 2 (1990), pp. 127–132.

—— 'Conflicting Territorial and Jurisdictional Claims in the South China Sea' (1979), reprinted in Hasjim Djalal. *Indonesia and the Law of the Sea.* Jakarta: Center for Strategic and International Studies (CSIS), 1995, pp. 364–383.

—— 'South China Sea Disputes'. Paper presented at the Annual Conference on Security Flashpoints: Oil, Sea Access and Military Confrontation, New York, February 1997.

—— 'Indonesia and the South China Sea Initiative'. *Ocean Development & International Law,* vol. 32, no. 2 (2001), pp. 97–105.

Djiwandono, Soedjati. 'ASEAN Solidarity, More Surface than Substance'. *Jakarta Post,* 27 July 1994.

Ding, Arthur S. 'The PRC's Military Modernization and a Security Mechanism for the Asia Pacific'. *Issues & Studies,* vol. 31, no. 8 (August 1995), pp. 1–18.

Dokken, Karin . 'Environment, Security and Regionalism in the Asia-Pacific: Is Environmental Security a Useful Concept?' *Pacifica Review,* vol. 14, no. 4 (2001), pp. 509–530.

Dorian, James P., David Fridley and Kristin Tressler. 'Multilateral Resource Cooperation among Northeast Asian Countries: Energy and Mineral Joint Venture Prospects'. *Journal of Northeast Asian Studies,* vol. XII, no. 1 (Spring 1993), pp. 3–35.

Downing, John. 'A Japanese Navy in All But Name'. *Jane's Navy International*, vol. 104, no. 3 (1 April 1999).

Downs, Erica and Philip Saunders. 'Legitimacy and the Limits of Nationalism. China and the Diaoyu Islands'. *International Security*, vol. 23, no. 3 (Winter 1998/99), pp. 114–146.

Dupont, Alan. 'The Environment and Security in Pacific Asia'. *Adelphi Paper 319* (1998).

Dyke, Jon M. Van and Mark J. Valencia. 'How Valid Are the South China Sea Claims under the Law of the Sea Convention?' *Southeast Asian Affairs 2000*. Singapore: Institute of Southeast Asian Affairs, 2000, pp. 47–63.

Dzurek, Daniel J. 'The Spratly Islands Dispute: Who's On First'. International Boundaries Research Unit's *Maritime Briefing*, vol. 2, no. 1 (1996).

—— 'Maritime Agreements and Oil Exploration in the Gulf of Thailand'. In Gerald Blake, Martin Pratt, Clive Schofield and Janet Allison Brown (eds), *Boundaries and Energy: Problems and Prospects*. London: Kluwer Law International, 1998, pp. 117–135.

—— 'Comments on Island Disputes in East Asia'. In Myron H. Nordquist and John Norton Moore (eds), *Security Flashpoints: Oil, Islands, Sea Access and Military Confrontation*. The Hague: Martinus Nijhoff, 1998, pp. 419–428.

Eikenberry, Karl W. 'Does China Threaten Asia-Pacific Regional Stability?' *Parameters*, vol. 25, (Spring 1995), pp. 82–103.

Elferink, Alex G. Oude. 'Clarifying Article 121(3) of the Law of the Sea: The Limits Set by the Nature of International Legal Processes'. *IBRU Boundary and Security Bulletin*, vol. 6, no. 2 (Summer 1998), pp. 58–68.

—— 'The Islands in the South China Sea: How Does Their Presence Limit the Extent of the High Seas and the Area and the Maritime Zones of the Mainland Coast?' *Ocean Development & International Law*, vol. 32, no. 2 (2001), pp. 169–190.

Evans, David C. and Mark R. Peattie. *Strategy, Tactics and Technology in the Imperial Japanese Navy*. Annapolis, Maryland: Naval Institute Press, 1997.

Far Eastern Economic Review (FEER). 'Drawn to the Fray'. Foreign Relations, (3 April 1997), pp. 14–16.

—— 'On the Backburner – Indonesia May Put Off Plans for Natuna Field'. *Business Energy*, 24 October (1996), p. 70.

Farrell, Espey Cooke. *The Socialist Republic of Vietnam and the Law of the Sea*. The Hague: Martinus Nijhoff, 1998.

Federation of American Scientists: 'People's Liberation Army Navy'. at http://www.fas.org/man/dod-101/ sys/ship/row/plan/index.html

Feigenbaum, Evan A. 'China's Military Posture and the New Economic Geopolitics'. *Survival*, vol. 41, no. 2 (Summer 1999), pp. 71–88.

Feng Chongyi. 'Seeking Lost Codes in the Wilderness: The Search for a Hainanese Culture'. *The China Quarterly*, no. 160 (December 1999), pp. 1036–1056.

Fernandez, Hermogenes C. *The Philippine 200-Mile Economic Zone. Sources of Possible Cooperation or Disputes with Other Countries.* Series One Monograph, no. 3 (October 1982). Makati, Metro Manila: Development Academy of the Philippine Press, for the Secretariat to the Cabinet Committee on the Law of the Sea Treaty.

Ferrer, Neil Frank R. (ed.). *The Philippines and the South China Sea Islands: Overview and Documents.* Metro Manila: Foreign Service Institute, 1993.

Fesharaki, Fereidun, Allen L. Clark and Duangjai Intarapravich (eds). *Pacific Energy Outlook: Strategies and Policy Imperatives to 2000.* Honolulu: East–West Center Occasional Papers, 1995.

Financial Times. 'Malaysia–Thai Gas Deal May Serve as Model for SE Asia'. 23 April 1998.

'First Meeting of the Malaysia–Philippines Joint Commission for Bilateral Cooperation. Speech by Foreign Minister of Malaysia'. *Foreign Affairs Malaysia* vol. 26, no. 4 (1993), pp.54–58.

Findlay, Trevor. 'South-East Asia and the New Asia-Pacific Security Dialogue'. In *SIPRI Yearbook 1994*, pp. 125–148.

—— 'Turning the Corner in Southeast Asia'. In Michael E. Brown (ed.), *The International Dimensions of Internal Conflict.* Cambridge, MA: MIT Press, 1996.

Finnish Foreign Ministry (Olli Ruohomäki and Timo Kivimäki). *Peaceful Solutions. Navigating Prevention and Mitigation of Conflicts.* Finland's Ministry for Foreign Affairs, Department for International Development Cooperation, Helsinki 2000.

Finon, Dominique et Pierre Jacquet (eds). *Énergie, développement et sécurité.* Paris: les cahiers de l'ifri (Institut francais Des relations internationales), no. 28, 1999.

Forbes, Vivian L. *Indonesia's Maritime Boundaries.* A Malaysian Institute of Maritime Affairs Monograph. Kuala Lumpur: Malaysian Institute of Maritime Affairs (MIMA), 1995.

Foreign Service Institute. 'The Philippines and the South China Sea Islands: Overview and Documents'. *CIRSS Papers*, no. 1 (December 1993).

Fukase, Emiko and Will Martin. 'The Effect of the United States' Granting Most Favoured Nation Status to Vietnam'. Development Research Group, World Bank, Washington, DC, USA (DATE?).

Furtado, Xavier. 'International Law and the Dispute over the Spratly Islands: Whiter UNCLOS?' *Contemporary Southeast Asia*, vol. 21, no. 3 (December 1999), pp. 386–404.

Galdorise, George V. and Kevin R. Vienna. *Beyond the Law of the Sea.* New York: Praeger, 1997.

Gallagher, Michael G. 'China's Illusory Threat to the South China Sea'. *International Security*, vol. 19, no. 1 (Summer 1994), pp. 169–194.

Gao, Mobo C.F. 'Sino-US Love and Hate Relations'. *Journal of Contemporary Asia*, vol. 30, no. 4 (2000).

Gao Zhiguo. 'The South China Sea: From Conflict to Cooperation?' *Ocean Development & International Law*, vol. 25, no. 3 (1994), pp. 345–359.

—— *Environmental Regulation of Oil and Gas in the Twentieth Century and Beyond: An Introduction and Overview.* Offprint from Environmental Regulation of Oil and Gas, London: Kluwer Law International, 1998.

Garver, John W. 'China Push through the South China Sea: The Interaction of Bureaucratic and National Interests'. *The China Quarterly,* no. 132 (December 1992), pp. 999–1028.

—— *Face Off: China, the United States, and Taiwan's Democratization.* Seattle: University of Washington Press, 1997.

Gill, Bates and Taeho Kim. 'China's Arms Acquisitions from Abroad: A Quest for "Superb and Secret Weapons"'. *SIPRI Research Report,* no. 11. Oxford: Oxford University Press, 1995.

Gjetnes, Marius. 'The Legal Regime of Islands in the South China Sea'. A thesis for the Cand. Jur. degree at the Department of Public and International Law, University of Oslo, Autumn 2000.

—— 'The Spratlys: Are They Rocks or Islands?' *Ocean Development & International Law,* vol. 32, no. 2 (2001), pp. 191–204.

Glaser, Bonnie S. 'China's Security Perceptions'. *Asian Survey,* vol. 33, no. 3 (March 1993), pp. 252–271.

Godwin, Paul H.B. 'Military Technology and Doctrine in Chinese Military Planning: Compensating for Obsolescence'. In Eric Arnett (ed.), *Military Capacity and the Risk of War. China, India, Pakistan and Iran.* Oxford: Oxford University Press, 1997, pp. 39–60.

Goh, B.P.L and Chou Loke Ming (eds). UNEP Regional Co-ordinating Unit/East Asian Seas Action Plan: Proceedings of the Second ASEAMS Scientific Symposium. Bangkok: UNEP. RCU/EAS Technical Reports Series no. 10. 1996.

Gomez, Edgardo D. 'Perspectives on Coral Reef Research and Management in the Pacific'. *Ocean Management,* vol. 8, no. 4 (1983), pp. 281–295.

—— 'Coastal Zone Management and Conservation in the South China Sea'. In B. Morton (ed.) *Proceedings of the Third International Conference on the Marine Biology of the South China Sea,* Hong Kong 28 October–1 November 1996. Hong Kong: Hong Kong University Press (abstract).

—— 'Achievements of the Action Plan for the East Asian Seas'. In UNEP, *Cooperation for Environmental Protection in the Pacific.* Bangkok: UNEP Regional Seas Reports and Studies no. 97, 1998.

—— 'Marine Scientific Research in the South China Sea and Environmental Security'. *Ocean Development & International Law,* vol. 32, no. 2, 2001.

Gomez, E.D. *et al.* 'A Review of the Status of Philippine Reefs'. *Marine Pollution Bulletin,* vol. 29, no. 1–3 (1994), pp. 62–68.

Goscha, Christopher E. 'The borders of Vietnam's Early Trade with Southern China: A Contemporary Perspective'. *Foreign Affairs,* vol. 40, no. 6 (2000).

Greenfield, Jeanette. *China's Practice in the Law of the Sea.* Oxford: Clarendon Press, 1992.

Gregor, A. James. 'East Asian Stability and the Defence of the Republic of China on Taiwan'. *Comparative Strategy,* vol. 16 (1997), pp. 321–335.

—— 'Qualified Engagement – US China Policy and Security Concerns'. *http://www.nwc.navy.mil/press/review/1996/spring/art3-sp9.htm.*

Grey, Jeffrey. *A Military History of Australia.* Cambridge: Cambridge University Press, 1999.

Grinter, Lawrence E. and Young Whan Kihl. *East Asian Conflict Zones – Prospects for Regional Stability and Deescalation.* Basingstoke: Macmillan Press, 1987.

Gu Xiaosong and Brantly Womack. 'Border Cooperation between China and Vietnam in the 1990s". *Foreign Affairs,* vol. 40, no. 6 (2000).

Gurtov, Mel and Byong-Moo Hwang, *China's Security: The New Roles of the Military.* Boulder, CO: Lynne Rienner, 1998.

Haas, Peter M. 'Prospects for Effective Marine Governance in the Northwest Pacific Region'. Commissioned for the ESENA workshop: Energy-Related Marine Issues in the Sea of Japan, Tokyo, Japan, 11–12 July 1998.

Hall, Marcus. 'Trouble Brewing in the South China Sea'. *http://psirus.sfsu.edu/IntRel/IRJournal/sp95/hall.html.*

Haller-Trost, R. 'Historical Legal Claims: A Study of Disputed Sovereignty over Pulau Batu Puteh (Pedra Branca)'. International Boundaries Research Unit's *Maritime Briefing,* vol. 1, no. 1 (1993).

—— 'The Brunei-Malaysia Dispute over Territorial and Maritime Claims in International Law'. International Boundaries Research Unit's *Maritime Briefing,* vol. 1, no. 3 (1994).

Hamzah, B.A. 'Jurisdictional Issues and Conflicting Claims in the Spratlys'. *Foreign Relations Journal,* vol. V, no. 1 (March 1990), pp. 1–26.

—— 'Jurisdiction Issues and the Conflicting Claims in the Spratly's'. *Indonesian Quarterly,* vol. 18, no. 2 (1990), pp. 133–153.

—— 'Possible Triggers of Conflict in the South China Sea'. Kuala Lumpur: Maritime Institute of Malaysia (MIMA) n.d.

—— 'The External Maritime Dimension of ASEAN Security'. *Journal of Strategic Studies,* vol. 18, no. 3 (September 1995), pp. 123–146.

Han Zhenhua. *Nanhai Zhudao Shidi Yanjiu* [History and Geography Studies on the South China Sea Islands], Beijing: Shehui Kexue Wenxian Chubanshe, 1996.

Hancox, David and Victor Prescott. 'A Geographical Description of the Spratly Islands and an Account of Hydrographic Surveys among those Islands'. International Boundary Research Unit's *Maritime Briefing,* vol. 1, no. 6 (1995).

—— 'Secret Hydrographic Surveys in the Spratly Islands'. Kuala Lumpur: Maritime Institute of Malaysia (MIMA), 1997.

Hänggi, Heiner. *Neutralität in Südostasien. Das Project einer Zone des Friedens, der Freiheit und der Neutralität.* Bern: Verlag Paul Haupt, 1993.

Hara, Kimie. 'Rethinking the "Cold War" in the Asia Pacific'. *Pacifica Review,* vol. 12, no. 4 (1995), pp. 515–536.

Harris, Stuart. 'The Economic Aspects of Pacific Security'. Working paper no. 6, Canberra: Australian National University, 1992.

Harrison, Selig. *China, Oil and Asia: Conflict Ahead.* New York: Columbia University Press, 1992.

Haseman, John. 'Indonesia, China Expand Co-operation'. *Jane's Defence Weekly,* vol. 33, no. 21 (24 May 2000).

Hawksley, Humphrey and Simon Holberton. *Dragonstrike. The Millennium War.* London: Sidgwick & Jackson, 1997.

Head, William P. and Edwin G. Clausen (eds). *Weaving a New Tapestry – Asia in the Post-Cold World War: Case Studies and General Trends.* London: Praeger, 1999.

Hearns, G.S. and Stormont W. G. 'Report: Managing Potential Conflicts in the South China Sea'. *Marine Policy,* vol. 20, no. 2 (1996), pp. 177–181.

Heinzig, Dieter. *Disputed Islands in the South China Sea. Paracels – Spratlys – Pratas – Macclesfield Bank.* Wiesbaden: Harrassowitz, 1976.

Herriman, Mx (Lieutenant Commander). 'China's Territorial Sea Law and International Law of the Sea'. *http://www.anu.edu.au/law/pub/ic/lawofsea/china.html.*

Herz, John M. 'Idealist Internationalism and the Security Dilemma'. *World Politics,* no. 2, 1950, pp. 157–180.

—— *Political Realism and Political Idealism. A Study in Theories and Realities.* Chicago: Chicago University Press, 1951.

Higgott, Richard. 'The Political Economy of Globalisation in East Asia – The Salience of Region Building'. In Kris Olds (ed.), *Globalisation and the Asia Pacific,* pp. 91–106.

Hill, R.D., Norman G. Owen and E.V. Roberts (eds). *Fishing in Troubled Waters. Proceedings of an Academic Conference on Territorial Claims in the South China Sea.* Hong Kong: University of Hong Kong, Centre of Asian Studies Occasional Papers and Monographs no. 97, 1991.

Hindley, Michael and James Bridge. 'South China Sea: the Spratly and Paracel Dispute'. *World Today,* vol. 50, no. 6 (June 1994), pp. 109–111.

Hollingsbee, Trevor. 'Spratlys Rivalry as Philippines Faces Malaysia'. *Jane's Intelligence Review,* vol. 11, no. 10 (1 December 1999).

Hollingsbee, Trevor. 'China Moves in on Mischief Reef'. *Jane's Intelligence Review,* vol. 11, no. 1 (1 January 1999), p. 5.

Holsti, Kalevi. *Peace and War: Armed Conflicts and International Order 1648– 1989.* Cambridge Studies in International Relations, vol. 14 (1991), Cambridge: Cambridge University Press.

Hu Wei-jen. 'View from Taiwan. In Search of National Security: Strategic Concepts of the Republic of China at a Crossroads'. *Comparative Strategy,* vol. 14 (1995), pp. 195–203.

Hua, Di. 'Threat Perception and Military Planning in China: Domestic Instability and the Importance of Prestige'. In Eric Arnett (ed.), *Military Capacity and the Risk of War. China, India, Pakistan and Iran.* Oxford: Oxford University Press, 1997, pp. 25–38.

Huber, Thomas M. *Strategic Economy in Japan.* Boulder, CO: Westview Press, 1994.

Hughesman, Miriam. 'China Moves In'. *Energy Economist,* vol. 129 (July 1992), pp. 2–4.

Hull, Richard E. 'The South China Sea: Future Source of Prosperity or Conflict in South East Asia?' National Defence University, Strategic Forum, Institute for National Strategic Studies, 1999.

Hutchison, Charles S. *Southeast Asian Oil, Gas, Coal and Mineral Deposits.* Oxford: Clarendon Press, 1996.

Huth, Paul K. 'Territorial Disputes and International Conflict: Empirical Findings and Theoretical Explanations'. Paper Presented at the 5th Annual Conference on the International Boundaries Research Unit, Borderlands Under Stress, IBRU, July 15–17 1998.

Huxley, Tim. 'A Threat in the South China Sea? A Rejoinder'. *Security Dialogue,* vol. 29, no. 1 (1998), pp. 113–118.

Huynh Minh Chinh. 'The Need for Managing Potential Conflicts in the Bien Dong Sea (South China Sea)'. Institute for International Relations SSRC-Macarthur Program on International Peace and Security, Workshop on New Approach to Peace and Security, Hanoi Daewoo Hotel, 26–28 August 1999.

Hyer, Eric. 'Special Issue: The South China Sea Territorial Disputes'. *American Asian Review,* vol. 12 (Winter 1994).

—— 'The South China Sea Disputes: Implications of China's Earlier Territorial Settlements'. *Pacific Affairs,* vol. 68, no. 1 (Spring 1995), pp. 34–54.

Ienaga, Saburo. 'The Glorification of War in Japanese Education'. *International Security,* vol. 18, no. 3 (Winter 1993–94), pp. 113–133.

Imai, Ryukichi. 'Ballistic Missile Defense, Nuclear Non-Proliferation, and a Nuclear Free World'. Special Report, 21.12.00, can be obtained from [NAPSNet@nautilus.org].

Institute for International Relations (IIR). Organisational Brochure (1996).

International Alert. *Code of Conduct. Conflict Transformation Work.* International Alert, London, n.d.

International Court of Justice. 'The Fisheries Case (United Kingdom vs Norway)'. *International Court of Justice, Year 1951.* 18 December 1951, General List no. 5.

International Herald Tribune. 'Drawing by Kal in The Sun (Baltimore)'. 20 February 1996.

—— 'China Is Slowly Winning a Long Game for the Sea'. 28 January 1999.

—— 'Work to Resolve the Maritime Conflict'. 17 December 1999.

International IDEA. *Democratic Institutions and Conflict Management.* Background Paper. IDEA, Stockholm 1999.

Inventory of Conflict and Environment (ICE) Case Studies (1997) 'Spratly Islands Dispute'. http://www.american.edu/projects/mandala/TED/ice/iceall.htm

ISSS. 'The Law of the Sea – Obstacle to an International Maritime Order'. *Law of the Sea,* vol. 5, no. 9 (November 1999).

Janssen, Joris. 'ASEAN Navies Extend their Maritime Reach'. *Jane's Defence Weekly,* vol. 26, no. 22 (27 Nov. 1996).

Jawhar bin Hassan, Mohamed. 'Disputes in the South China Sea: Approaches for Conflict Management'. In Derek Da Cunha (ed.), *Southeast Asian Perspectives on Security.* Singapore: Institute of Southeast Asian Studies (ISEAS), 2000.

Jenisch, Uwe. 'The Future of the UN Law of the Sea Convention'. *Aussenpolitik,* no. 1 (1988), pp. 46–60.

Ji Guoxing. 'The Spratlys Disputes and Prospects for Settlement'. *ISIS Issue Paper,* Kuala Lumpur: Institute of Strategic and International Studies, 1992.

——— 'China Versus South China Sea Security'. *Security Dialogue,* vol. 29, no. 1 (March 1998), pp. 101–112.

Ji Guoxing. 'China Versus Asian Pacific Energy Security'. *The Korean Journal of Defense Analysis,* vol. X, no. 2 (Winter 1998), pp. 109–141.

Ji, You. *The Armed Forces of China.* London: I.B. Tauris, 1999.

Jie Chen. 'China's Spratly Policy. With Special Reference to the Philippines and Malaysia'. *Asian Survey,* vol. 34 (1994), pp. 893–903.

Johnson, Stewart. 'Territorial Issues and Conflict Potential in the South China Sea'. *Conflict Quarterly,* vol. 14, no. 4 (Fall 1994), pp. 26–44.

Johnston, Douglas. 'Environmental Management in the South China Sea: Legal and Institutional Developments'. *East–West Environment and Policy Institute Research Report,* no. 10 (May 1982).

——— *The Theory and History of Ocean Boundary Making.* Kingston: McGill-Queen's University Press, 1988.

Jones, Daniel M., Stuart A. Bremer and J. David Singer. 'Militarized Interstate Disputes, 1816–1992: Rationale, Coding Rules, and Empirical Patterns'. *Conflict Management and Peace Science.* vol. 15, no. 2 (Fall 1996), pp. 163–213.

Jones, Howard P. *Indonesia, a Possible Dream.* Mas Aju: Singapore, 1974.

Joyaux François. *Géopolitique de l'Extrême Orient* (2 vols). Brussels: Editions Complexe, 1991.

Joyner, Christopher C. 'The Spratly Dispute: Rethinking the Interplay of Law, Diplomacy, and Geo-politics in the South China Sea'. *The International Journal of Marine and Coastal Law,* vol. 13, no. 2 (May 1998), pp. 193–236.

——— 'The Spratly Islands Dispute: What Role for Normalizing Relations between China and Taiwan?' *New England Law Review,* vol. 32, no. 3 (Spring 1998), pp. 819–854.

——— 'The Spratly Island Dispute in the South China Sea'. *Integrated Coastal Zone Management* (Spring 2000), pp. 85–90.

Kamarulzaman Askandar, 'ASEAN and Conflict Management: The Formative Years of 1967–1976'. *Pacifica Review,* vol. 6, no. 2 (1994).

Kang Wu and Binsheng Li. 'Energy Development in China'. *Energy Policy,* vol. 23, no. 2 (1995), pp. 167–178.

Karmel, Solomon M. 'The Maoist Drag on China's Military'. *Orbis,* vol. 42, no. 3 (summer 1998), pp. 374–386.

Karniol, Robert. 'Briefing: Military Modernisation in Asia'. *Jane's Defence Weekly,* vol. 32, no. 21 (24 November 1999).

Kayahara, Ikuo. 'China as a Military Power in the Twenty-first Century'. *Japan Review of International Affairs,* vol. 12, no. 1 (Spring 1998), pp. 49–68.

Khatab, Ali. 'The Kancil, the Panda and the Blue Lagoon: Simulating a Dyadic Asymmetry in the Spratlys'. *International Studies,* vol. 34, no. 2 (1997), pp. 145–162.

Kim, Samuel. 'Mainland China in a Changing Asia-Pacific Regional Order'. *Issues & Studies* vol. 30, no. 10, 1994.

Kirkpatrick, Jane. 'A Question of Intent: What Is China up to in the South China Sea?' *American Enterprise,* vol. 5 (1994), pp. 64–75.

Kittichaisaree, Kriangsak. *The Law of the Sea and Maritime Boundary Delimitation in Southeast Asia.* New York: Oxford University Press, 1987.

—— 'A Code of Conduct for Human and Regional Security around the South China Sea'. *Ocean Development & International Law,* vol. 32, no. 2 (2001), pp. 131–148.

Kivimäki, Timo. 'The Long Peace of ASEAN'. *Journal of Peace Research,* vol. 38 (January 2001), p. 1.

—— '"Reason" and "Power" in the South China Sea Disputes'. A paper at the Panel on the South China Sea in honour of Professor Michael Leifer, Third European Association of Southeast Asian Studies Conference, London School of Economics and Political Science, 6–8 September 2001.

—— (ed.). *Territorial Disputes in the South China Sea.* A study commissioned by the Finnish Foreign Ministry undertaken by the Nordic Institute of Asian Studies. Helsinki and Copenhagen: CTS-Conflict Transformation Service, 2001.

Klintworth, Gary. 'Taiwan's Asia-Pacific Policy and Community'. *Pacifica Review,* vol. 7, no. 4 (1994), pp. 447–455.

Klintworth, Gary. 'China and Taiwan – From Flash Point to Redefining One China'. *Taipei Review,* vol.. 51, no. 3 (March 2001), pp. 46–53.

Knudsen, Olav F. 'The South China Sea and the East Asian Region'. *NUPI Report,* no. 205. Oslo: NUPI, 1996.

Kondapalli, Srikanth. 'China's Naval Equipment Acquisition'. *Strategic Analysis,* vol. 23, no. 9. New Delhi: IDSA (December 1999), pp. 1509–1530.

—— *China's Military. The PLA in Transition.* New Delhi: Knowledge World and Institute for Defense Studies and Analyses, 1999.

Kunihiro, Masao. 'The Decline and Fall of Pacifism'. *The Bulletin of the Atomic Scientists,* vol. 53, no. 1 (January/February 1997).

Kurus, Bilson. 'The BIMB-EAGA: Developments, Obstacles and Future Direction'. *Borneo Review,* vol. 8, no. 1 (1997), pp. 1–13.

—— 'Understanding ASEAN: Benefits and Raison d'Être'. *Asian Survey,* vol. 33, no. 8, (1993).

Labrecque, Georges. 'Les frontières internationales. Essai de classification pour un tour du monde géopolitique'. Paris: l'Harmattan, 1998.

Labrousse, Henri. 'Les ambitions Maritimes de la Chine'. *Défense Nationale* (1994), pp. 131–141.

—— 'Les tensions insulaires en Asie du sud-est'. *La Revue Maritime* (1996), pp. 72–79.

Lake, David A. and Patrick M. Morgan (eds). *Regional Orders. Building Security in a New World.* University Park, PA: Pennsylvania State University Press, 1997.

Lam Peng Er. 'Japan and the Spratlys Dispute'. *Asian Survey,* vol. XXXVI, no. 10 (October 1996), pp. 995–1010.

Lasserre, Frédéric. *Le Dragon et la Mer: Stratégies géopolitiques chinoises en mer de Chine du Sud.* Montréal: l'Harmattan, 1996.

La Vina, Antonio G.M. 'A Critique of Joint Implementation: A Southern Perspective'. *World Bulletin,* vol. 10, no. 5/6 (September–December 1994), pp. 1–10.

Lawson, Stephanie. 'Culture, Relativism and Democracy: Political Myths about "Asia" and the "West"'. In Richard Robison (ed.), *Pathways to Asia: The Politics of Engagement.* St Leonard's: Allen & Unwin, 1996.

Lee Lai To. 'Managing Potential Conflicts in the South China Sea: Political and Security Issues'. *Indonesian Quarterly,* vol. 18, no. 2 (1990), pp. 154–163.

—— 'ASEAN and the South China Sea Conflicts'. *Pacifica Review,* vol. 8, no. 3 (1995), pp. 531–543.

—— 'Introduction'. *Pacifica Review,* vol. 8, no. 3 (1995), pp. 417–423.

—— 'The South China Sea – China and Multilateral Dialogues'. *Security Dialogue,* vol. 30, no. 2 (1999), pp. 165–178.

—— *China and the South China Sea Dialogues.* Westport, CO: Praeger, 1999.

—— 'China, the US and the South China Sea Conflicts'. A keynote speech delivered at the Panel on the South China Sea in honour of Professor Michael Leifer, Third European Association of Southeast Asian Studies Conference, London School of Economics and Political Science, 6–8 September 2001.

Lee Seok-Soo. 'The Anatomy of the Korean Conflict'. Unpublished PhD Dissertation, University of Kentucky, Lexington, 1993.

Leifer, Michael. 'The Maritime Regime and Regional Security in East Asia'. *Pacifica Review,* vol. 4, no. 2 (1991), pp. 126–137.

—— 'Chinese Economic Reform and Security Policy: The South China Sea Connection'. *Survival,* vol. 37, no. 2 (1996), pp. 44–59.

—— 'The ASEAN Regional Forum: Extending ASEAN's Model of Regional Security'. *Adelphi Paper,* no. 302 (1996).

—— 'The ASEAN Peace Process: A Category Mistake'. *Pacifica Review,* vol. 12, no. 1 (1999), pp. 25–38.

—— *Singapore's Foreign Policy. Coping with Vulnerability.* London: Routledge, 2000, pp. 108–124.

Lewis, John Wilson and Xue Litai. *China's Strategic Seapower. The Politics of Force Modernization in the Nuclear Age.* Stanford CA: Stanford University Press, 1994.

Li Guoqiang and Kou Junmin (eds). *Hainan ji nanhai zhudao shidi lunzhu ziliao suoyin* [Documents Index on the South China Sea and Studies on its Islands]. Zhengzhou (Henan Province): Zhongzhou Guji Chubanshe, 1994.

Li Ma. 'China and Vietnam: Coping with the Threat of Peaceful Evolution'. In Carlyle A. Thayer and Ramses Amer (eds), *Vietnamese Foreign Policy in Transition.* Singapore: Institute of Southeast Asian Studies, 1999.

Li, Rex. 'China and Asia-Pacific Security in the Post-Cold War Era'. *Security Dialogue,* vol. 26, no. 3 (1995), pp. 331–344.

—— 'The Taiwan Strait Crisis and the Future of China–Taiwan Relations'. *Security Dialogue,* vol. 27, no. 4 (1996), pp. 449–458.

—— 'China in Transition: Nationalism, Regionalism and Trans-nationalism'. *Contemporary Politics,* vol. 3, no. 4 (1997), pp. 365–380.

—— 'China's Investment Environment: The Security Dimension'. *Asia Pacific Business Review,* vol. 4, no. 1 (Autumn 1997), pp. 39–62.

—— 'Unipolar Aspirations in a Multipolar Reality: China's Perceptions of US Ambitions and Capabilities in the Post-Cold War World'. *Pacifica Review,* vol. 11, no. 2 (June 1999), pp. 115–149.

—— 'Partners or Rivals? Chinese Perceptions of Japan's Security Strategy'. *Journal of Strategic Studies,* vol. 22, no. 4 (September 1999), pp. 1–25.

Liao Wen-Chung. 'China's Blue Waters Strategy in the 21st Century'. Occasional Paper Series by the Chinese Council of Advanced Policy Studies, Taipei, September 1995.

Lim Joo-jock. *Geo Strategy and the South China Sea Basin.* Singapore, 1979.

Lim, Robyn. 'The ASEAN Regional Forum: Building on Sand'. *Contemporary Southeast Asia,* vol. 20, no. 2 (1998), pp. 115–136.

Lin Cheng-yi. 'Taiwan's South China Sea Policy'. *Asian Survey,* vol. 37, no. 4 (April 1997), pp. 323–339.

Lin, Chong-Pin. 'Chinese Military Modernization: Perceptions, Progress, and Prospects'. *Security Studies,* vol. 3, no. 4 (Summer 1994), pp. 718–753.

Lin Piao. 'Long Live the Victory in the People's War'. In Walter Lacqueur (ed.), *The Guerilla Reader. A Historical Anthology.* London: Wildwood House, 1978, pp. 197–202.

Lo Chi-Kin. *China's Policy towards Territorial Disputes. The Case of the South China Sea Islands.* London: Routledge, 1989.

Lombard, Denys. 'Une autre "Méditerranée" dans le Sud-Est asiatique'. *Hérodote, revue de géographie et de géopolitique,* vol. 88, no. 1 (1998), pp. 184–193.

Low, Jeffrey K.Y., Beverly P.L. Goh and L.M. Chou. 'Regional Cooperation in Prevention and Response to Marine Pollution in the South China Sea'. Paper presented to the Second ASEAMS Scientific Symposium, UNEP, Bangkok, 1996.

Lowry, Rober.: *The Armed Forces of Indonesia.* London: Allen & Unwin, 1996.

Lu Ning. *Flashpoint Spratlys*. Singapore: Dolphin Trade Press, 1995.

Lu Yiyan (ed.). *Nanhai zhudao dili lishi zhuquan* [The South China Sea Islands. Geography, History, Sovereignty]. Harbin: Heilongjiang Jiaoyu Chubanshe, 1992.

Luu Van Loi. Cuôc tranh châp Viêt-Trung vê hai quân dao Hoàng Sa và Truong Sa [The Sino-Vietnamese Dispute over the Hoang sa and Truong Sa Island., Hanoi: Công an nhân dân [People's Security Forces], 1995.

—— *The Sino-Vietnamese Difference on the Hoang Sa and Truong Sa Archipelagos.* Hanoi: The Gioi Publishers, 1996.

Ma Ping. 'The Strategic Thinking of Active Defence and China's Military Strategic Principle'. *International Strategic Studies*, no. 1. Beijing: China Institute for International Strategic Studies, March 1994.

McDorman, Ted L. 'Thailand's Fisheries: A Victim of 200-Mile Zones'. *Ocean Development & International Law,* vol. 16, no. 2 (1986), pp. 183–209.

—— 'Implementation of the LOS Convention: Options, Impediments and the ASEAN States'. *Ocean Development & International Law,* vol. 18, no. 3 (1987), pp. 279–303.

—— 'International Fishery Relations in the Gulf of Thailand'. *Contemporary Southeast Asia,* vol. 12, no. 1 (June 1990), pp. 40–54.

—— 'The South China Sea Island Dispute in the 1990s – a New Multilateral Process and Continuing Friction'. *The International Journal of Marine and Coastal Law,* vol. 8, no. 2 (1993).

—— and Panat Tasneeyanond. 'Increasing Problems for Thailand's Fisheries: Malaysia's New Fisheries Law'. *Marine Policy* (July 1987), pp. 205–216.

McGrew, Anthony and Christopher Brook. *Asia-Pacific in the New World Order.* London: The Open University, 1998.

McGwire, Michael: *Military Objectives in Soviet Foreign Policy.* Washington, DC: The Brookings Institution, 1987.

McManus, John W. 'The Spratly Islands: A Marine Park?' *Ambio,* vol. 23, no. 3 (May 1994), pp. 181–186.

McVadon, Rear Admiral Eric A. 'China: An Opponent or an Opportunity?' *http://www.nwc.navy.mil/press/review/1996/autumn/chna-a96.htm.*

Magno, Francisco. 'Environmental Security in the South China Sea'. *Orbis,* vol. 28, no. 1 (Summer 1996), pp. 97–112.

Mahan, Alfred T. *The Influence of Sea Power upon History 1660–1783.* [1st edn 1894] New York: Dover Publications, 1987.

Mathahir bin Mohammad. *Regionalism, Globalism and Spheres of Influence.* Singapore: ISEAS, 1989.

Mak, J.N. 'The Chinese Navy and the South China Sea. A Malaysian Assessment'. *Pacifica Review,* vol. 4, no. 2 (1991), pp. 150–161.

—— 'The ASEAN Naval Buildup: Implications for the Regional Order'. *Pacifica Review,* vol. 8, no. 2 (1995), pp. 303–326.

Mak, J.N. and B.A. Hamzah. 'The External Maritime Dimension of ASEAN Security'. In Desmond Ball (ed.), *The Transformation of Security in the Asia/Pacific Region*. London: Frank Cass, 1996, pp. 123–146.

Mangahas, Maria F. 'Traditional Marine Tenure and Management in ASEAN'. *World Bulletin*, vol. 10, no. 5–6 (September–December 1994), pp. 29–40.

Manguin, Pierre Yves. 'Trading Ships of the South China Sea'. *Journal of the Economic and Social History of the Orient*, vol. 36, no. 3 (August 1993), p. 253.

Manning, Robert A. *The Asian Energy Factor.* New York: Palgrave, 2000.

Marston, Geoffrey. 'Abandonment of Territorial Claims: The Cases of Bouvet and Spratly Islands'. *British Yearbook of International Law* (1986), pp. 337–356.

Mearsheimer, John J. 'A Strategic Misstep: the Maritime Strategy and Deterrence in Europe'. *International Security*, vol. 11, no. 2 (Fall 1986), pp. 3–57.

Metzger, Thomas A. and Ramon H. Myers. 'Chinese Nationalism and American Policy'. *Orbis* (Winter 1998), pp. 21–36.

Miles, James. 'Chinese Nationalism, US Policy and Asian Security'. *Survival*, vol. 42, no. 4 (Winter 2000).

Ministry of Foreign Affairs. Joint Press Statement. *The Third Malaysia-Singapore Meeting to Submit the Case of Pedra Branca/Pulau Batu Puteh to the International Court of Justice, Kuala Lumpur, 14 April 1988*. Kuala Lumpur: Press Release, Ministry of Foreign Affairs Malaysia, 14 April 1998.

Miyoshi, Masahiro. 'The Joint Development of Offshore Oil and Gas in Relation to Maritime Boundary Delimitation'. International Boundary Research Unit's *Maritime Briefing*, vol. 2, no. 5 (1999).

Mochizuki, Michael M. 'Review Essay: The Past in Japan's Future. Will the Japanese Change?' *Foreign Affairs*, vol. 73, no. 5 (Sept–Oct 1994), pp. 126–134.

Møller, Bjørn. 'Restructuring the Naval Forces towards Non-Offensive Defence'. In Marlies ter Borg and Wim Smit (eds), *Non-provocative Defence as a Principle of Arms Control and its Implications for Assessing Defence Technologies*. Amsterdam: Free University Press, 1989, pp. 189–206.

—— 'Introduction: Defence Restructuring in Asia'. In B. Møller (ed.), *Security, Arms Control and Defence Restructuring in Asia*. Aldershot: Ashgate, 1998), pp. 1–36.

—— *Security, Arms Control and Defence Restructuring in Asia*. Aldershot: Ashgate, 1998.

—— 'From Arms to Disarmament Races: Disarmament Dynamics after the Cold War'. In Ho-Won Jeong (ed.), *The New Agenda for Peace Research*. Aldershot: Ashgate, 1999, pp. 83–104.

Möller, Kay. 'East Asian Security: Lessons from Europe'. *Contemporary Southeast Asia*, vol. 17, no. 4 (1996).

Momoki Shiro. 'Dai Viet and the South China Sea Trade from the 10th to the 15th. Century'. *Crossroads: An Interdisciplinary Journal of South East Asian Studies*, vol. 12, no. 1 (1998), pp. 1–34.

Moon Chung-in. 'Political Economy of East Asian Development and Pacific Economic Cooperation'. *Pacifica Review,* vol. 12, no. 2 (1999), pp. 199–224.

Munro, Ross H. 'Eavesdropping on the Chinese Military: Where It Expects War – Where It Doesn't'. *Orbis,* vol. 38, no. 3 (Summer 1994), pp. 355–372.

Nan Li. 'The PLA's Evolving Warfighting Doctrine, Strategy and Tactics, 1985–95: a Chinese Perspective'. *The China Quarterly,* no. 146 (June 1996), pp. 443–464.

Narine, Shaun. 'ASEAN and the ARF. The Limits of the "ASEAN Way"'. *Asian Survey,* vol. 37, no. 10 (October 1997), pp. 961–979.

—— 'ASEAN and the Management of Regional Security'. *Pacific Affairs,* vol. 11, no. 2 (Summer 1998), pp. 195–214.

Nathan, Andrew J. and Robert S. Ross. *The Great Wall and the Empty Fortress: China's Search for Security.* New York: W.W. Norton, 1997.

National Defence Report 1993–94. Taipei: Ministry of National Defence, 1994.

Nayan, Md Hussin. 'Openness and Transparency in the ASEAN Countries'. *Disarmament,* vol. 18, no. 2 (1995), pp. 135–144.

Ness, Peter Van. 'Alternative US Strategies with Respect to China and the Implications for Vietnam'. *Contemporary Southeast Asia,* vol. 20, no. 2 (August 1998), pp. 154–170.

Nghia, Quang. 'Vietnam–Kampuchea Border Issue Settled'. *Vietnam Courier,* no. 4 (1986).

Nguyen Hong Thao. 'Vietnam's First Maritime Boundary Agreement'. *Boundary and Security Bulletin,* vol. 5, no. 3 (1997).

—— *Nhung dieu can biet ve Luat Bien.* Hà Noi: Nhà Xuat Ban Công An Nhân Dân, 1997.

—— 'Vietnam and Thailand Settle Maritime Disputes in the Gulf of Thailand'. *The MIMA Bulletin,* vol. 2/98 (1998).

—— *Le Vietnam face aux problèmes de l'extension maritime dans la mer de Chine mériodinale.*Villeneuve d'Ascq: Presses Universitaires du Septentrion, 1998 (2 vols).

—— 'Exploitation conjointe dans le golfe de Thaïlande'. *Annuaire du droit de la mer 1998,* tome III. Paris: Pédone, 1999, pp. 221–234.

—— 'The China–Vietnam Border Delimitation Treaty of 30 December 1999'. *Boundary and Security Bulletin,* vol. 8, no. 1 (Spring 2000), pp. 87–90.

—— 'Vietnam and the Code of Conduct for the South China Sea'. *Ocean Development & International Law,* vol. 32, no. 2 (2001), pp. 105–130.

Noer, John H. 'Chokepoints: Maritime Economic Concerns in Southeast Asia'. Washington: National Defense University Press, 1996.

Nordhaug, Kristen. 'Explaining Taiwan's Policies in the South China Sea, 1988–1999'. *Pacifica Review,* vol. 14, no. 4 (2001), pp. 487–508.

—— (ed.). 'Konflikten om Sørkinahavet'. *Working Paper* no. 2. Oslo: Centre for Development and the Environment (SUM), 1998.

Nossum, Johan Henrik. *Straight Baselines of Vietnam.* Oslo: Centre for Development and the Environment (SUM). Dissertations & Thesis series, no. 12, 2000.

Næss, Tom. 'Environment and Security in the South China Sea Region: The Role of Experts, Non-governmental Actors and Governments in Regime Building Processes'. A thesis for the Cand. Polit. Degree at the Department of Political Science, University of Oslo, Autumn 1999. Published in the SUM Dissertations & Thesis series as no. 1/2000 (ISSN 0806-475X).

—— 'Environmental Cooperation Around the South China Sea: the Experiences of the South China Sea Workshops and the UNEP's Strategic Action Programme', *Pacifica Review,* vol. 14, no. 4(2001), pp. 553-575.

Odgaard, Liselotte. 'The Reconstruction of the East Asian Regional Order: An Analysis of the Sovereignty Disputes in the South and East China Sea'. Context paper for the 5th NEWAS at the Centre for Asian Studies, Amsterdam, 18–20 April 1997.

—— 'The Spratly Dispute and Southeast Asian Security – Towards a Pluralist Order?' Paper presented at the Fifth International Conference of International Boundaries Research Unit 'Borderlands Under Stress'. 16 July 1998.

—— 'Deterrence and Cooperation in the South China Sea. An Analysis of the Spratly Dispute and the Implications for Regional Order between the PRC and Southeast Asia after the Cold War'. PhD dissertation: Department of Political Science, University of Aarhus, Denmark, December 1999.

—— 'Deterrence and Cooperation in the South China Sea'. *Contemporary Southeast Asia,* 23: 2, August 2001, pp. 292–306.

—— 'The South China Sea: A Source of Internal Fracture or Unity in ASEAN?'. A paper presented at the Panel on the South China Sea in honour of Professor Michael Leifer, Third European Association of Southeast Asian Studies Conference, London School of Economics and Political Science, 6–8 September 2001.

—— *Maritime Security between China and Southeast Asia: Conflict and Cooperation in the Making of Regional Order.* Aldershot: Ashgate 2002.

OECD/DAC. *Conflict Peace and Development Cooperation on the Threshold of the 21st Century.* Policy statement, May 1997. Paris: OECD, 1997.

OECD/DAC 1997. *DAC Guidelines on Conflict, Peace and Development Cooperation.* Paris: OECD, 1997.

Ögütcü, Mehmet. 'China in World Energy. Its Energy Security and Evolving Links with Other Major Regional Players'. In Dominique Finon and Pierre Jacquet (eds), *Énergie, développement et sécurité.* Paris: Les cahiers de l'ifri (Institut français des relations internationales), no. 28, 1999, pp. 95–132.

Olds, Kris, Peter Dicken and Philip F. Kelly (eds). *Globalisation and the Asia-Pacific: Contested Territories.* London: Routledge/ Warwick Studies in Globalisation, 1999.

Olsen, Willy. 'What Will Be China's Oil Consumption?' Outline and facts of talk held at Centre for Development and the Environment, June 1999.

Olson, Theodore. 'Thinking Independently about Strategy in Southeast Asia'. *Contemporary Southeast Asia*, vol. 11, no. 3 (December 1989), pp. 257–282.

O'Neill, Robert. 'The Balance of Naval Power in the Pacific'. *Pacifica Review*, vol. 1, no. 2 (1998), pp. 151–163.

Østreng, Willy. 'The Politics of Continental Shelves: The South China Sea in a Comparative Perspective'. *Cooperation and Conflict*, vol. 20, no. 4 (1985), pp. 253–277.

Oxman, Bernhard H. 'Law of the Sea'. In Oscar Schachter and Christopher C. Joyner (eds), *United Nations Legal Order*. Cambridge: Grotius Publications/Cambridge University Press, 1995, vol. 2, pp. 671–714.

Paal, Douglas H. 'The Regional Security Implications of China's Economic Expansion, Military Modernization, and the Rise of Nationalism'. In Hung-mao Tien and Tun-jen Cheng (eds), *The Security Environment in the Asia-Pacific*. Armonk, NY: M.E. Sharpe, 2000, pp. 79–91.

Paik Keun-Wook and Jae-Yong Choi. 'Pipeline Gas in Northeast Asia: Recent Developments and Regional Perspective'. *Briefing Paper, The Royal Institute of International Affairs, Energy and Environmental Programme*, no. 39 (January 1998).

Pan Shiying. 'The Nansha Islands: A Chinese Point of View'. *Window* (3 September 1993).

—— *The Petropolitics of the Nansha Islands. China's Indisputable Legal Case.* (in Chinese and English). Beijing: Economic Information and Agency, 1996.

Park Choon-Ho. 'The South China Sea Disputes: Who Owns the Islands and the Natural Resources?' *Ocean Development & International Law*, vol. 5, no. 1 (1978), pp. 27–59.

—— *East Asia and the Law of the Sea*. Seoul: Seoul National University Press, 1983.

—— 'Oil Development in the China Seas'. *Asian Economies*, (September 1984), pp. 5–26.

Park Choon-Ho and Hungdah Chiu. 'Legal Status of the Paracel and Spratly Islands'. *Ocean Development & International Law Journal*, vol. 3, no. 1 (1995), pp. 1–28.

Park Hee Kwon. *The Law of the Sea and Northeast Asia*. The Hague: Kluwer, 2000.

Picault, Raoul. *L'honorable partie de Vietnam*. Paris: l'Harmattan, 1997.

Pilcher, N., S. Oakley and G. Ismail. *Layang Layang: A Drop in the Ocean*. Borneo: Natural History Publications, 1999.

Pluvier, Jan. 'The Silence of the South China Sea'. *Partisan Scholarship Essays in Honour of Renato Constantino*, (1989), pp. 382–393.

Pollack, Jonathan D. 'The Future of China's Nuclear Weapons Policy'. In John C. Hopkins and Weixing Hu (eds), *Strategic Views from the Second*

Tier. The Nuclear Weapons Policies of France, Britain and China. New Brunswick: Transaction Publishers, 1996, pp. 157–166.

Pratt, Martin. 'Whose Oil Is It Anyway? International Boundaries and Hydrocarbon Production'. *Petroleum Review* (February 1998), pp. 34–36.

Prescott, J.R.V. *Boundaries and Frontiers.* London: Croom Helm, 1978:132–166.

—— *The Maritime Political Boundaries of the World.* London: Methuen, 1985, pp. 209–233.

—— *The South China Sea: Limits of National Claims,* MIMA Paper. Kuala Lumpur: Maritime Institute of Malaysia (MIMA), 1996.

—— *The Gulf of Thailand.* Kuala Lumpur: Maritime Institute of Malaysia (MIMA), 1998.

Ptak, Roderich. 'Die Paracel- und Spratly-Inseln in Sung-, Yüan- und frühen Ming-Texten: Ein maritimes Grenzgebiet?' In Sabine Dabringham and Roderich Ptak (eds), *China and Her Neighbours: Borders, Visions of the Other, Foreign Policy. 10th to 19th Century.* Wiesbaden: Harrassowitz Verlag, 1997.

—— 'From Quanzhou to the Sulu Zone and Beyond: Questions Related to the Early Fourteenth Century'. *Journal of Southeast Asian Studies,* vol. 29, no. 2 (September 1998), pp. 269–294.

Pugh, Michael. 'Maritime Disputes in the China Seas'. The World in Conflict 1994/95, *Jane's Intelligence Review Yearbook,* pp. 107–110.

Punal, Antonio Martinez. 'The Rights of Land-Locked and Geographically Disadvantaged States in Exclusive Economic Zones'. *Journal of Maritime Law and Commerce,* vol. 23, no. 3 (July 1992), pp. 429–459.

Quan Lan and Keun-Wook Paik. *China Natural Gas Report.* China OGP, Xinhua News Agency and Royal Institute of International Affairs, Selwood Printing, Great Britain, 1998.

Raisson, Virginie. 'Eaux troubles entre Jakarta et Pékin: la question des Natuna'. *Hérodote, revue de géographie et de géopolitique,* no. 88, 1/1998, pp. 109–124.

Rajendran, M. *ASEAN's Foreign Relations. The Shift to Collective Action.* Kuala Lumpur: Arenabuku Sdn. Bhd., 1985.

Rappai, M.V. 'China's Quest for Blue Waters'. *Strategic Analysis* (December 1998), pp. 1329–1340.

—— 'South China Sea: Conflict and Cooperation'. *Asian Strategic Review 1996–97.* New Delhi: IDSA, 1997.

Rau, Robert. 'Present and Future Maritime Security Issues in the Southeast Asian and the South China Seas'. *Contemporary Southeast Asia,* vol. 8, no. 1 (June 1986), pp. 37–55.

Reid, Anthony. 'Marchands et hommes d'affaries asiatiques dans l'Océan Indien et la Mer de Chine' (book review), *Journal of Southeast Asian Studies* (March 1990), pp. 202–204.

Renwick, Neil and Jason Abbott. 'Piratical Violence and Maritime Security in Southeast Asia'. *Security Dialogue,* vol. 30, no. 2 (1999), pp. 183–196.

Republic of China. 'Law on the Territorial Sea and the Contiguous Zone of the Republic of China'. Promulgated on January 21, 1998.

Rice University. 'China and Long-range Asia Energy Security: An Analysis of the Political, Economic and Technological Factors Shaping Asian Energy Markets'. *Working Paper April 1999*. Prepared in conjunction with the Center for International Political Economy and the James A. Baker III Institute for Public Policy. *http://riceinfo.rice.edu/projects/baker/*.

Richardson, Michael. 'In Asia, a New Mutual Defense – US to Offer Aid in Return for Access to Local Bases'. *International Herald Tribune,* 3 December 1998, pp. 1, 4.

—— 'Philippines is Stymied in Dispute with China'. *International Herald Tribune,* 21 January 1999, p. 4.

—— 'On Eve of Annual Talks, ASEAN Members Are Split over Spratly Dispute'. *International Herald Tribune,* 23 July 1999, p. 6.

Riedel, Eibe. 'Standards and Sources. Farewell to the Exclusivity of the Sources Triad in International Law?' *European Journal of International Law,* vol. 2, no. 2 (1991).

Rodell, Paul A. 'Historical Legacies and Contemporary ASEAN–PRC Relations'. In William P. Head and Edwin G. Clausen (eds), *Weaving a New Tapestry – Asia in the Post-Cold War World: Case Studies and General Trends.* London: Praeger, 1999.

Roper, Christopher T. 'Sino–Vietnamese Relations and the Economy Of Vietnam's Border Region'. *Foreign Affairs,* vol. 40, no. 6 (2000).

Rosen, Stephen Peter. *Societies and Military Power: India and Its Armies.* Ithaca: Cornell University Press, 1996.

Rosenberg, David. 'Environmental Pollution around the South China Sea: Developing a Regional Response'. *Contemporary South East Asia,* vol. 21, no. 1 (April 1999), pp. 119–145.

Ross, Robert S. 'The Geography of the Peace: East Asia in the Twenty-first Century'. *International Security,* vol. 23, no. 4 (Spring 1999).

Ross, Robert S. and Andrew J. Nathan. *The Great Wall and the Empty Fortress.* New York: Norton, 1997.

Rothwell, Donald R. 'International Straits and UNCLOS: An Australian Case Study'. *Journal of Maritime Law and Commerce,* vol. 23, no. 3 (July 1992), pp. 461–483.

Roy, Danny. 'Tensions in the Taiwan Strait'. *Survival,* vol. 42, no. 1 (2000), pp. 76–96.

Rozman, Gilbert. 'China's Quest for Great Power Identity'. *Orbis,* vol. 43, no. 3 (Summer 1999), pp. 383–402.

—— 'A New Sino-Russian-American Triangle?' *Orbis,* vol. 44, no. 4 (Fall 2000).

Salameh, Mamdouh. 'China, Oil and the Risk of Regional Conflict'. *Survival,* vol. 37, no. 4 (Winter 1995–96), pp. 133–146.

Samuels, Marwyn. *Contest for the South China Sea.* New York: Methuen, 1982.

Samuels, Richard J. *'Rich Nation, Strong Army'. National Security and the Technological Transformation of Japan.* Ithaca, NY: Cornell University Press, 1994.

Sandvand, John E. 'Seks land krangler om retten til forblåste skjær i Sør-Kina-havet'. *Aftenposten,* 2 June 2000.

Sanger, Clyde. *Ordering the Oceans. The Making of the Law of the Sea.* Toronto: University of Toronto Press, 1987.

Sarasin Viraphol and Werner Pfenning (eds), *ASEAN–UN Cooperation in Preventive Diplomacy.* Bangkok: Ministry of Foreign Affairs, 1995.

Sasae, Kenichiro. 'Rethinking Japan–US Relations'. *Adelphi Paper,* no. 292 (1994).

Schelling, Thomas. *The Strategy of Conflict.* Cambridge, MA: Harvard University Press, 1960.

Scherer, Sabine. 'La stratégie expansioniste chinoise en mer de Chine du Sud'. *Défense Nationale* (1997), pp. 105–122.

Schofield, Clive. 'A Code of Conduct for the South China Sea?' *Jane's Intelligence Review* (1 November 2000).

—— 'Sea of Plenty? The "Oil Factor" in the South China Sea and Prospects for Joint Development'. A paper at the Panel on the South China Sea in honour of Professor Michael Leifer, Third European Association of Southeast Asian Studies Conference, London School of Economics and Political Science, 6–8 September 2001.

Schultz, Clifford J. and William J. Ardrey. 'The Future Prospects of Sino–Vietnamese Relations: Are Trade and Commerce the Critical Factors for Sustainable Peace?' *Contemporary Southeast Asia,* vol. 17, no. 2 (September 1995), pp. 126–146.

Schwennesen, Olaf. *China sticht in See: Die Spratly-Inseln als Konfliktherd im südchinesischen Meer.* Frankfurt a.M.: Lang, 1996.

Scobell, Andrew and Larry M. Wortzel. *The Asia-Pacific in the U.S. National Security Calculus for a New Millenium.* Carlisle, Pennsylvania: Strategic Studies Institute (March 2000). http://carlisle-www.army.mil/usassi/welcome.htm.

Scovazzi, Tullio. 'Historic Waters, Marine Environment, Scientific Research and Settlement of Disputes'. *Publications on Ocean Development,* Volume 19 (1993), pp. 321–331.

SEAPOL International Conference: Report of the Rapporteurs on the Technical Workshop (26–28 April 1987). *Marine Policy.* (January 1988), pp. 55–66.

Setboonsargn, Suthad. 'ASEAN Economic Cooperation: Adjusting to the Crisis'. *Southeast Asia Affairs 1998.* Singapore: Institute of Southeast Asian Affairs, 1998, pp. 18–36.

Segal, Gerald. 'The Coming Confrontation between China and Japan?'. *World Policy Journal,* vol. 10, no. 2 (Summer 1993), pp. 27–32.

—— 'Tying China to the International System'. *Survival,* vol. 37, no. 2 (Summer 1995), pp. 60–73.

Shambaugh, David. 'China's Military Views the World: Ambivalent Security'. *International Security,* vol. 24, no. 3 (Winter 1999/2000), pp. 52–79.

—— 'Sino-American Strategic Relations: From Partners to Competitors'. *Survival,* vol. 42, no. 1 (2000), pp. 97–115.

Shaw, Malcolm N. *International Law.* Third Edition. Cambridge: Grotius Publications, 1991, pp. 337–392.

Shee Poon Kim. 'China's Strategic Thinking and Policies towards the South China Sea'. Paper prepared for the World Congress of the International Political Science Association, Seoul, 17–21 August 1997.

—— 'The South China Sea in China's Strategic Thinking'. *Contemporary Southeast Asia,* vol. 19, no. 4 (March 1998), pp. 368–387.

—— 'Is China a Threat to the Asia-Pacific Region?' In Wang Gungwu and John Wong (eds), *China's Political Economy.* Singapore: Singapore University Press, 1998, pp. 339–359.

—— 'Cross-Strait Impasse: One Country Two Systems or One Country Three Systems?' *EIA Working Paper,* no. 25. Singapore: National University of Singapore, 1999.

Shee Poon Kim and Zou Keyuan. 'The Scarborough Reef: Political, Strategic, Security and Legal Implications for Sino-Philippine Relations'. *East Asian Institute Background Brief,* no. 22 (29 September 1998).

Sheng Lijun. *China's Policy towards the Spratly Islands in the 1990s.* Working Paper, no. 287. Canberra: Strategic and Defence Studies Centre, The Australian National University, June 1995.

—— 'Beijing and the Spratlys'. *Issues & Studies,* vol. 31, no. 7 (July 1995), pp. 18–45.

—— 'Ice Across the Taiwan Strait'. *Far Eastern Economic Review,* 29 January 1998, p. 28.

—— 'China Eyes Taiwan: Why Is a Breakthrough So Difficult?' *The Journal of Strategic Studies,* vol. 21, no. 1 (March 1998), pp. 65–78.

—— 'China and the United States: Asymmetrical Strategic Partners'. *The Washington Quarterly,* vol. 22, no. 3 (Summer 1999), pp. 147–164.

Shepard, Allan. 'Maritime Tensions in the South China Sea and the Neighborhood: Some Solutions'. *Studies of Conflict and Terrorism,* vol. 17 (April–June 1994), pp. 181–211.

Shichor, Yitzhak. 'Demobilization: The Dialectics of PLA Troop Reduction'. In Brömmelhörster, Jörn and John Frankenstein (eds), *Mixed Motives, Uncertain Outcomes. Defense Conversion in China.* Boulder, CO: Lynne Rienner, 1997, pp. 336–359.

Shulong Chu. 'The PRC Girds for Limited, High-Tech War'. *Orbis,* vol. 38, no. 2 (Spring 1994), pp. 177–191.

Simon, Sheldon W. 'Security Prospects in Southeast Asia: Collaborative Efforts and the ASEAN Regional Forum'. *Pacifica Review,* vol. 11, no. 2 (1998), pp. 195–212.

—— 'Davids and Goliaths: Small Power – Great Power Relations in Southeast Asia'. *Asian Survey,* vol. 23, no. 3 (1983), pp. 302–315.

—— 'US Strategy and Southeast Asian Security: Issues of Compatibility'. *Contemporary Southeast Asia,* vol. 14, no. 4 (1993), pp. 301–313.

—— 'Asian Armed Forces: Internal and External Tasks and Capabilities'. *NBR Analysis,* vol. 11, no. 1 (May 2000).

Simone, Vera. 'Economic Reform and China as a Regional Power with Global Aspirations'. Paper prepared for the World Congress of the International Political Science association, Seoul, 17–21 August 1997.

Singh, Jasjit. 'Future Directions of India's Defence Policy'. *Strategic Digest.* New Delhi: Institute for Defence Studies and Analyses, vol. 26, no. 5 (May 1996), pp. 605–612.

Singh, Swaran. 'Sino-Myanmar Military Ties: Implications for India's Security'. *U.S.I. Journal*, vol. 125, no. 521 (July–September 1995), pp. 348–357.

Singh, Udai Bhanu. 'Vietnam's Security Perspectives'. *Strategic Analysis*, vol. 23, no. 9 (December 1999), pp. 1489–1491.

—— 'Recent Trends in Relations between Myanmar and China'. *Strategic Analysis*, vol. 18, no. 1 (April 1995), pp. 61–72.

Smith, Chris. *India's ad hoc Arsenal. Directions or Drift in Defence Policy?* Oxford: Oxford University Press/SIPRI, 1994.

Smith, Esmond. 'China's Aspirations in the Spratly Islands'. *Contemporary Southeast Asia*, vol. 16, no. 3 (December 1994), pp. 274–294.

Smith, Robert W. and Bradford L. Thomas. 'Island Disputes and the Law of the Sea: An Examination of Sovereignty and Delimitation Disputes'. International Boundaries Research Unit's *Maritime Briefing*, vol. 2, no. 4 (1998).

Snildal, Knut. 'Petroleum in the South China Sea – a Chinese National Interest?' A thesis for the Cand. Polit. Degree at the Department of Political Science, University of Oslo, 2000.

—— 'Petroleum in the South China Sea – a Chinese National Interest?' SUM Dissertation and Thesis Series, No 8/2000.

Snitwongse, Kusuma. 'Achievements through Cooperation'. *Pacifica Review*, vol. 11, no. 2 (1998), pp. 183–194.

—— 'ASEAN's Security Cooperation: Searching for Regional Order'. *Pacifica Review*, vol. 8, no. 3 (1995), pp. 518–530.

Sogiarto, Aprilani. 'The South China Sea: Its Ecological Features and Potential for Developing Cooperation'. *Indonesian Quarterly*, vol. 18, no. 2 (1990), pp. 116–126.

Soligo, Jaffe. 'China and Long-range Asia Energy Security: An Analysis of the Political,Economic and Technological Factors Shaping Asian Energy Markets'. hhttp://riceinfo.rice.edu/projects/naker/publications/claes/CPIs/cpis.html.

Song Yann-Huei. 'China's "Historic Waters"' in the South China Sea: An Analysis From Taiwan, ROC'. *American Asian Review*, vol. 12, no. 4 (Winter 1994), pp. 83–101.

—— 'Indonesia in the New Asia Pacific Order'. *The Indonesian Quarterly*, vol. XXV, no. 3 (third quarter 1997), pp. 316–334.

—— 'Managing Potential Conflicts in the South China Sea. Taiwan's Perspective'. *East Asian Institute Occasional Paper*, no. 14 (1999).

Song Yann-Huei, Billy. 'China's Marine Policy: EEZ and Marine Policy'. *Asian Survey*, vol. 24, no. 10 (1989), pp. 983–998.

—— 'Shipping and Shipbuilding Policies in PR China'. *Marine Policy* (January 1990), pp. 53–70.

South China Morning Post. 'New Vietnamese Decree Fuels Territorial Disputes', 12 June 1999.

South China Sea Informal Working Group. 'The First Meeting of the Technical Working Group on Marine Environmental Protection in the South China Sea'. Hangzhou, 6–8 October 1994.

—— 'The First Group of Experts Meeting on Biological Diversity in the South China Sea'. Cebu, Philippines, 18–20 July 1996.

—— 'The Second Meeting of the Technical Working Group on Safety of Navigation, Shipping and Communication in the South China Sea'. Bandar Seri Begawan, Brunei, Darussalam, 29 October–2 November 1996.

—— 'The Second Meeting of the Technical Working Group on Marine Environmental Protection in the South China Sea'. Haikou, 13–16 October 1997.

St John, Ronald Bruce. 'The Land Boundaries of Indochina: Cambodia, Laos and Vietnam'. International Boundary Research Unit's *Boundary and Territory Briefing*, vol. 2, no. 6 (1998).

Statement by the ASEAN Foreign Ministers on the Recent Development in the South China Sea, 18 March 1995. Available at http://www.aseansec.org.

Stenseth, Leni. *Nationalism and Foreign Policy: The Case of China's Nansha Rhetoric.* A thesis for the Cand. Polit. Degree at the Department of Political Science, University of Oslo, December 1998.

—— 'The Imagined Threat of China in the South China Sea: A Rejoinder'. *Security Dialogue*, vol. 30, no. 3 (September 1999), pp. 347–351.

Stone, Eric. 'The Good Life is Slow to Come to Hainan'. *Asian Finance*, 15 August 1989, pp. 52–57, 70.

Storey, Ian James. 'Creeping Assertiveness: China, the Philippines and the South China Sea Dispute'. *Contemporary Southeast Asia*, vol. 21, no. 1 (April 1999), pp. 95–118.

—— 'Manila Looks to USA for Help over Spratlys'. *Jane's Intelligence Review*, vol. 11, no. 8 (August 1999), pp. 46–50. http://www.janes.com/geopol/editors/china/china_manilla.html

—— 'Living with the Colossus: How Southeast Asian Countries Cope with China'. *Parameters* , vol. XXIX, no. 4 (Winter 1999), pp. 111–125. Downloaded from http://carlisle-www.army.mil/usawc/parameters/99winter/storey.htm

—— 'Indonesia's China Policy in the New Order and Beyond: Problems and Prospects'. *Contemporary Southeast Asia*, vol. 22, no. 1 (April 2000), pp. 145–174.

Stormont, W.G. 'Managing Potential Conflicts in the South China Sea'. Report, *Marine Policy*, vol. 18, no. 4 (July 1994), pp. 353–356.

Studeman, Lieutenant Michael. 'Calculating China's Advances in the South China Sea – Identifying the Triggers of "Expansionism"'. http://www.nwc.navy.mil/press/Review/1998/spring/art5-sp8.htm.

Suárez, Thomas. *Early Mapping of Southeast Asia.* Singapore: Periplus, 1999.

Suisheng Zhao. 'Chinese Intellectuals' Quest for National Greatness and Nationalistic Writing in the 1990s'. *The China Quarterly,* no. 152 (1997), pp. 725–745.

—— 'China's Periphery Policy and Its Asian Neighbors'. *Security Dialogue,* vol. 30, no. 3 (1999), pp. 335–346.

Sukma, Rizal. 'Indonesia and South China Sea Interests and Policies'. *Indonesian Quarterly,* vol. 20, no. 4 (1992), pp. 395–404.

Sun Kuan-Ming. 'Policy of the Republic of China towards the South China Sea. Recent Developments'. *Marine Policy,* vol. 19, no. 5 (1995), pp. 401–409.

—— 'Freeze the Tropical Seas. An Ice-cool Prescription for the Burning Spratly Issues!' *Marine Policy,* vol. 20, no. 3 (1996), pp. 199–208.

—— 'The Republic of China's Policy Towards the South China Sea: A Review'. *Issues & Studies* (March 1996).

Sutter, Karen M. 'China's Vietnam Policy: The Road to Normalization and Prospects for the Sino-Vietnamese Relationship'. *Journal of Northeast Asian Studies,* vol. XII, no. 2 (Spring 1993), pp. 21–47.

Swaine, Michael D. and Ashley J. Tellis. *Interpreting China's Grand Strategy. Past, Present, and Future.* Santa Monica, CA: RAND, 2000.

Swedish Foreign Ministry 1999. *Preventing Violent Conflict – A Swedish Action Plan.* Ds. 1999:24, The Printing Works of the Government Offices, Stockholm.

Symmons, Clive. 'Some Problems Relating to the Definition of "Insular Formations" in International Law: Islands and Low-tide Elevations'. International Boundaries Research Unit's *Maritime Briefing,* vol. 1, no. 5 (1995).

Sæther, Elin. 'Nasjonalisme og bruk av *de andre* i kinesisk identitets-konstruksjon'. [Nationalism and the use of *the others* in Chinese construction of identity]. Dissertation for the Cand. Polit degree at the University of Oslo, 2000.

Tamamoto, Masaru. 'The Japan That Wants to Be Liked: Society and International Participation'. In Danny Unger and Paul Blackburn (eds), *Japan's Emerging Global Role.* Boulder, CO: Lynne Rienner, 1993, pp. 37–54.

Tangsubkul, Phiphat. 'The Spratlys Dispute: Is there a Multilateral Solution?' Paper prepared for the Conference on Comprehensive Security and Multilateralism in the Post-Cold War East Asia, Seoul, Korea, 12–14 November 1998.

Tanji, Miyume and Stephanie Lawson. '"Democratic Peace" and "Asian Democracy": A Universalist-Particularist Tension'. *Alternatives,* vol. 22 (1997), pp. 133–155.

Thayer, Carlyle A. 'Sino-Chinese Relations: The Interplay of Ideology and National Interests'. *Asian Survey,* vol. 34, no. 6 (1994), pp. 513–528.

Thongchai Winichakul. *Siam Mapped. A History of the Geo-body of a Nation.* Honolulu: University of Hawaii Press, 1994.

Tien Hung-Mao and Cheng Tun-jen (eds). *The Security Environment in the Asia-Pacific*. Studies of the Institute for National Policy Research. Armonk: East Gate Book, 2000.

Till, Geoffrey. 'China, Its Navy and the South China Sea'. *The RUSI Journal*, vol. 141, no. 2 (April 1996), pp. 45–51.

Tønnesson, Stein. 'Konflikten i Sør-Kina-havet'. *Hvor hender det?* no. 29–30 (1997–98).

—— 'Resolving the South China Sea Conflict'. Paper presented at the Workshop on the South China Sea Conflict, Centre for Development and the Environment, University of Oslo, 24–26 April 1999.

—— 'Can Conflicts Be Solved by Shelving Disputes? A Rejoinder'. *Security Dialogue*, vol. 30, no. 2 (June 1999), pp. 179–182.

—— 'Vietnam's Aim in the South China Sea: National or Regional Security?' *Contemporary Southeast Asia*, vol. 22, no. 1 (April 2000), pp. 199–220.

—— 'An International History of the South China Sea'. *EIA Working Paper*, no. 71. Singapore: National University of Singapore, 2000.

—— 'Human and Regional Security around the South China Sea'. Report on workshop held in Oslo, 2–4 June 2000.

—— 'Can China Resolve the Conflict in the South China Sea?' Singapore: East Asian Institute Working Paper, no. 39 (2000).

—— 'Here's How to Settle Rocky Disputes in the South China Sea'. *International Herald Tribune*, 6 September 2000.

—— 'Settling South China Sea Disputes'. *The Straits Times*, 7 September 2000.

—— 'China and the South China Sea: a Peace Proposal'. *Security Dialogue*, vol. 31, no. 3 (September 2000), pp. 307–326.

—— 'Det Sydkinesiske Hav, historie'. *Den Danske Nationalencyklopædi*, vol. 18 (2000), pp. 399–400.

—— 'Introduction'. Special issue of *Ocean Development & International Law*, vol. 32, no. 2 (2001), pp. 93–96.

—— 'Sino-Vietnamese Relations and the South China Sea'. A paper at the Panel on the South China Sea in honour of Professor Michael Leifer, Third European Association of Southeast Asian Studies Conference, London School of Economics and Political Science, 6–8 September 2001.

Townsend-Gault, Ian. 'Has There Been an Inadvertent Abandonment of Historically-based Jurisdictional Claims in the South China Sea?'. A paper at the Panel on the South China Sea in honour of Professor Michael Leifer, Third European Association of Southeast Asian Studies Conference, London School of Economics and Political Science, 6–8 September 2001.

—— 'Legal and Political Perspectives on Sovereignty over the Spratly Islands'. Paper prepared for the Workshop on the South China Sea Conflict, organised by the Centre for Development and the Environment, University of Oslo, 24–26 April 1999.

—— 'Testing the Waters: Making Progress in the South China Sea'. *Harvard International Review*, vol. 16, no. 2 (1994), pp. 16–19.

—— 'Preventive Diplomacy and Pro-activity in the South China Sea'. *Contemporary Southeast Asia*, vol. 20, no. 2 (1998), pp. 171–189.

—— 'Letters to the Editor – Oil and the Lack of it in the South China Sea'. *Contemporary South East Asia*, vol. 21, no. 1 (April 1999), pp. 153–156.

'Treaty on the Southeast Asia Nuclear-Weapon-Free Zone'. *Strategic Digest*, vol. 26, no. 3. New Delhi: IDSA, 1996), pp. 320–328.

Tréglodé, Benoît de. 'UN théâtre d'ombres: le Vietnam entre la Chine et l'ASEAN au lendemain de la crise asiatique'. Paris: Les Études du CERI (Centre d'études et de recherches internationales), no. 68 (August 2000).

Tretiak, Daniel. 'The Sino-Japanese Treaty of 1978: The Senkaku Incident Prelude'. *Asian Survey*, vol. 18, no. 12 (December 1978), pp. 1235–1249.

Trood, Russell. 'The Asia Pacific Region, Economics and New Concepts of Security'. In Hadi Soesastro and Anthony Bergin (eds.), *The Role of Economic Cooperation Structures in the Asia Pacific Region*. Jakarta and Canberra: CSIS and ADSC (1996), pp. 119–120.

Tuan, Hoang Anh. 'ASEAN Dispute Management: Implications for Vietnam and an Expanded ASEAN'. *Contemporary Southeast Asia*, vol. 18, no. 1 (June 1996), pp. 61–80.

—— 'Vietnam Membership in ASEAN: Economic, Political and Security Implications'. *Contemporary Southeast Asia*, vol. 16, no. 3 (December 1996), pp. 259–273.

UNDP. *UNDP in Crisis, Post-Conflict and Recovery Situations*. UNDP, New York, forthcoming.

UNEP. Strategic Action Programme for the South China Sea, Draft Version 3. http://www.roap.unep.org/easrcu/publication/sapV3.doc [03.01.2001].

UNCLOS (United Nations Convention on the Law of the Sea). Den Norske Stat, Det Kgl. Norske Utenriksdepartement. 'Overenskomster med fremmede stater – De Forente Nasjoners havrettskonvensjon'. *Overenskomster med fremmede stater 1996*, pp. 670–1130.

United Nations, Office for Ocean Affairs and the Law of the Sea. *Baselines: An Examination of the Relevant Provisions of the United Nations Convention on the Law of the Sea*. New York: United Nations, 1989.

—— *Baselines: National Legislation with Illustrative Maps*. New York: United Nations, 1989.

US Department of State. 'Straight Baselines: Vietnam'. *Limits in the Seas*, no. 99 (12 December 1983).

—— 'Developing Standard Guidelines for Evaluating Straight Baselines'. *Limits in the Seas*, no. 106 (31 August 1987).

—— 'Straight Baseline Claim: China'. *Limits in the Seas*, no. 117 (9 July 1996).

—— 'The United States Security Strategy for the East Asia-Pacific Region 1998'. *Defense Link*, http://www.defenselink.mil/pubs/east98/.

Usman, Asnani and Rizal Sukma. *Konflik laut Cina Selatan. Tantangan bagi ASEAN.* Jakarta: Centre for Strategic and International Studies, 1997.

Utrikesdepartementet. *Framtid med Asien: Förslag till en Svensk Asienstrategi, pp. 81–82,* Stockholm: Utrikesdepartementet, 1998.

Valencia, Mark J. 'Vietnam: Fisheries and Navigation Policies and Issues'. *Ocean Development & International Law,* vol. 21 (1990), pp. 431–445.

—— *Malaysia and the Law of the Sea.* Kuala Lumpur: Institute of Strategic and International Studies Malaysia (ISIS), 1991.

—— 'Spratly Solution Still at Sea'. *Pacifica Review,* vol. 6, no. 2 (1993), pp. 155–170.

—— 'Troubled Waters: Disputes in the South China Sea'. *Harvard International Review,* vol. 16, no. 2 (1994), pp. 12–15.

—— 'China and the South China Sea Dispute. Conflicting Claims and Potential Solutions in the South China Sea'. *Adelphi Paper,* no. 298. Oxford: Oxford University Press, 1995.

—— 'The Spratly Imbroglio in the Post-Cold War Era'. In David Wurfel and Bruce Burton (eds.), *South East Asia in the New World Order; The Political Economy of a Dynamic Region.* New York: St Martin's Press, 1996, pp. 244–269.

—— 'Troubled Waters: Oil is Only One Reason for Asia's Many-sided Dispute over Tiny, Uninhabitable Islands'. *Bul-Atomic Scientists,* vol. 53 (Jan/Feb 1997), pp. 49–54.

Valencia, Mark. 'Joining up with Japan to Patrol Asian Waters'. *International Herald Tribune,* 28 April 2000.

Valencia, Mark. 'Beijing Is Setting the Stage for Trouble in the South China Sea'. *International Herald Tribune,* 3 July 2000.

Valencia, Mark. 'Regional Maritime Regime Building: Prospects in Northeast and Southeast Asia'. *Ocean Development & International Law,* no. 31 (2000), pp. 223–247.

Valencia, Mark and George Kent. *Marine Policy in Southeast Asia.* Berkeley: University of California Press, 1985.

Valencia, Mark J. and James Barney Marsh. 'Access to Straits and Sea-lanes in Southeast Asian States: Legal, Economic and Strategic Considerations'. *Journal of Maritime Law and Commerce,* vol. 16, no. 4 (October 1985), pp. 513–551.

Valencia, Mark J. and Jon M. Van Dyke. 'Vietnam's National Interest and the Law of the Sea'. *Ocean Development & International Law,* vol. 25 (1994), pp. 217–250.

—— 'Comprehensive Solutions to the South China Sea Disputes: Some Options'. In Gerald Blake, Martin Pratt, Clive Schofield and Janet Allison (eds), *Boundaries and Energy: Problems and Prospects.* London: Kluwer Law International, 1998, pp. 85–117.

Valencia, Mark, Jon Van Dyke and Noel Ludwig. *Sharing the Resources of the South China Sea.* The Hague: Martinus Nijhoff, 1997. (paperback edition: University of Hawaii Press, 1999).

Valero, Gerardo M.C. 'Spratly Archipelago Dispute. Is the Question of Sovereignty Still Relevant?' Queson City: Institute of International Legal Studies, 1993.

—— 'Spratly Archipelago Dispute. Is the Question of Sovereignty Still Relevant?' *Marine Policy*, vol. 18, no. 4 (1994), pp. 314–344.

Vanderzwaag, Davis and Douglas M. Johnston. 'Toward the Management of the Gulf of Thailand: Charting the Course of Cooperation'. In Douglas M. Johnston (ed.), *SEAPO Integrated Studies of the Gulf of Thailand*, vol. 1. Bangkok: Innomedia, 1998.

Väyrynen, Raimo. 'Regional Conflict Formations: An Intractable Problem of International Relations'. *Journal of Peace Research*, vol. 21, no. 4 (1984), pp. 337–359.

Vietnam, Socialist Republic of. *The Truth About Vietnam–China Relations over the Past 30 Years – Unofficial translation.* Ministry of Foreign Affairs, October 1979.

—— *Vietnam's Sovereignty over the Hoang Sa and Truong Sa Archipelagoes.* Hanoi: Information and Press Department, Ministry of Foreign Affairs, 1979.

—— *On the Vietnamese Foreign Ministry's White Book Concerning Vietnam–China Relations. By Peoples Daily and Xinhua News Agency Commentators.* Beijing: Foreign Languages Press, 1979.

—— *The Hoang Sa and Truong Sa Archipelagoes (Paracels and Spratlys).* Hanoi: Vietnam Courier, 1981.

—— *The Hoang Sa and Truong Sa Archipelagoes and International Law.* Hanoi: Ministry of Foreign Affairs, April 1988.

—— *For a Negotiated Settlement of the Hoang Sa Truong Sa (Paracels – Spratly) Affair.* Published by Vietnamese Studies, Hanoi 1988.

—— 'Joint Statement on the Fourth Annual Bilateral Consultations between the Republic of the Philippines and the Socialist Republic of Vietnam'. Hanoi, 7 November 1995.

Vinita Sukrasep. *ASEAN in International Relations.* Bangkok: Institute of Security and International Studies, Faculty of Political Science, Chulalongkorn University, 1989.

Wain, Barry. 'A Code of Conduct in the South China Sea'. *Asian Wall Street Journal*, 10–11 March 2000.

—— 'At Loggerheads with Beijing. A regional code of conduct would do little to change the volatile relations that make the South China Sea a potential flashpoint'. *Asian Wall Street Journal*, 6 October 2000.

Wallensteen, Peter and Niklas Swanström. 'Asien: Framtid i fred eller konflikt?' *Asian Studies*, no. 13. The Asia Strategy Project, Ministry for Foreign Affairs, April 1998.

Walt, Stephen M. *The Origins of Alliances.* Ithaca, NY: Cornell University Press, 1979.

Wanandi, Jusuf. 'The Future of ARF and CSCAP in the Regional Security Architecture'. In Jusuf Wanandi (ed.), *Regional Security Arrangements.* Jakarta: CSIS, 1996.

Wang Gungwu. *The Nanhai Trade. The Early History of Chinese Trade in the South China Sea*. Singapore: Times Academic Press, 1998 (reprint of the 1958 edition).

Wang, Haijiang. 'China's Oil Policy and its Impact'. *Energy Policy*, vol. 23, no. 7 (1995), pp. 627–635.

Wang Kuang-Hsiung. 'Bridge Over Troubled Waters: Fisheries Cooperation as a Resolution to the South China Sea Conflicts', *Pacifica Review*, vol. 14, no. 4(2001), pp. 531–551.

Wang Liyu and Peter H. Pearse. 'The Legal Regime for China's Territorial Seas'. *Ocean Development & International Law*, vol. 25 (1994), pp. 431–442.

Wang Peiyun and Liang Hongguang. 'The Wealth of Our Nansha' [Chinese text].

Wang, Shaoguang: 'The Military Expenditure of China, 1989–98'. *SIPRI Yearbook 1999*, 2000, pp. 334–350.

Wang Yixuan and Wei Taoyuan. 'The Energy Account in China – A Technical Documentation'. *Statistics Norway*, vol. 7 (February 1999).

Weeks, Stanley B. and Charles A. Meconis. *The Armed Forces of the USA in the Asia-Pacific Region*. London: I.B. Tauris, 1999.

Weatherbee, Donald E. 'The South China Sea: From Zone of Conflict to Zone of Peace?' In Lawrence Grinter and Young Whan Kihl (eds), *East Asian Conflict Zones – Prospects for Regional Stability and Deescalation*. Basingstoke: Macmillan, 1987, pp. 123–148.

—— *ASEAN and Pacific Regionalism*. Bangkok: ISIS, 1989.

White Paper Defense of Japan 1996, available at http://www.jda.go.jp/pab/8aramasi/defcont.htm.

Whiting, Allen S. 'Chinese Nationalism and Foreign Policy after Deng'. *The China Quarterly*, no. 142 (June 1995), pp. 299–322.

—— 'ASEAN Eyes China – The Security Dimension'. *Asian Survey*, vol. 37, no. 4 (April 1997), pp. 295–316.

—— 'The PLA and China's Threat Perceptions'. In David Shambaugh and Richard H. Yang (eds), *China's Military in Transition*. Oxford: Oxford University Press, 1997, pp. 332–352

Whiting, Allen S. and Xin Jianfei: 'Sino-Japanese Relations. Pragmatism and Passion'. *World Policy Journal*, vol. 8, no. 1 (Winter 1990–91), pp. 107–136.

Winterford, David. 'Chinese Naval Planning and Maritime Interests in the South China Sea: Implications for US and Regional Security Policies'. *The Journal of American–East Asian Relations*, vol. 2, no. 4 (Winter 1993), pp. 369–398.

Wohlstetter, Albert. 'The Delicate Balance of Terror'. In Henry M. Kissinger (ed.), *Problems of National Strategy*. New York: Praeger, 1965, pp. 34–58.

Womack, Brantly. 'International Relationships at the Border of China and Vietnam: An Introduction'. *Foreign Affairs*, vol. 40, no. 6 (2000).

World Bank, Post-Conflict Unit and Belgian Ministry of Foreign Affairs 1999. *Security, Poverty Reduction and Sustainable Development, Challenges for the New Millennium*, September 1999.

Wortzel, Larry M. 'China's Military'. *The Asia-Pacific Magazine*, no. 12 (September 1998), pp. 17–21.

Wortzel, Larry M. (ed.). *The Chinese Armed Forces in the 21st Century*. Carlisle, Pennsylvania: Strategic Studies Institute (December 1999). http://carlisle-www.army.mil/usassi/welcome.htm.

Wu Chunguang. *PRC Environment, Maritime Security Examined in New Book*. A January 1998 Report from the US Embassy in Beijing. http://www.usembassy-china.gov/english/sandt/paccpca.htm.

Wu, Samuel and Bruce Bueno de Mesquita. 'Assessing the Dispute in the South China Sea: A Model of China's Security Decision Making'. *International Studies Quarterly*, vol. 38, no. 3 (September 1994), pp. 379–404.

Wu Shicun. *Nansha zhengduan de youlai yu fazhan* [Origin and Development of the Nansha Disputes]. Beijing: Haiyang chubanshe [Marine Publishing House], 1999.

Wu Yu-Sham. 'Theories and Analogies in the Study of Cross-straits Relations'. Paper prepared for the World Congress of the International Political Science Association, Seoul, 17–21 August 1997.

Wurfel, David. 'Between China and ASEAN: The Dialectics of Recent Vietnamese Foreign Policy'. In Charlyle A. Thayer and Ramses Amer (eds), *Vietnamese Foreign Policy in Transitio.*, Singapore: Institute of Southeast Asian Studies, 1999.

Wurfel, David and Bruce Burton. *Southeast Asia in the New World Order; the Political Economy of a Dynamic Region*. New York: St Martin's Press, 1996.

Xu Guangqiu. 'The Chinese Anti-American Nationalism in the 1990's'. *Asian Perspective*, vol. 22, no. 2 (1998), pp. 193–218.

Xu Xin. 'China's Defence Strategy Under New Circumstances'. *Asian Perspective*, no. 3 (September 1993), pp. 1–6.

Xue, Litai. 'Evolution of China's Nuclear Strategy'. In John C. Hopkins and Weixing Hu (eds), *Strategic Views from the Second Tier. The Nuclear Weapons Policies of France, Britain and China*. New Brunswick: Transaction Publishers, 1996, pp. 167–189

Yahuda, Michael. *The International Politics of the Asia-Pacific, 1945–1995*. New York: Routledge, 1996.

—— 'The International Politics of Asia: The Post Cold War Period and Beyond'. *Asian Studies*, no. 10, The Asia Strategy Project, Ministry for Foreign Affairs, February 1998.

Yang, Andrew N.D. 'Threats across the Taiwan Strait: Reaching out for the Unreachable'. *The RUSI Journal*, vol. 141, no. 2 (April 1996), pp. 52–56.

Yee, Herbert. 'Beijing Policies towards Southeast Asia and Spratly Islands in the Post Cold War Era'. *Issues & Studies*, vol. 31, no. 7 (July 1995), pp. 46–65.

Yorac, Haydee. 'The Philippine Claim to the Spratly Islands Group'. *Philippine Law Journal*, vol. 58 (1983).

You Ji. 'A Test Case for China's Defense and Foreign Policies'. *Contemporary Southeast Asia*, vol. 16, no. 4 (March 1995), pp. 375–403.

——— *The Armed Forces of China*. Sydney: Allen & Unwin, 1999.

——— 'The Revolution in Military Affairs and the Evolution of China's Strategic Thinking'. *Contemporary Southeast Asia*, vol. 21, no. 3 (December 1999), pp. 344–364.

You Ji and You Xu. 'In search of Blue Water Power: The PLA Navy's Maritime Strategy in the 1990's'. *Pacifica Review*, vol. 4, no. 2 (1991), pp. 137–149.

Yu, Peter Kien-hong. 'Protecting the Spratlys'. *Pacifica Review*, vol. 3, no. 1 (1990), pp. 78–83.

——— 'Issues on the South China Sea: A Case Study'. *Chinese Yearbook of International Law and Affairs*, vol. 11 (1991–92), pp. 138–200.

——— 'Itu Aba Island and the Spratlys Conflict'. In Carl Grundy-Warr (ed.), *World Boundaries*, vol. 3 *Eurasia*. London: Routledge, 1994, pp. 183–195.

——— 'A Critique of the Three Proposals for "Solving" the Spratly Dispute: A Chinese View from Taiwan'. *Issues & Studies*, vol. 31, no. 1 (1995), pp. 63–76.

——— 'The Choppy Taiwan Strait: Changing Political and Military Issues'. *The Korean Journal of Defense Analysis*, vol. XI, no. 1 (Summer 1999), pp. 39–66.

Yuan, Jing Dong. 'China's Defence Modernization: Implications for Asian Pacific Security'. *Contemporary Southeast Asia*, vol. 17, no. 1 (June 1995), pp. 67–84.

——— *Asia-Pacific Security: China's Conditional Multilateralism and Great Power Entente*. Carlisle, Pennsylvania: Strategic Studies Institute, January 2000. http://carlisle-www.army.mil/usassi/welcome.htm.

Yue Feng. 'Trade, FDI and Economic Integration in the South China Sea Region'. A thesis for the Cand. Econ. Degree at the Department of Economics, University of Oslo, 2000.

Zalamea, Lieutnant Commander Ulysses O. 'Eagles and Dragons at Sea: the Inevitable Strategic Collision between the United States and China'. http://www.nwc.navy.mil/press/Review/1996/autumn/eagl-a96.htm.

Zha Daojiong. 'Security in the South China Sea'. *Alternatives*, vol. 26, no. 1 (Jan–Mar 2001), pp. 33–51.

——— 'Localizing the South China Sea Problem: The Case of China's Hainan', *Pacifica Review*, vol. 14, no. 4 (2001), pp. 575–598.

Zhan Jun. 'China Goes to the Blue Waters: The Navy, Seapower Mentality and the South China Sea'. *Journal of Strategic Studies*, vol. 17, no. 3 (September 1994), pp. 180–208.

Zou Keyuan. 'The Chinese Traditional Maritime Boundary Line in the South China Sea and Its Legal Consequences for the Resolution of the Dispute over the Spratly Islands'. *The International Journal of Marine and Coastal Law*, vol. 14, no. 1 (March 1999), pp. 27–54.

——— 'Implementing Marine Environmental Protection Law in China: Progress, Problems and Prospects'. *Marine Policy*, vol. 23, no. 3 (1999), pp. 207–225.

—— 'Maritime Boundary Delimitation in the Gulf of Tonkin'. *Ocean Development & International Law*, no. 30 (1999), pp. 235–254.

—— 'Scarborough Reef: A New Flashpoint?' *Boundary and Security Bulletin*, vol. 7, no. 2 (1999), pp. 71–81.

—— 'Enforcing the Law of Piracy in the South China Sea'. *Journal of Maritime Law and Commerce*, vol. 31, no. 1 (January 2000), pp. 107–117.

—— 'Piracy at Sea and China's Response'. *Lloyd's Maritime and Commercial Law Quarterly* (August 2000), pp. 364–382.

—— 'Redefining the Legal Status of the Taiwan Strait'. *The International Journal of Marine and Coastal Law*, vol. 15, no. 2 (2000), pp. 245–268.

—— 'Maritime Legislation of Mainland China and Taiwan: Developments, Comparison, Implications, and Potential Challenges for the United States'. *Ocean Development & International Law*, vol. 31 (2000), pp. 303–345.

—— 'Curbing Marine Environmental Degradation: China's New Legislation'. *East Asian Institute Working Paper*, no. 66 (29 January 2001).

—— 'Historic Rights in International Law and in China's Practice'. *Ocean Development & International Law*, vol. 32, no. 2 (2001), pp. 149–168.

INDEX

Amboyna Cay 9–10, 12
Anambas Islands 28,31
ASEAN, 17–21, 46–47, 50–51, 63–
    65, 70–74, 88–107, 122–125,
    135–139, 148–151, 158–160,
    167–169
    ASEAN Experts' Group on
        Environment 50
    ASEAN Ministerial Meeting
        (AMM) 50, 99
    ASEAN Post–Ministerial
        Conference (PMC) 77
    ASEAN Regional Forum (ARF)
        19, 77–78, 86, 122, 129
    ASEAN Senior Officials on
        Environment 50, 52
Australia 12, 21, 48, 52, 54, 58, 63,
    74, 76–78, 85
Badas Islands 25, 28
biodiversity 45–47
    coral reefs 43–46, 54, 55, 154,
        158, 166
    estuaries 44–45
    mangroves 43–46
    seagrass 43, 45
    wetlands 45
Borneo 7–9, 12, 14–15, 31–32, 54,
    101, 102
Brunei Darussalam 12, 17, 24, 27,
    29, 31–32, 25, 27, 55, 57–58, 63,
    99, 102, 120, 124, 142, 154, 167
    claims 17, 27, 31–32,
    disputes 31
Cam Ranh Bay 17, 19, 76
Cambodia 8, 9, 15, 17–18, 25, 27,
    32–34, 37, 39, 46–49, 78, 88, 99,
    102, 114, 118, 127, 136, 142, 165

    claims 27
    disputes 32–34, 37, 103
China 7–10
    Chinese claim 10, 16, 27–32
    China, People's Republic of
        (PRC) 1, 11, 13, 15–17,
        19–21, 24, 27–31, 34–38,
        40, 44, 46–49, 51, 55–60,
        62–68, 70, 72–7, 87–89,
        91–96, 102, 107–8, 118–
        124, 126, 134–50, 158,
        166–167
    disputes 27–8, 31–37, 102,
        118–120, 121–122
    China, Republic of (Taiwan), 9–
        15, 17, 19–21, 27–32, 34–
        37, 58–59, 62–64, 68–70,
        76, 78, 87–89, 91, 93–94,
        108, 123, 144–146, 154,
        166, 169
    disputes 29–30, 34–37,
conflict containment 134–151
    Code of Conduct 120–121, 135–
        136, 147–151
    deterrence 139–147
conflict resolution 151–158
    mediation 98, 106, 112, 117, 153
conflict transformation 158–160
    Joint Development 33–34, 37,
        58, 101, 118, 125–126,
        129, 150, 152, 163
    confidence-building measures
        (CBM) 49, 63, 78, 89,
        106, 124–125, 151
continental shelf 14–15, 17–18, 20,
    25, 27–36, 55, 101–102, 119–
    120, 126, 153–155, 168

Council for Security Cooperation in the Asia Pacific (CSCAP) 124–125
fisheries 1–3, 7, 9, 12, 14, 18, 20–21, 43–46, 48, 54–55, 60, 63, 121–122, 138, 150–152, 154, 155, 158, 166–167
France 9–13, 81
gas 15, 20, 54–57, 59–60, 151, 155
Great Britain 10, 14
Gulf of Thailand 3, 6, 9, 15, 17–18, 23, 25, 27–28, 30–34, 36–39, 58, 101, 117–118, 120, 125–126, 152, 167
Gulf of Tonkin 6, 8, 17–18, 21, 24–25, 27, 29–31, 34–36, 55, 118–120, 149, 154
Hainan Island 8–13, 20, 25, 46, 55, 154–157
India 54–55, 60, 62–63, 73–76, 78, 145, 156
Indonesia 2, 17–20, 25, 28, 31–32, 34–37, 42–48, 55–60, 63, 72–73, 76, 78, 88–89, 92–96, 99–105, 107–108, 110, 118, 124, 135, 141–142, 146, 152, 154, 160, 165–167
  claims 28, 31–32
  disputes 34–37, 101–103, 118
International Court of Justice (ICJ) 14, 104
Itu Aba 10–11, 13, 15, 30, 36, 144
Japan 2, 8–10, 12–13, 15, 17, 59–60, 62–64, 66, 73–78, 136, 141, 145–147, 156, 166–167
Kampuchea, People's Republic of (PRK) 33
Kien Giang 33
Ligitan Island 92–94, 102, 104
Louisa Reef 27, 29, 32, 36
Luzon 7, 20, 59, 154
Macclesfield Bank 6, 155
Malaysia 2, 12, 15, 17–19, 21, 24–25, 27–29, 31–37, 43–49, 55–64, 72, 76, 78, 88–89, 92–96, 99–105, 108, 118, 120, 123, 124–126, 128, 135, 137, 140–142, 146, 152, 154, 156, 160, 165–167
  claims 28–29, 31–34,
  disputes 34–37, 101–105, 118, 120–122
Malaysia–Thailand Joint Authority 33

Mischief Reef 18–19, 63, 72, 95, 121, 137–138, 140
Natuna Islands 25, 27–29, 31–32, 36, 55, 92, 108
Oil 14–15, 17, 20, 43, 54–56, 58–60, 65, 119–120, 125–126, 143, 151, 155, 157–158
Paracel Islands 6–13, 16, 20, 25, 27–30, 32, 34–37, 92, 119–120, 149, 151–152, 154–155, 168
Peoples Republic of China (PRC). *See* China
Philippines 8, 10–11, 13–15, 17–20, 24, 27, 29, 31–32, 35–38, 43–49, 55–59, 63–64, 72, 76, 78, 88–89, 91, 94–96, 99–100, 102–103, 107, 121–124, 128, 135, 137–138, 140–142, 144, 149, 154, 166
  claims 29, 31–32
  disputes 35–38, 102–103, 121–124
Royal Charlotte Reef 29
Russia 56, 63, 65–66, 74, 76–77, 134, 146
Scarborough Reef & Shoal 6, 20, 121–122, 154–155
sea lines of communication (SLOC) 63, 165
Sipadan Island 92, 94, 102, 104, 160
Soviet Union 12, 17, 88–89, 134–136, 138, 145, 165
Spratly Islands 2, 6–20, 24–25, 27–30, 32, 34–37, 56–57, 59, 62–65, 68, 72–73, 95, 117, 119–120, 122–126, 137–140, 142, 144, 147, 149, 151–155, 157, 168
Swallow Reef 29
Taiwan Strait 20, 59, 70, 75–76, 144, 147, 166
Taiwan. *See* China, Republic of
Tambelan Islands 25, 28
Thailand 8, 15, 17–18, 25, 30–34, 36–37, 44–49, 58, 76, 78, 88, 95–96, 100–103, 118, 123, 125–126, 135, 142, 144, 152, 166–167
  claims 30, 31–34
  disputes 34–37, 101–103,
United Nations 14–15, 21, 27, 69, 97, 121, 152,
  UN Convention on the Law of the Sea (UNCLOS) 14, 15, 27–31, 71, 120–121

UN Conference on Human
Environment
(UNCED), 50
UN Environmental Programme
(UNEP) 21, 46–51, 152
UNEP Strategic Action
Programme for the South
China Sea, 46–51
United States 1–2, 10–17, 19–21,
56–57, 59–60, 62–64, 67, 72–
77, 92, 94, 134–136, 138–147,
149–150, 156, 165–167.
military presence 139–147
US Commander–in–Chief
Pacific (CINCPAC) 20

Vietnam 7, 9–12,
Vietnam, Democratic Republic
of 2, 7, 10–18, 20, 24–5,
30–31, 31–37, 44, 46–49,
55–60, 63–64, 66, 70,
72–73, 76, 78, 87–89, 92,
94, 96, 99, 102–103,
117–126, 136, 138, 142,
145, 149, 152, 154–156
claims 30–31, 31–34
disputes 34–37, 118–120,
121–122
Vietnam, Republic of 7, 9, 11–
16,
Woody Island 11, 13